MEDIATED POLITICAL REALITIES

MEDIATED POLITICAL REALITIES

DAN NIMMO

University of Oklahoma

JAMES E. COMBS

Valparaiso University

Longman
New York & London

Mediated Political Realities, second edition

Copyright © 1990, 1983 by Longman,
a division of Addison-Wesley Publishing Co., Inc.

Longman 95 Church Street, White Plains, N.Y. 10601
A division of Addison-Wesley Publishing Co., Inc.

Associated companies:
Longman Group Ltd., London
Longman Cheshire Pty., Melbourne
Longman Paul Pty., Auckland
Copp Clark Pitman, Toronto

Executive editor: David J. Estrin
Production editor: Marie-Josée Schorp
Cover design: Susan J. Moore
Cover photo: Dome, Washington, D.C. by Hill Frost ©.
Production supervisor: Kathleen M. Ryan

Library of Congress Cataloging-in-Publication Data

Nimmo, Dan D.
    Mediated political realities / Dan Nimmo, James E. Combs.—2nd ed.
        p.   cm.
    Includes indexes.
    ISBN 0-8013-0220-X
    1. Communication in politics.   I. Combs, James E.   II. Title.
    JA74.N54   1990
    302′. 72—dc20   89-8288
                                                            CIP

ABCDEFGHIJ–MA–99 98 97 96 95 94 93 92 91 90 89

In remembrance of Dutton Peabody,
pioneer of fantasy journalism,
who taught:
"When the legend becomes fact,
print the legend."

Man is essentially a dreamer,
wakened sometimes for a
moment by some peculiarly
obtrusive element in the outer
world, but lapsing again quickly
into the happy somnolence of
imagination.

Bertrand Russell
Sceptical Essays

Contents

Preface

In the Preface to the first edition of this book, published in 1983, the authors recalled the instructions urged upon political scientists by one of the founders of that discipline. Specifically, we recalled what Arthur F. Bentley had to say that is relevant to understanding the basic subject of this text, namely, the mediation of political realities through communication. Bentley wrote in the first decade of this century, a period when he spoke of a "dead political science" that had "the very breath of life left out." What was that breath? Said Bentley, "He who writes of the state, of law, or of politics without first coming to close quarters with public opinion is simply evading the very central structure of his study."

We pointed out in 1983 that since Bentley's writing of *The Process of Government* in 1908 political science had changed and that the study of public opinion was far from ignored.[1] But the analysis of public opinion did not evolve along the lines recommended by Bentley, who thought that the primary focus of political inquiry generally, and of public opinion specifically, should be what he called "language activity." More precisely, he argued that "it is what is reflected in language that demands primary attention." As a working journalist for 15 years, he had learned a lesson: There is a vital relationship between communication and politics, so vital that to study politics without making communication a key feature of the political is, indeed, to take the "breath" out of political science.

This is not to say that "language activity" has had no attention from political scientists. The highly diverse and insightful contributions of such political scientists as David V. J. Bell, Lance Bennett, William Connolly, Paul Corcoran, Murray Edelman, Doris Graber, David Paletz, Michael Shapiro, and others offer testimony to the contrary. Especially in the past decade, political scientists have made the relationship of politics and communication an important—although certainly not the "very central"—structure of political inquiry, to use Bentley's words.

Increasingly, political scientists have heeded Bentley's advice to examine public opinion and particularly "language activity" in politics. They have been considerably more reluctant (only slightly less so than in 1983) to attend to another of Bentley's recommendation. Writing of "the raw material of government," Bentley asked in *The Process of Government,* "Ought we not to draw a distinction in advance between it and other varieties of social activity, so that we can have our field of study defined and delimited at the outset?" He answered with a resounding "No." He said that political scientists should not be like children making paper toys, using their scissors too confidently, thus cutting themselves off from the material they need. Rather, they should "plunge into any phenomena or set of phenomena belonging to the roughly recognized field of government."

Although the "roughly recognized field of government" now includes communication for political scientists, political communication *per se* has been relatively narrowly defined to include communication in electoral campaigns, political journalism, and presidential communication, but little else. Excluded for the most part from political scientists' studies have been a key set of phenomena—namely, elements of popular culture such as entertainment programming on radio and television, popular pageantry and celebration, the popular film industry, celebrity magazines, amateur and professional sports, televangelist movements and their celebrity leaders, popular music, the use of leisure time, and the like. Popular communication in all its diverse forms, so important to the populace in a polity, has been deemed largely nonpolitical by the bulk of political scientists. The study of popular communication as a mediator of politics has instead been left to sociologists, communication scientists, and scholars in the humanities.

As recent published scholarship attests, the relationship of popular to political communication is well established. Although one does not find relevant studies in political science journals, they abound elsewhere. For example, consider *Critical Studies in Mass Communication,* a quarterly journal founded in 1984. Recent issues contain studies of the political relevance of popular music, visitors to the Vietnam Veterans Memorial, TV movies such as *The Day After,* cable TV, "60 Minutes," "Star Trek," horror films, sportswriting, and many more.[2] Similarly, scholarly studies in popular culture focus increasingly on the link between "pop" culture and political culture. And book-length treatises on the mediation of politics by popular communication appear with greater frequency than they did a decade ago.

This volume is an effort to heed Bentley's advice in the study of politics generally and in the study of language activity as a mediator of politics; like the 1983 edition it remains a "plunge into any phenomena or set of phenomena belonging to the roughly recognized field of government."[3] Our argument remains that of the first edition: Few people learn about politics through direct experience. For most persons, political realities are mediated through mass and group communication, a process that results as much in the creation, transmission, and adoption of political fantasies as it results in independently validated views of what happens. However, this edition differs from the first in two major respects. First, in 1983 there were relatively few studies providing insights into how various media portray politics to Americans, especially through popular communication. As noted, that is no longer the case. We must warn, however, that as in 1983 there are still relatively few studies of how Americans respond on the basis of media portrayals. So, although this edition can take greater advantage of published research into political mediation by diverse media than did the first, we must still turn primarily to speculation in discussing the consequences of that mediation.

Second, although each of the authors did receive a few of the by now obligatory dismissals that the first edition was "just another of his textbooks," many, many people who actually did read the work before judging—teachers, students, colleagues, friends, adversaries, and enemies—took it seriously, liked it, and provided evaluations and suggestions for revision. We are very thankful to them. We have heeded their advice when possible. Because we have done so, and because of studies published since 1983, this edition is not simply old wine in a new bottle. The basic organization of the text remains the same, as does the message of each chapter. Many of those chapters have been more than merely updated, however; they have been extensively revised and rewritten.

The Preface of the first edition acknowledged our debts to individuals who contributed to its publication. We remain indebted to them but shall not repeat their names here. They know who they are and of our gratitude. As noted, this revision depends on the evaluations and advice of numerous individuals, too numerous to acknowledge here. They too know who they are; they too know of our gratitude. We do single out David Estrin of Longman Inc. for his encouragement and enthusiasm in the publication of a revised edition. Understanding baseball as he does, he thereby understands the heart and mind of America.

We believe that people live in a shared world, an all-too-often common, single reality mediated for them. Each person reaches different personal judgments about what mediated political reality *means,* but the tendency is to accept the mediated world as *real* without question. We invite—nay, encourage—readers to take a skeptical approach. The task of the skeptic is not to question meanings only but the common reality itself from which those meanings derive, on grounds that political reality is but one of many fantasies that may or may not serve us well. We hope that a new generation of readers will find the contents useful, especially in recognizing and evaluating their own political fantasies—no matter what the source.

Dan Nimmo
James E. Combs

NOTES

1. Arthur F. Bentley, *The Process of Government* (Cambridge, MA: The Belknap Press of Harvard University Press, 1967; first published in 1908 by Chicago University Press, Chicago, IL).
2. See all of the following: Karen A. Foss and Stephen W. Littlejohn, *"The Day After*: Rhetorical Visions in an Ironic Frame," *Critical Studies in Mass Communication,* 3 (September 1986): 317–336; Thomas Streeter, "The Cable Fable Revisited: Discourse, Policy, and the Making of Cable Television," *Critical Studies in Mass Communication,* 4 (June 1987): 174–200; Richard Campbell, "Securing the Middle Ground: Reporter Formulas in '60 Minutes'," *Critical Studies in Mass Communication,* 4 (December 1987): 325–350; Henry Jenkins III, " 'Star Trek' Rerun, Reread, Rewritten: Fan Writing as Textual Poaching," *Critical Studies in Mass Communication,* 5 (June 1988): 85–107; Barry Brummett, "Electric Literature as Equipment for Living: Haunted House Films," *Critical Studies in Mass Communication,* 2 (September 1985): 247–261: Nick Trujillo and Leah R. Ekdom, "Sportswriting and American Cultural Values: The 1984 Chicago Cubs," *Critical Studies in Mass Communication,* 2 (September 1985): 262–280. See also Harry W. Haines, " 'What Kind of War?': An Analysis of the Vietnam Veterans Memorial," *Critical Studies in Mass Communication,* 3 (March 1986): 1–20.
3. Bentley, *The Process of Government,* p. 199.

How Real Is Politics?
The Mediation of Political Realities

Miss Sherwin of Gopher Prairie never lived, yet she is immortal. Her name is unknown to most, yet her fame is enduring. Her residence is fictional, yet we all live there. She will never die because, at least in politics, each of us is Miss Sherwin of Gopher Prairie.

Writing in 1922 after the close of World War I, journalist Walter Lippmann reflected on Miss Sherwin and her understanding of that great conflict.[1] Miss Sherwin, he wrote, borrowing from the 1920 novel of Sinclair Lewis, *Main Street,* "is aware that a war is raging in France and tries to conceive it." But she has never been to France and "certainly she has never been along what is now the battle front." All she has seen are pictures of soldiers, and it is impossible for her to imagine three million of them. "No one, in fact, can imagine them, and the professionals do not try," wrote Lippmann. Instead, "they think of them as, say, two hundred divisions." Miss Sherwin thinks not of masses of soldiers but of a personal duel between the French General Joffre and the German Kaiser. Her mind's eye pictures an 18th-century painting of a great soldier, a hero: "He stands there boldly unruffled and more than life size, with a shadowy army of tiny little figures winding off into the landscape behind." Miss Sherwin is not alone in this fantasy. Indeed, great men themselves are not "oblivious to these expectations." A photographer visits the French General Joffre and finds him in a drab office at a worktable without papers where he is preparing to sign his name to a single document. Someone notes that there are no maps on the walls. Surely it is impossible to think of a general without maps! So, aides hastily put maps in place. The photograph is snapped, the maps immediately removed.

There is a moral in this little tale about innocent Miss Sherwin of Gopher Prairie. Lippmann believed that people act on the basis of pictures they carry around in their heads, pictures of the way they think things are. These pictures derive from, and are changed by, two different sources or a combination thereof. One is direct experience. People's daily lives consist of direct, first-hand experiences of events, places, other people, objects, and so on. They eat and sleep, work and play, argue and relent, worry and relax. The pictures in their heads help them to make sense of it all, and in large measure the pictures comprise what is "real" for each of them. But a lot of things happen that people do not experience directly. They hear, read, or see pictures of these things, imagine what took place, make sense of them, and incorporate these indirectly experienced things into their pictures of the world as another bit of their "real" world.

For Miss Sherwin of Gopher Prairie, direct experience of the war in France was impossible. She could conceive of the war only on the basis of what she was told or what she expected to be told. Her reality was not a first-hand, direct involvement in the Great War but a product of secondhand, indirect accounts. It was a *mediated,* not an experienced reality. Miss Sherwin was not alone in this respect. Unable to conceive of three million soldiers, each plagued by the agonies of combat, the professional military imagined them instead as 200 depersonalized, faceless divisions. Nor could the mediated realities of Miss Sherwin or the generals differ from popular expectations. We expect generals to have battle maps; so supply them, take the photograph, remove them. Mediated realities are thereby self-fulfilling: Accounts of the way things are conform to the pictures people have of those things, the way they imagine them, and thus the accounts reinforce instead of challenging the pictures in our heads.

This book is about such mediated realities, specifically, the mediated realities of politics. Its argument is straightforward—the pictures we have of politics are rarely the products of direct involvement. Instead, they are perceptions focused, filtered, and fantasized by a host of mediators. Some are found in the mass media—the press or in entertainment programming on television, in movies, popular magazines, songs, and so on. Others consist of group efforts in election campaigns, political movements, religious causes, and government policymaking. To introduce the argument, we first pose the question "How real is politics?" by considering how real is real, how real is fantasy, and by considering the logic of mediated politics—real and fantastic.

HOW REAL IS REAL?

There is a Japanese fable so venerable that over the course of many centuries it has been related in song, narrative, and dramatic form. It is the fable of *Rashomon.* The lesson the fable teaches goes far beyond the boundaries of Japan. Indeed, by transferring its setting to the American West, an enterprising producer made it into a moderately successful movie (*The Outrage*) featuring William Shatner, who later starred in TV and movies as Captain James T. Kirk of *Star Trek*. *Rashomon* involves a group of people who cross paths after separately witnessing a common event. Each renders an account of what he or she saw. Although each person saw precisely the same things happen, each interprets those happenings in such different ways that no two persons' accounts are the same. Each person's imagination results in a different picture in his or her head. The point of the story is that we all live in a common world, but no two people live in the same one. Each of us forges our own reality. What is real to one of us may be illusion to another, and vice versa.

How real, then, is real? Philosophers have debated that question for centuries and are probably no closer to a consensus than on that first day when one of them stubbed a toe on a rock and pondered whether the pain came from a real stone or an imaginary one. For purposes of our discussion, there is little gain in summarizing the many philosophic arguments about the nature of reality. Rather, we shall simply state a position on that question that is in keeping with our basic purpose of describing mediated political realities.

Our view derives from a line of thinking summarized in a provocative, anecdotal book by Paul Watzlawick entitled *How Real Is Real?*[2] Watzlawick's training and professional experience are in the fields of psychiatry and psychotherapy. His studies have led him to conclude that many alleged mental, emotional, and social disorders grow out of faulty communication between people, discourse that places people in different worlds and causes them constantly to talk past one another. *How Real Is Real?* argues simply that "communication creates what we call reality." At first, one may dismiss that proposition as obvious, even trivial. After all, humans must communicate with one another; it stands to reason that they will influence one another's views by doing so. Hence, is it not obvious that one's impressions of things flow from communication? Perhaps, but Watzlawick is saying something more. He is saying that insofar as things make any difference to us at all—that is, real things, or reality—communication creates them. Watzlawick admits this is a "most peculiar" view, "for surely reality is what is, and communication is merely a way of expressing or explaining it." Not at all, he urges, and then summarizes his position neatly:

> [O]ur everyday, traditional ideas of reality are delusions which we spend substantial parts of our daily lives shoring up, even at the considerable risk of trying to force facts to fit our definition of reality instead of vice versa. And the most dangerous delusion of all is that there is only one reality. What there are, in fact, are so many different versions of reality, some of which are contradictory, but all of which are the results of communication and not reflections of eternal, objective truths.[3]

There are three points here: (1) Our everyday, taken-for-granted reality is a delusion; (2) reality is created, or constructed, through communication—not expressed by it; (3) for any situation there is no single reality, no one objective truth, but multiple, subjectively derived realities. The world is *Rashomon*.

There are some discomforting implications in all of this when one thinks about it. Granted, we are generally willing to accept limits to our understanding, that there are few things we can really know. But does that deny that there is a concrete, palpable "real world" that exists and is knowable? Watzlawick implies as much. The trouble, as he understands it, is that whether a real world exists or not, the only way we can know it, grasp it, make sense of it, is through communication. Even when we are directly involved in things, we do not apprehend them directly. Instead, media of communication intervene, media in the form of language, customs, symbols, stories, and so forth. That very intervention is a process that creates and re-creates (constructs and reconstructs) our realities of the moment and over the proverbial long haul. Communication does more than report, describe, explain: it creates. In this sense all realities—even those emerging out of direct, firsthand experience with things—are mediated. Looking back we can speculate that Miss Sherwin's reality of Gopher Prairie was no less mediated than was her conception of the war raging in France.

One other point should be emphasized: In any situation there is more than one reality, or version of reality; some versions are contradictory. We scarcely need reminding that countless millions have died extending or defending a particular version of reality in the face of other versions and seeking to impose a single objective truth on all. More peaceful political debates are also clashes of competing versions of what is real. Every four years the Republican and Democratic presidential candidates debate each other, each offering a contrasting vision of the state of the country and of the world and how it should be. Is one clearly right, correct, and honest? Is the other wrong, stupid, and evil? Avid supporters of either candidate might think so. It is more likely, however, that the pictures of the world dancing through each candidate's head are contradictory, not disconfirming.

What accounts for multiple, contradictory realities? If we accept Watzlawick's basic premise, that communication creates multiple realities (i.e., all realities are mediated), then any means of communication that intervenes in human experience is a potential mediator of reality. Our focus in this book, however, is not on all such means but only on two. One is the role that group communication plays in mediating realities (what we refer to as *group-mediated politics*); the other is the part mass communication plays (what we speak of as *mass-mediated politics*).

Whether birds of a feather flock together or opposites attract, we know not which, if either, adage is correct. We do know that it is characteristic of the human species to congregate in groups of all kinds: families, neighborhoods, villages, work groups, play groups, churches, crowds, and many others. Rewarding or not, group life apparently serves needs for companionship, camaraderie, cooperation, defense, and so forth. Certainly one attribute of any group is communication among its members. Through communication members define situations, problems, and the means of coping with difficulties. Communication simply makes living together possible. And in the process, the members create realities for the group. Differing groups (and differing groups within groups) frequently create contrasting pictures of the world. As we argue in Part II, group-mediated politics lends a special quality to political realities in this nation, particularly in defining relationships between politics and policymaking, elites, religious leaders, and alleged conspirators.

In an earlier era, groups were the center of life for people. Tightly bonded, intimate family gatherings, for instance, were important in defining the realities for several generations of Americans. Today, however, there is another reality-creating means of communication, sometimes complementing and sometimes competing with groups. That is mass communication, or what we often refer to as *mass media*. "Social reality is constituted, recognized, and celebrated with media," write the authors of an insightful work on how mass media shape American understandings of the way things are.[4] We share the view that much of what passes for social realities in contemporary America is what the mass media fashion. We examine the quality of mass-mediated politics in Part I.

Before discussing the specific sources of mediated political realities, we need to consider a problem thus far brushed aside in asking "How real is real?" To say that communication creates realities, that there are different versions of what is real in a given situation, that commonsense notions of eternal, objective truths are deluding, implies that reality is an iffy matter. Few of us, however, care to live our lives in a continuous state of doubt. Indeed, we would be regarded as strange if we went around constantly asking: "What did you really mean by that?" "Did I really see what I think I saw?" "Do you see what I see?" In our everyday lives we simply take certain things for granted. If not reality, then what?

WELCOME TO FANTASYLAND:
IT'S NOT ALL MICKEY MOUSE!

Humans are not passive creatures. Things that reach them in their everyday lives—whether through direct, firsthand experience or indirectly by way of groups and mass media—have no inherent meaning. People pay heed to some things, ignore others; the messages that they heed, they interpret and act on. Some things impress people, others they forget, others they avoid. People are active mediators, or interpreters, of their worlds. They are in, and constitute, a communication process that creates realities.

Human imagination is essential to that process. We employ our imaginations for every conceivable purpose. It surely helps us to frame a picture of the way the world is and all possible objects are which we deal with in our daily lives. But imagination does more. As philosopher David Hume wrote, "Imagination extends experience."[5] Lacking imagination, the pictures in our heads would be limited, but with imagination we can conceive of things that we have never experienced. Indeed, perhaps no one has ever experienced what can sometimes be imagined.

Imagination can take many forms. Suppose one plans to take an extended vacation in a foreign land. Hardheaded planning is needed to decide what clothes to take, to arrange lodging, to prepare or buy meals, to schedule transportation, perhaps to learn a language, and to attend to a myriad of other details—not to mention financing the whole expedition. A person must anticipate the problems that can come up in such a venture. Not having made the trip before, one's experience is only a partial guide to what can happen. Imagination is indispensable in adjusting to and formulating expectations of possible happenings. But not everyone carefully plans. Some daydream, which is another form of imagining. The planning of concrete activities takes second place to drifting off into a dream world of what the trip will be like—visits to exotic places, encounters with exciting strangers, titillating experiences.

Whatever form imagination takes—planning, anticipating, forming expectations, dreaming, *déjà vu* experiences, extrasensory perception, remembering, and so on—the process is essential to the construction of our realities, the pictures of the world in our heads. In dealing with sources of mediated realities, especially the group and mass communication sources of political realities, we single out a particular type of imaginative activity, that of fantasy. As this book will show, the vast bulk of political reality that most of us take for granted (whether we are private citizens or public officials) consists of a combination of fantasies created and evoked by group and mass communication.

We are not the only ones to single out fantasy as a form of imaginative activity worthy of attention. Advertisers of commercial products hawk their wares by catering to the imagination through fantasy. Pick up any magazine. Thumb through the advertising. One ad pictures a fantasy for "people who like to smoke": Select the advertised cigarette and, by implication, enjoy witty conversation with affluent, bright, beautiful people. Would you like to go to "all corners of the earth"? An ad for an airline promises "London's jolly cheer," "Frankfurt's frosty beer," and "Cancun's water so clear." Do you fancy earning money for college? Then, "Be all you can be" and join the U.S. Army so that you too can be hugged by Mom after graduation from basic training, just like the recruit in the full-page ad.

As another case, consider the leisure industry. In 1955 Walt Disney Productions, Inc. opened its theme park, Disneyland, in California. The enterprise was so well received that another opened in 1971, Disney World, in Florida. Both parks feature "Fantasyland," areas wherein hundreds of thousands of tourists have indulged their imaginations to the full over the years. The wide appeal of Fantasyland has not gone unnoticed. One of the world's largest hotel chains, heretofore noted for its hotels designed around lavish atriums, has embarked upon another venture, the opening of "fantasy resorts." Inspired by the Fantasyland notion, the resorts provide vacationers with opportunities to fulfill their fantasies—driving race cars over competitive courses, playing golf with star professionals, scuba diving in a tropical pool, hunting for big game in an African setting, floating on a raft in a tropical rain forest, watching the heavens alongside professional astronomers, even fighting a bull in the ring—at an average cost of $2,500 per week and up. Noted the president of the hotel chain: "We'll be selling an experience. We are, in effect, becoming entertainers and therapists as well as hoteliers. We're creating stage sets where our guests can step out of their everyday hectic life and live out their fantasies."[6]

The hotel chain is but cashing in on a growth industry—that is, the market for a form of fantasy known as "designed experiences."[7] A designed experience is not something one normally does in everyday life but an event planned, constructed, and conducted by an "experience broker." Suppose, for example, that a professor of English has always held the secret desire to be in TV soap opera. The professor saves up meager earnings and goes to an experience broker. The broker shops around and, using the professor's money, purchases a designed, one-week experience: The professor not only visits the set of, say, "All My Children," but rehearses with the cast, has a nonspeaking walk-on, kisses the serial's star, and, as part of the plotline, dies at the hands of terrorists who are kidnapping the leading character. The English professor has had a designed experience, a dream vacation that has allowed escape from classroom routine, flirtation with a new lifestyle, attention, challenge, learning, entertainment, and fulfillment of a fantasy.

Is a world of advertised fantasies, fantasy resorts, and designed experiences remote from the harsh realities of politics? We think not. Fantasy is one of the chief ways that the mediation of political realities occurs. It may be argued that politics is itself a designed experience. Preliminary to that argument, we need first to delve more into the nature of fantasy, its necessity, and its origins.

How Real Is Fantasy, How Fantastic Reality?

In common usage the word *fantasy* has many meanings. If it is perplexing to try to decide how real is reality, consider any standard dictionary's efforts to state how real is fantasy. Several definitions of fantasy found in typical dictionaries follow:

- The realm of vivid imagination, reverie, depiction, illusion, and the like; the natural conjuring of mental invention and association; the visionary world; make-believe.

- A mental image, especially a disordered and weird image; an illusion; phantasm.
- A capricious or whimsical idea or notion.
- Literary or dramatic fiction characterized by highly fanciful or supernatural elements.
- An imagined event or condition fulfilling a wish.
- Literally apart from reality, but more often describes what seems to have slight relation to the real world because of strangeness or extravagance.

In sum, fantasy involves imagination, its relationship to reality is problematic, and it is often dramatic in content. It may be vivid or illusory, natural or supernatural, visionary or capricious, believable or make-believe, real or unreal.

Where does reality end and fantasy begin? Many researchers and scholars try to distinguish fantasy as a way of thinking. Psychologists, for example, contrast fantasizing with reality-testing. Fantasy involves imagining events or conditions, usually pleasant and satisfying experiences, that permit a person to achieve wants and wishes blocked in the "real" world. The person escapes into a world of imagination. Reality-testing involves exploring and experimenting with one's environment to learn the nature of things, people, and events—in short, probing for evidence to support one's thoughts. Psychosis thus consists of an impairment of reality-testing and a retreat into a world of fantasy.[8] Because all of us fantasize to some degree, the activity extends well beyond the psychotic.

Other scholars endeavor to distinguish between serious and nonserious activity.[9] Taking something seriously demands concentration, application of acquired skills, and work. Nonserious activity is more playful, demanding less focused attention and permitting reverie. A similar contrast is that between directed thought and fantasy thought.[10] Directed thought concerns immediate goals formed in coping with the environment (such as whether to carry an umbrella if it is cloudy). It involves both short-term memory (Has it rained a lot lately?) and long-term memory (Have I been wet without an umbrella under similar conditions in the past?). Directed thought rouses a person to action, to a decision—to take the umbrella or to leave it. Finally, directed thought can be tested, checked for its accuracy or inaccuracy: Did I need the umbrella or not? Directed thought, then, is volitional. That is, it is the serious activity in which one voluntarily focuses attention on the problem at hand and does something about it.

Fantasy differs in several respects. Fantasy concerns goals that are less immediate, perhaps extending to wishes and desires that one has had for a long time but whose fulfillment was interrupted by the demands of everyday life. Attention to the immediate external environment is much more perfunctory in fantasizing than in directed thought. Fantasy is more internally focused, more self-centered. Research suggests that during fantasizing this self-centered concern is reflected in ocular fixation that is, a tendency to ignore other people and one's surroundings, to acquire the blank stare that we have all experienced in talking with someone whose attention is miles away from the conversation. Fantasizing relies largely on long-term memory, on a reliving of the past, and on imagining how things will be the same or different in the future. Fantasizers act on the basis of what is running through their heads more rarely than do persons in directed thought; the thought it not father to the deed but enjoyed purely for its own sake. Finally, because fantasy seldom rouses one to act, the correctness of the fantasy cannot be checked against what happened when one behaved in accordance with it. More frequently, the fantasy's accuracy is gauged by whether holding it yields satisfaction, not what happens by living it out. A nonvolitional reverie substitutes for a voluntary focusing of attention and effort.

Living in Fantastic Worlds

Such distinctions are useful. They assist in formulating an understanding of fantasy that flows throughout our discussion, but they do not directly answer the question, "What then is fantasy?" A fantasy is a credible picture of the world created when one interprets mediated experiences as the way things are and takes for granted the authenticity of the mediated reality without checking against alternative, perhaps contradictory, realities so long as the fantasy itself offers dramatic proof of one's expectations. Consider the main points in this definition. First, a person has a fantasy not because it is demonstrably true or false but because it is believable, that is, credible. The young man fantasizing he is a handsome, desirable lover or the young lady visualizing herself as a femme fatale may not be easily dissuaded, acne or bad breath notwithstanding. Or, if both fantasize that a facial lotion or a mouthwash will correct the fatal flaw disrupting their love life, contradictory results go ignored. Second, if communication creates realities, given the fine line between the real and the fantastic, it is no shock to think that communication creates fantasies as well. Third, the delusion that there is a single reality for any given event rather than many different versions of reality is precisely the substance on which fantasy feeds. A fantasy world substitutes a simplified, single reality for the complex, overlapping, and contradictory versions possible through communication. Fourth, the proof of a fantasy's worth (i.e., whether it is true for its holder) lies not in its correspondence to what happens in the world but whether it conforms to what one expects, perhaps even wants, to be so. Finally, a fantasy has dramatic qualities; for the person creating it, the fantasy is a story with a plot, actors, scene, and ways of expressing things, acts, and motives. Either in the mind or with other people, fantasies are rehearsed and enacted—a key point we return to later in this chapter.

There are several reasons why people frequently cling to fantasies. As Eric

S. Rabkin writes in *Fantastic Worlds,* what we take to be the real world "is a messy place where dust accumulates and people die for no good reason and crime often pays and true love doesn't conquer much."[11] In the real world things make no sense, occurring randomly; they are "indifferent to the shape we try to sense in our lives."[12] Fantasy is an alternative. Our fantasies can be neat and tidy. Through them we can impose an order on the messy, dirty, chaotic world. We can bend things to our liking through imagination or, if not to our liking, at least to our understanding. Fantasy provides a way out of grappling with contradictory realities. We transcend the here-and-now, relieve our boredom, and substitute a single reality for multiple ones. Finally, in addition to simplifying and perhaps comforting us, fantasies offer a way for each of us to know who we are; they provide a self-identity and, if we try to live our fantasies, a way of expressing it. Even in the face of refuting evidence from our daily lives, we reluctantly yield the fantasy of a self-image, even avoiding or ignoring the contradictory claims of others' alleged realities.

There is evidence that we begin to employ fantasies to cope with the world at a very early age. Vivian Paley teaches 3–5-year-old preschoolers in a Chicago nursery school. Over several years she has observed the preschoolers' fantasy play. She says children spend about three-fourths of their time in fantasy play that consists of making up stories about parents and babies, good guys and bad guys, animals, superheroes, and so on.[13] The children then act out the stories. The key, reports Paley, is getting to be Superman, Batman, or Robin fighting Plutar or the Joker *in front of your friends.* Roughly the same themes reappear with each new nursery school class, especially stories from younger children about conquering evil. Through fantasy play, children feel powerful and in control of their environment; they overcome fears of being away from home for the first time. By telling stories about themselves through imaginary characters (say, Barbie and Ken), they avoid revealing directly things about themselves that they don't wish to expose.

Thus, for a variety of reasons and whether we are adults or not, we all share Miss Sherwin's penchant for imagining what the world is like. We cannot be everywhere, taking part in everything firsthand. Even if we could, we often shy away from confronting things directly, accepting instead mediated, secondhand accounts of what happens. Because we are unable to check the authenticity of those accounts, we unconsciously take most of them for granted. As Rabkin suggests, a good portion of the time we inhabit fantastic worlds.

You Know What "Really" Happened?

We have all known people who are willing to confide "what really happened" regarding a person, event, or situation. But did it really happen, or is this but one of many fantastic accounts of what might have been the case? This raises the corollary questions of how fantasies come into being and how they get to be shared by large numbers of people.

As our definition implies, fantastic realities flow from the work of human imagination interpreting mediated accounts. The social construction of fantasy involves an interplay of group and mass communication. The sequence runs roughly as follows: Something happens that people find sufficiently novel, perplexing, threatening, amusing, or interesting to take note of it. It may be something seen firsthand—an auto accident, bank robbery, political speech, someone scaling the side of a skyscraper—indeed, anything. Or it may be something reported in the news. In either case, it is sufficiently provocative, out of the ordinary, and untoward to cause people to want to know about it and to understand it. The American philosopher Charles S. Peirce believed that humans confronted with novel situations or problems experience an "irritation of doubt" and engage in a natural process of relieving the tensions produced by the ambiguities and anxieties in such a state.[14] If Peirce is correct, this is the beginning of fantasy.

Normally one's striving for clarification leads to personal sampling—an unsystematic process of sorting through one's own thoughts and comparing them to what other people think by gleaning tidbits from conversations with friends, acquaintances, co-workers, and others as well as from following the news, watching TV talk shows, and perhaps simply overhearing random comments.[15] Gradually a picture emerges as to what others think and what they are talking about.

Different people offer different accounts of what happens, however. Diverse clusters and groups of people exchange ideas but have no way of knowing whether the version of reality they have fashioned matches that of other groups. They may think everyone shares their version, or they may think reality is unique to them, that they alone know the truth. In either case, a state of "pluralistic ignorance" emerges, a "situation in which individuals hold unwarranted assumptions about the thoughts, feelings, and behavior of other people."[16] Pluralistic ignorance promotes a tendency for individuals to share their private fantasies, form group fantasies, and then either communicate those fantasies more broadly under the assumption that other groups share them or hide them for fear people holding contradictory pictures of the world will be critical, even threatening.

Because it is shared, a group fantasy takes on an aura of truth that the private fantasies of individuals do not. To have one's private views shared by others constitutes a social validation of a person's image of things. Laboring under the deceptive assumption that, "if others believe what I believe, it must be true," the proof of the validity of a group fantasy lies simply in the fact that it is shared. Similarly, when group members think other groups hold an identical picture of the world, that is added proof that the fantasy is valid.

A person need only reflect on everyday life to spot examples of this fantasy-building process. There is a strong impulse in most of us to want to get along with others. When we come in contact with them—in casual conversation, classroom discussion, working together, playing, or whatever—we seek common ground. Strangers thrust together, for example, probe for a common interest to break the ice. Add to this another impulse: to entertain one another, usually by relating stories of personal experiences or of things happening in the world. If, for instance, family members at dinner hear a tale of political scandal, this may inspire other anecdotes about public morality that conjure up a fantasy of corrupt politicians, the underworld, disliked social groups, even the decline and fall of civilization. The group's fantasy sharing enlivens the dinner by interweaving exploits of heroes, villains, fools, ironic twists in the plot, an ending, and a moral.

Ernest Bormann, a communication scholar, studies the process of group fantasizing and believes that "dramatizing communication creates social reality for groups of people."[17] Such dramatizing (akin to the tales and stories of Vivian Paley's preschoolers) occurs in all types of groups. When it begins, the tempo of the conversation picks up, people get excited, are less self-conscious, and the tone of the group meeting becomes lively, intense, interesting. Dramatizing promotes fantasy building, sharing, and "chaining," that is, the spread of the fantasy to all group members. The result is a group fantasy; its "content consists of characters, real or fictitious, playing out a dramatic situation in a setting removed in time and space from the here-and-how transactions of the group." (Again like Vivian Paley's preschoolers.)

So people encounter situations (either directly or indirectly) that pique their interest. They sample thoughts of others, paint a picture frequently shared with others, and, then, assume that other groups either do or do not share the same understanding. Out of pluralistic ignorance, however, groups have no way of knowing how widely their versions of reality extend. If what provoked the fantasizing in the first place is of sufficiently widespread interest, conditions are ripe for another key stage in fantasy development where mass communication enters, spreading a single fantasy shared by broad segments of a population to mass audiences.

Bormann does not limit his argument to small, face-to-face groups. Fantasy building and fantasy "chaining," as he calls it, occur in larger, less intimate groups in which people do not even know one another, as in an audience listening to a public speech or viewers scattered nationwide watching TV news or entertainment. Masses of people can enter the fantasy process. "Fantasy themes," Bormann's designation of the dramatic elements of a group's fantasy, constitute the reality for a group faced with a problematic situation. That reality, or fantasy theme, is replete with symbols describing the actors, means of expression, acts, scenes, and motives of the drama that constitutes the fantasy. As people get caught up in the symbolic reality, they share a "rhetorical vision"—that is, they all respond the same way emotionally to the key symbols that make up fantasies:

> A rhetorical vision is constructed from fantasy themes that chain out in face-to-face interacting groups, in speaker-audience transactions, in viewers of television broadcasts, in listeners to radio programs, and in all diverse set-

tings for public and intimate communication in a given society. . . . [More-over,] once such a rhetorical vision emerges it contains dramatis personae and typical plot lines that can be alluded to in all communication contexts and spark a response reminiscent of the original emotional chain.[18]

This process completes the sequence of building fantastic worlds. Something happens. Individuals take account of it, try to make sense of it. They sort out their own thoughts and sample those of others. They exchange notes or thoughts with others in small groups. They spin tales; some strike a common responsive chord. They grow excited and involved, a shared symbolic reality builds, a single fantasy filled with *dramatis personae* spreads to all group members. To relieve a state of pluralistic ignorance, the group goes public, communicating the rhetorical vision to larger audiences. Some visions reach the mass media. These visions penetrate other small groups and stimulate conversation, storytelling, and more fantasy. The fantasy spreads to even larger audiences and, if potent enough, constitutes the single symbolic reality created for an entire population.

Thus are fantasies created and propagated. *For those who share them, fantasies are real, the fantasy is reality.* So described, the process of group and mass fantasizing is similar to the spread of rumor. Like fantasy, a rumor is a story in general circulation without certainty as to its truth. Rumors help us to explain confusing situations and relieve uncertainties; they supply neat, tidy, simplified accounts. And like fantasy, the more important people deem the topic of the rumor to be and the more ambiguous the situation that stimulated it, the wider the spread of the rumor. Unlike fantasies, however, there frequently are efforts to check the authenticity of rumors. If verified, rumors take on the aura of fact; if contradicted with concrete evidence, they die out. When a rumor cannot be verified or lives on despite mountains of contradictions, it is scarcely distinguishable from fantasy. It fulfills deeply felt emotional needs shared by large numbers of people; hence, it is real for them.

The Great Cabbage Hoax exemplifies a rumor of fantastic proportions.[19] In the 1940s a rumor started that a federal agency in Washington, DC, had issued a memo on the regulation of cabbage prices—a memo of 26,911 words. The memo embarrassed bureaucrats setting food prices during World War II. With the close of the war, the rumor died out, or so it seemed. In 1951 a toastmaster at a gathering where the director of a federal price-regulating agency was to speak again related the tale, drawing odious comparisons between the rumored memo and the Gettysburg Address (266 words), the Ten Commandments (297), and the Declaration of Independence (1,348). The rumor spread to newspapers, sometimes substituting the price of fog horns for cabbages. Then the rumor apparently died. But no, in 1977 a major oil company in an advertisement in the nation's leading newspapers resurrected the cabbage version of price regulation. This caught the attention of "CBS Evening News," which reported it as fact. An international version reached the

London Times; this time the alleged memo was a European Common Market directive on duck eggs, 26,911 words long. In 1980, Republican congressional candidate Lynn Martin of Illinois made a televised commercial that pictured her looking across a field of soybeans. She told viewers how her district's soybean farmers had been damaged by a federal "regulation on soybean gradations 18,000 words long. Why, the Declaration of Independence had only 463 words, the Ten Commandments but 165!" (Apparently these were abridged versions of the latter two documents.) The hoax has been reborn most recently in a published book as follows: "Lincoln's Gettysburg Address contained 266 words. A recent federal regulation to regulate the price of cabbage contains 26,911 words."[20] The Great Cabbage Hoax is a fantasy rumor that seemingly will not die.

Many fantasies that will not die, that endure through generations of chaining, enter the realm of myth. A myth is a credible, dramatic, and socially constructed picture that people accept as permanent, fixed, unchanging reality. The genius of the Founding Fathers, the greatness of Abraham Lincoln, the Manifest Destiny of America are all examples of myths. Fantasy themes may combine to support enduring myths; at the same time, fantasies conforming to a nation's mythology endure and continue chaining out because of that mythology. In our concluding chapter, we list several recurrent fantasies discussed throughout the book that have become the taken-for-granted, unquestioned stuff of politics.

SOAP OPERA POLITICS: THE LOGIC OF MEDIATED, FANTASTIC REALITY

The creation and chaining out of fantastic worlds from individuals to groups to mass audiences involve storytelling. When something happens that is ambiguous in meaning, provokes people's interest, and raises doubts demanding resolution, the popular urge is to represent what "really happened" in dramatic ways. Dramatic representation of what goes on in the world constitutes the inherent logic of mediated realities, whether those realities are the products of group or mass communication. In the chapters that follow, we explore how the media of group and mass communication portray reality in dramatic ways through news and entertainment programming on television, popular magazines, movies, art, sports, popular movements, and group life. It will help us to clarify at this point the logic of dramatic representation.

To say something is logical is simply to note that its parts relate to one another and to the whole in a reasonable, systematic fashion. A scientific account—for example, Einstein's theory of relativity—has a logic; each portion of the explanation complements and does not contradict the other portions. Similarly, the classic example of syllogistic reasoning (all men are mortal; Socrates was a man; therefore, Socrates was mortal) is logical. Dramatic communication also has a logic. Think of any story, movie, or stage play. What are its elements?

- *Dramatis personae,* or actors: the characters of the drama, frequently portrayed as heroes, villains, and fools.
- *Acts:* what the actors do and say.
- *Style:* the way the actors portray themselves through their tone of voice, gestures, expressions, and so on.
- *Plot line, or scenario:* the unfolding story that relates what is happening, to whom, and how.
- *Scene:* the setting wherein the drama takes place.
- *Motives:* the aims and purposes attributed to the actors that allegedly cause them to do what they do.
- *Sanctioning agent:* the principal source that justifies the events, actions, and conclusion of the drama.[21]

One or more of these elements may be emphasized, others minimized. For instance, the plot lines of the exploits of Superman have always been less important to the drama than the heroic qualities of the lead character and the virtue of the sanctioning agent, "Truth, justice, and the American way." In horror films, acts (usually violent) take meaning largely from the leading character's motives and style—say, Freddy Kruger in the *Nightmare on Elm Street* series.

Regardless of emphasis, however, dramatic logic requires a sense of unity in the relationship of these elements that is achieved primarily through the unfolding of the drama itself, a progression that conforms to the necessities of developing dramatic conflict. Conflict is the struggle emerging from the interplay of opposing forces in the plot—for example, between the villainous J. R. Ewing and virtually every other character in the popular nighttime TV soap opera "Dallas." The ancients, Greeks and Romans, who originated drama, compared the plot, or logical sequence, of a drama to the tying and untying of a knot.[22] The tying and untying has a five-part structure: introduction, rising action (or complication), crisis (or turning point), falling action, and denouement (or resolution). The introduction creates the tone, sketches the characters, details the setting, establishes opening events, and supplies nuances necessary for understanding the drama. The pace of the plot picks up, action rises, and opposing forces join the dramatic conflict (the Southern gentry ride off to war in *Gone with the Wind*). Then something happens (as when the temptress Delilah coaxes from Samson the secret of his strength) to provoke a crisis. Action subsides (even Crocodile Dundee cannot be witty and innovative throughout the entire film). But there must be a final resolution in keeping with the overall rhetorical vision evoked by the drama (as when, in TV situation comedies, after laughing for 20 minutes, crying for five, we smile through our tears at the end).

Such are the basics of dramatized communication. One other point: Mediated realities unfold before audiences in a particular dramatic format, melodrama. Melodrama emerged as the most popular dramatic form of the 19th century. As attested to by soap operas on television ("General Hospital," "All My Children," "Guiding Light" in the daytime, "Dallas," and "Dynasty" at night), comic strips ("Apartment 3G," "Mary Worth"), adventure novel series (James Bond), and movies (*Superman*), the popularity of melodrama is undiminished. Moral justice is at the heart of most melodrama—trials of the virtuous, calumny of the villainous, good rewarded, evil punished. Suspense is the key—from certain death to miraculous safety, disgrace to vindication, paradise lost to paradise regained, vanquished to victor. Anxiety reigns—unrelenting dangers, unexpected threats, hairbreadth escapes. And characters' traits are clear-cut: Good are good, bad are bad. Finally, happy endings are preferred but not essential (once things have been put right again on the ranch, we ask, "Who was that masked man, anyway?") Tragic endings suffice; as trivia buffs know, even John Wayne died in many (but how many?) of his movies! Or there may be no clear-cut resolution at all. This is especially the case in serialized melodrama for, as the durability of "Dallas" demonstrated, the audience left hanging is the audience kept, even enlarged.

These characteristics are more than qualities of melodrama; they are requirements. Related as they are to the elements and structure of dramatic logic, they define what an account must have to be melodramatic. They add up to a "melodramatic imperative."[23] That imperative is a set of requirements frequently imposed by people on events as they try to account for what really happened. Those requirements fix the content and structure of fantasy themes and rhetorical visions. Mediated realities, thus, often carry the aura of soap operas. Is this the case with mediated *political* realities?

The chapters that follow contend that this is precisely the case. The political world that unfolds daily before our eyes is presented in group and mass communication in melodramatic ways. Other observers have come to similar, albeit not identical, conclusions. Almost four centuries ago Niccolo Machiavelli, a hardheaded observer credited with founding the realist view of what politics is all about, noted that the "majority of men delude themselves with what seems to be rather than with what actually is; indeed they are more often moved by things that seem to be rather than by things that are."[24] For most of us, he argued, political reality is imagined, being constituted of nothing else but "seemings." He called this product of imagination *fantasia*.

More contemporary political observers have suggested that all those persons actively and directly engaged in politics—politicians, journalists, spokespersons for causes, and so on—take advantage of the popular propensity to believe in things as they seem rather than as they are and jointly construct politics as a *spectacle*.[25] Much like a designed experience, a political spectacle is enjoyed for its own sake, the excitement it offers, the reassurance it provides that all is well, that things will turn out all right in the end, and that all problems—no matter how intractable—are solved by the pleasure of the spectacle. For instance, a summit meeting between the president of the United States and the president of the Soviet Union is a complex, conflict-laden set of overlapping and contradictory realities. The public vision of the two leaders reaching agreement on armament reductions is both spectacular and reassuring, however.

I. S. Eliot wrote that we understand nothing until it is dramatized before our eyes. Shakespeare wrote that "the play's the thing." When politics is presented as fantasia, spectacle, and melodrama, we add that mediated politics is soap opera politics. Keep in mind, however, that in some cases—again to quote Shakespeare—the fantastic realities may be tales "told by an idiot, full of sound and fury, signifying nothing."

MEDIATING THE REALITIES OF MEDIATED POLITICS

As noted, the idea that political realities are mediated through communication is not new. It did not originate with Lippmann's concern over Miss Sherwin of Gopher Prairie. It is a theme that runs through much of political theory. An American social scientist, Arthur F. Bentley, argued decades ago that the principal raw materials of political inquiry are linguistic. Bentley was interested in describing government as the activities of people, not as static institutions nor as the hidden motives of men. Government for Bentley was always in process—changing, dynamic, in flux. The only way to observe that process was by studying the activities of the politically involved. And the key activity was communicaton: "Actions, not of individual men, but as wave motions of the linguistic behaviors of men, advancing and receding across the centuries."[26]

In the chapters that follow, we examine these "wave motions" as they manifest themselves in political fantasies, rhetorical visions, and melodramas. We look first at mass mediated political realities. Our focus turns initially to the principal source of mediated politics for most Americans: television news (Chapter 1) and the mediated world of the election campaigns (Chapter 2). Political history was once something people read about in textbooks. They still do. But political history is also mediated through the art forms of popular culture (Chapter 3). Americans love to celebrate their heroes and heroines, political as well as any other; in Chapter 4 we describe the national soap opera of political celebration. Consciously or not, countless people fashion their images of politics as it is depicted in the movies; Chapter 5 deals with Hollywood's mediation of politics. Chapter 6 closes the discussion of mass-mediated politics by examining politically relevant rhetorical visions in popular sports. Then we shift our attention to four areas of group-mediated political fantasies. In Chapter 7 the topic is groupthink—the tendency of people to fantasize in coming to a group consensus on courses of action. Chapter 8 examines the political pundits, the trend setters in fantasy creation and chaining. The overlap of religion and politics, and the politico-religious visions that result, is the subject of Chapter 9. Chapter 10 examines the recurring tendency of many groups to explain our politics in conspiratorial ways, fashioning fantasy worlds of friends and enemies. In the concluding chapter, we look back on the fantasyland that is Americans' mediated politics.

In his *Republic,* Plato relates the tale of prisoners in an underground den, bound so that they cannot turn their heads. They can see nothing that goes on around them, only the shadows of those things that the fire throws on the cave wall. When they converse, they give names to and talk about the shadows of things, thinking they are naming the real things and not shadows. Suddenly one prisoner is released. The objects that produced the shadows are passed before his eyes. He is perplexed. He thinks the shadows he formerly saw are truer than the objects shown to him. Compelled to look at the piercing light of the fire, he turns away from the objects to the images on the wall. The shadows are clearer than the objects, again more real. Finally, hauled out to the sunlight, slowly the prisoner adjusts to seeing the objects for what they are. Yet, pushed back into the cave, blinded by the sudden darkness, he sees even less than his fellow prisoners who were not released. The prisoners conclude it is better not to ascend to the light and vow to kill anyone forcing them to do so.

Mediated, secondhand reality is our politics, and there is little we can do about it. But we can examine our own and others' political fantasies with an air of skepticism, learning to be wary of what we might otherwise take for granted. There is at least some liberation from the cave of fantasy in that. But what if no one wants to ascend? We think the risk worth taking in spite of the fate of Plato's prisoner. We hope readers will find that to be the case as well. Otherwise they may get restless, a prospect not too bright in the light of Plato's little tale.

NOTES

1. Walter Lippmann, *Public Opinion* (New York: Macmillan, 1922), pp. 12–13.
2. Paul Watzlawick, *How Real Is Real?* (New York: Random House, Vintage Books, 1976).
3. Ibid, p. xi.
4. David L. Altheide and Robert P. Snow, *Media Logic* (Beverly Hills, CA: Sage, 1979), p. 12. Emphasis in the original.
5. David Hume, *A Treatise of Human Nature* (London: Noon, 1739).
6. Stanley Ziemba, "Hyatt Ties Its Future into Fantasy Resorts." *Chicago Daily Tribune,* May 2, 1988.
7. Philip Kotler, "'Dream Vacations': The Booming Market for Designed Experiences," *The Futurist* (October 1984): 7–13.

8. Robert M. Goldenson, *The Encyclopedia of Human Behavior* (Garden City, NY: Doubleday, 1970), s.v. "fantasy"; George A. Theodorson and Achilles G. Theodorson, *A Modern Dictionary of Sociology* (New York: Crowell, 1969), s.v. "fantasy." These definitions exemplify the contrast between fantasy and reality-testing.

9. Dennis K. Davis and Stanley J. Baran, *Mass Communication and Everyday Life* (Belmont, CA: Wadsworth, 1981), Chap. 5. A full discussion of the distinction between serious and nonserious activity.

10. Thomas L. Lindlof, "Fantasy Activity and the Televiewing Event," in *Communication Yearbook 4,* ed. Dan Nimmo (New Brunswick, NJ: Transaction Books, 1980), pp. 277–291.

11. Eric S. Rabkin, ed., *Fantastic Worlds* (New York: Oxford University Press, 1979).

12. Ibid., p. 3.

13. Vivian Paley, *Bad Guys Don't Have Birthdays: Fantasy Play at Four* (Chicago: University of Chicago Press, 1987).

14. Charles S. Peirce, "The Fixation of Belief," in Philip P. Wiener, ed., *Values in a Universe of Chance: Selected Writing of Charles S. Peirce* (Garden City, NY: Doubleday, Anchor Books, 1958), pp. 91–112.

15. W. Phillips Davison, "The Public Opinion Process," *Public Opinion Quarterly* 22 (Summer 1958): 93.

16. Hubert J. O'Gorman, "Pluralistic Ignorance and White Estimates for Racial Integration," *Public Opinion Quarterly* 39 (Fall 1975): 314; Robert K. Merton, *Social Theory and Social Structure* (Glencoe, IL: Free Press, 1957), p. 377; Floyd H. Allport, *Social Psychology* (Boston: Houghton Mifflin, 1924).

17. Ernest G. Bormann, "Fantasy and Rhetorical Vision: The Rhetorical Criticism of Social Reality," *Quarterly Journal of Speech* 58 (December 1972): 397.

18. Ibid., p. 398.

19. Ralph L. Rosnow and Allan J. Kimmel, "Lives of a Rumor," *Psychology Today* (June 1979): 88–92. The definition of rumor used in this discussion is that of Rosnow and Kimmel. See also Tamototsu Shibutani, *Improvised News* (Indianapolis, IN: Bobbs Merrill, 1966).

20. Bill Gordon, ed., *How Many Books Do You Sell in Ohio?: A Quote Book for Writers* (Akron, OH: North Ridge Books, 1986).

21. Donald C. Shields, "A Dramatistic Approach to Applied Communication Research," in John F. Cragan and Donald C. Shields, eds., *Applied Communication Research* (Prospect Heights, IL: Waveland Press, 1981), pp. 5–13; Kenneth Burke, "Dramatism," in Lee Thayer, ed., *Communication: Concepts and Perspectives* (Washington, DC: Hayden, Sparton Books, 1967).

22. William Flint Thrall, Addison Hibbard, and C. Hugh Holman, *A Handbook to Literature* (New York: Odyssey Press, 1960).

23. Paul H. Weaver, "Captives of Melodrama," *New York Times Magazine,* April 29, 1979, p. 6.

24. Peter Nondanella and Mark Musa, eds., *The Portable Machiavelli* (New York: Penguin Books, 1979), p. 231. See also K.R. Minogue, "Theatricality and Politics: Machiavelli's Concept of Fantasia," in B. Parehk and R.N. Berti, eds., *The Morality of Politics* (London: George Allen and Unwin, 1972), pp. 148–162.

25. Bruce Miroff, "The Presidency and the Public: Leadership as Spectacle," in *The Presidency and the Political System,* ed. Michael Nelson (Washington, DC: Con-

gressional Quarterly, 1988), pp. 271–291; Murray Edelman, *Constructing the Political Spectacle* (Chicago: University of Chicago Press, 1988).

26. Arthur F. Bentley, "Epilogue," in Richard W. Taylor, ed., *Life, Language, Law: Essays in Honor of Arthur F. Bentley* (Yellow Springs, OH: Antioch Press, 1957), p. 212.

PART I

Mass-Mediated Politics

As individuals, people live in the private world of their own hopes and dreams, fears and anxieties, joys and sorrows. Few people exist as isolated individuals. Most of us also live in groups, sharing with others the pleasures and discomforts of group life. In both their private and group life, people depend on the mass media—to inform, entertain, guide, and yield a sense of a larger world than the everyday experiences that private and group matters offer. A large portion of their daily lives thus derives from the mediation of mass communication as well as from their personal and group contacts. As noted in our introduction, it is not always clear just how much of the mass-mediated world is real, how much fantasy. In Part I we deal with several of the mass-mediated worlds where Americans reside—worlds of newsworthy events, electoral conflict, the historical past, filmland fiction, celebrities, and sports. Obviously, some of these worlds are of explicit political importance. Others may seem less so, yet readers will find that they too mediate realities of political relevance.

In 1922 noted political journalist Walter Lippmann wrote, "Universally it is admitted that the press is the chief means of contact with the unseen environment."[1] Perhaps, but certainly no longer exclusively. People look beyond the news media to contact the unseen environment. TV news and entertainment programming, Hollywood films, celebrity magazines, and popular sports create and mediate politically relevant worlds, real and fantastic. The state of the art in the political and communication sciences now gives rise to an ever-increasing number of studies of the sources and consequences of our mediated world. There remains, however, a larger body of speculation than of tested propositions. Some of our assertions in Part I—especially in Chapters 3 through 6—are of that nature. They speak not to the effects of the mass media but to the content of media messages that bring to individuals and group members visions of the unseen environment of politics. The legitimate scientific enterprise consists of paired activities—that is, the proposing of plausible explanations and the testing of such ideas. One does not proceed without the other. It is to that initial task that we now turn.

NOTE

1. Walter Lippmann, *Public Opinion* (New York: Macmillan, 1922), p. 396.

CHAPTER 1

What's Happening?
TV News Lights the Way

In 1929 people called it "Black Thursday." In 1987 they called it "Black Monday." In 1929 it was October 24. In 1987 it was October 19. Two dates separated by 58 years and a few days. What could they have in common to make them so dark, so ready to be labeled black?

Black Thursday, 1929, was the day of the Great Crash on the New York Stock Exchange. It heralded the end of unprecedented prosperity. Throughout the day stock prices fell. The crash threatened, then destroyed fortunes. Black Thursday foreshadowed the beginning of the Great Depression—$50 billion in stock losses by 1931, the failure of 85,000 businesses, and unemployment for 12 million Americans, 25 percent of the workforce. So grim were the times that the direct and mediated realities of Black Thursday have remained in the memories of generations of its victims for decades. Could such a crash happen again?

Black Monday, 1987, was a jolting reminder that another crash could occur. One economist, predicting a major economic depression in the 1990s, called Black Monday "a preliminary tremor, a mild preview of the greater upheaval yet to come."[1] In the "tremor" of October 19 the New York stock market, after falling almost 23 percent, suffered its largest loss in 73 years. It was larger, in fact, than the worst single day fall in the market in 1929. By weeks' end 5,000 companies traded on U.S. exchanges had suffered a drop of $490 billion in value. Even more than in 1929, millions of Americans faced diminished life savings, threatened pension plans and retirement schemes, and severe losses in income.

The Great Crash of 1929 was a reality mediated for Americans by newspapers and radio. Both continued to have a major part in reporting the crash of '87 (for example, "Crash" headlined the *New York Post,* "Panic" said the *New York Daily News*), but in 1987 they were joined by television, that glowing, one-eyed companion found in 98 percent of American households. What light did TV news throw on the darkened hours of Black Monday, 1987? In many respects TV's light conformed to what political scientist Doris Graber calls the three stages in reporting a crisis.[2] When unexpected events occur, notes Graber, the news first transmits uncoordinated messages about them. As reporters gather more information and begin to discern patterns in events, they develop a coherent story. This constitutes the second stage. In a third and final stage, reporters try to put the events into larger perspectives, probing causes and long-range consequences.

All three national TV news networks (ABC, CBS, and NBC) and CNN, the Cable News Network, gave extended coverage to the events of Black Monday and their aftermath. Initial messages of fact were coordinated—all news networks reported the record one-day drop of 95 points in the Dow Jones industrial average. But TV journalists and networks were not coordinated in interpreting the drop: ABC scarcely tried, NBC demanded action from official Washington, and CBS prophesied that Black Monday could well be followed by Black Tuesday. Market volatility viewed as "staggering" (being a record drop) to one network was "standard" to another, a mere "market correction." As the stock market seemed to snap back on Tuesday, October 20, TV news became more reassuring, but at the closing hour of trading there was another 57-point drop in the Dow. Network reports turned more alarming. Wednesday ushered in Graber's second stage of crisis coverage with another record drop, this time of 108 points in the Dow. The TV news quickly coordinated a coherent story—the market fall was "staggering" rather than "standard."

Less coordinated in TV news reporting of the Crash of 1987 were reports of the causes for the crash and prospects for recovery. Depending on what TV news network they relied on, viewers received a laundry list of causes: an international financial situation seriously out of balance; the "huge" U.S. federal budget deficit and/or debt; the U.S. foreign trade imbalance; the "sagging" U.S. dollar on foreign exchanges; threats of inflation in Japan, West Germany, and the United States; increases in long-term interest rates; "erratic" buy-and-sell practices by large institutional investors, such as mutual funds; and "high-tech mischief making" caused by automatic, computer-programmed sell-offs in stocks. Also depending on what sources the networks relied on for their information, TV viewers saw fantasies of disaster, warning, reassurance, or recovery. Thus, they learned from one "investment analyst" that coping with the crash was "like trying to catch a falling knife"; from a member of the Chicago Board Options Exchange that "if you don't time it just right" to sell or buy, "you can lose a lot of money"; from the U.S. Secretary of the Treasury that economic conditions "do not warrant 'Apocalypse

Now' worries or scenarios;" and from a corporate executive that "stocks will rebound smartly. Right now there's a buying opportunity."

In short, the fantasies in TV coverage of the Crash of '87 were sometimes confusing, sometimes contradictory, sometimes chaotic. This is not an indictment. Coverage of complex events requires quick, often questionable judgments. There is no leisure to verify all sources and information. The key is not *why* certain fantasies derive and chain out from such coverage but the *content* of the fantasies that are presented to TV viewers.

TV NEWS IN FANTASYLAND

Americans are indeed exposed to TV news. Findings from opinion polls indicate that since 1963 a higher proportion of Americans have named television as their news source than have named newspapers, radio, magazines, or other people. Four in 10 consider TV to be a sole source of news. Moreover, Americans regard television as a believable news medium. A nationwide poll asked people to rate "how much you think you can believe" each of several news organizations. More than 80 percent of respondents rated ABC, CBS, NBC, and CNN "highly believable or believable." Another survey reported seven of every 10 Americans expressed "a great deal" or "some" confidence in the press, radio, and TV.[3] Being exposed to and believing TV news are quite different from being informed by it. After examining a host of studies of how much people learn from TV news, a research group concluded that no study "indicated superior news information gain by television viewers when compared to the gain by users of the other media." In fact, in some cases "TV news viewers emerged as less well informed than nonviewers," a finding particularly applicable to "those who claim that TV is their main source of news."[4]

So we have an anomaly. The medium most Americans rely on, the one they find believable, does not inform them. Why do people use and believe yet are not informed by TV news? We think the answer lies in the content of TV news as fantasy. To explore that possibility, first we review briefly why people rely on the mass media for information generally, and second, we explore the characteristics of TV news that make it used and believable but not necessarily informative.

Media Dependency

In the introductory chapter, we noted that people are increasingly dependent on the mass media for their versions of reality. This is a major tenet of the dependency theory of mass communication.[5] Proponents of this theory argue that in simple cultures people's realities stem from their life histories, personal experiences, and social connections. As society grows more complex, opportunities for firsthand experiences with social and political institutions decrease;

moreover, resources for direct involvement are scarce. People have little direct awareness of what happens outside their immediate surroundings. Mass media become the chief source of information about society at large. People grow increasingly dependent on mass communication for visions of what is real and unreal. Under such conditions of media dependence, it follows that:

- The more dependent people are on mass media for information, the more likely they will change their opinions as a result of that information.
- The more mass-mediated information meets people's needs, the more dependent they are on it and, hence, the more influential the media.
- The more developed a society's media, the more people rely on it during periods of social conflict, crisis, and change.

Television has developed rapidly in the past three decades, with many consequences, two of which are especially noteworthy. First, as noted, people have grown increasingly dependent on TV as a news source. Second, the logic of television has become the logic of much of the mass media. But what is television's logic? Recall that we designated the logic of mediated realities as essentially a dramatic logic. Within that context each medium possesses a logic of its own, that is, a format for "how material is organized, the style in which it is presented, the focus or emphasis of particular characteristics of behavior, and the grammar of media communication . . . a perspective that is used to present as well as interpret phenomena."[6] We can readily see that TV's logic, or format, conforms to the melodramatic imperative described previously. That format also increasingly pervades newspaper and newsmagazine design. Think, for example, of newspapers with open designs—layouts that appeal to the eye, a clean look, color photographs, compact articles. *USA Today* is a prime example but so also are many metropolitan dailies. Or consider content. The logic of *People* magazine is largely that of television. The political men and women of *People,* like so many of the political figures covered on TV, are celebrities, people not known necessarily for achievements but "known for well-knownness."[7]

Does the melodramatic logic of TV apply to news programming as well as to entertainment programming? Is not TV news informative and true, TV entertainment fanciful and fictional? Our view is that the logic of TV news is every bit as melodramatic as that of television entertainment programming. It is the melodramatic logic of TV news that attracts audiences. It makes TV a major source of news for most Americans, the sole source for a plurality and a believable source to a vast majority. It is also the melodramatic aspects that contribute to TV news in "priming" its audiences. When people judge complex events, such as the Crash of 1987, they don't do so on the basis of everything they know. To apply everything one knows in making judgments is difficult, time-consuming, and costly. Instead, people economize; they consider what comes to mind, those bits and pieces of political memory that are accessible. Through fantasies portrayed in melodramatic ways, TV news is a key influence on what pops into the viewer's mind and what does not. Thus, even though it may not inform people (that is, provide them with factual details of events, and point out all the complexities and consequences surrounding them), TV news offers simplified visions *"priming certain aspects of national life while ignoring others,"* and thereby setting *the terms by which political judgments are rendered and political choices made."*[8]

TV News as Storytelling

In remarking on the mediated realities of Miss Sherwin of Gopher Prairie, journalist Walter Lippmann distinguished between news and truth. They are "not the same thing," he said. Wrote Lippmann, "The function of news is to signalize an event, the function of truth is to bring to light the hidden facts, to set them into relation with each other, and make a picture of reality on which men can act."[9] Hence, "journalism is not a firsthand report of raw material, . . . [but a] report of that material *after it has been stylized."*[10] And unless it can be clearly demonstrated that news deals with "accomplished fact, news does not separate itself from the ocean of possible truth."[11]

If news is not truth, what is it? The American philosopher George Herbert Mead provided one answer. He argued that journalism reports "situations through which one can enter into the attitude and experiences of other people." In that respect news is like drama. It picks "out characters which lie in men's minds," then expresses "through these characters situations of their own time but which carry the individuals beyond the actual fixed walls which have arisen between them."[12] For Mead most journalism was not information journalism, which deals with facts and truth, but story journalism, which gives us accounts of events we find emotionally exciting, aesthetically pleasing, and personally meaningful in our daily lives.[13]

If most journalism is story journalism, then TV news is certainly so. It is storytelling. Television news employs the logic of dramatic narrative through verbal and nonverbal symbols, sound, and visual imagery. Reuven Frank, former producer of "NBC Nightly News," has often been quoted as saying that every news story should "without sacrifice of probity or responsibility, display the attributes of fiction, of drama." Like drama, "it should have structure and conflict, problem and *dénouement,* rising action and falling action, a beginning, a middle and an end." For Frank these are "essentials of drama" and "essentials of narrative."[14]

TV news thus imposes on reported events a thematic unity consistent with the demands of dramatic logic, a unity that makes those events real-fictions. Real-fictions are compositions of sight and sound that select and organize facts in ways yielding a sense of purpose not otherwise present without the thematic unity imposed by the TV story.[15] The resulting real-fiction is at the same time an entertaining, larger-than-life drama that sparks people's interests, yet one that permits them to relate the larger-than-life to their everyday lives. Television news thus performs the task Mead assigned journalism, one of giving people the opportunity to soar "beyond the actual fixed walls which have arisen between them."

Hence, TV reporting is a literary act, a continuous search for story lines.[16] Such story lines may incorporate the metaphors and plots of novels, folk traditions, and myths. Some scholars argue that TV news stories appeal to broadcasters and viewers alike because of "mythic adequacy," that is, the degree that stories are deeply rooted in cultural mythology and exploit appealing aesthetic qualities.[17] Conformity to the requirements imposed by the melodramatic imperative, more than precision of informational content, is a key way that producers of TV news, anchors, and correspondents achieve mythic adequacy. The same melodramatic formats available to entertainment programmers are options for producers of TV news: Adventure, mystery, romance, pathos, nightmare, comedy, and the like pervade children's programs, sports coverage, soap operas, situation comedies, and docudramas. Faced with an event that requires prolonged storytelling—for example, a presidential campaign, the seizure of hostages in a foreign country, a threat of war, and so on—a variety of melodramatic formats can be adapted to news coverage, thus imposing a thematic unity (a story) on what might otherwise seem unrelated events.

TV news contains mythic elements. Communication scholar Robert Rutherford Smith analyzed the weekday evening newscasts of ABC, NBC, a public broadcast station, and a local TV station. He discovered patterns that constituted mythical narratives. Among them were the following:

- TV reports social reality by creating stories with men as the key actors; in most instances these men are government officials.
- Government, more frequently than any other group, is the actor in TV narratives.
- Government is also the group most frequently acted on.
- Women are treated as members of a mythical chorus, neither acting nor acted on.
- The actors are portrayed as making decisions, suffering through discomfort, and sometimes catching villains.
- The emphasis in the stories is on injustice, corruption, and the testing of strength—all common mythical themes.[18]

Smith observed that in the "place of sirens, demons, sensations of flying or falling," common elements in mythic tales, "we have a new narrative: political leaders as an omnipotent elite, beyond both marketplace and law, struggling with each other to determine the rules under which the rest of us must live." Concluded Smith, "The Greek gods on Mount Olympus were no less remote and only slightly more powerful."[19]

Different TV news networks may, of course, seek mythic adequacy by adopting different melodramatic formats. Hence, different news organizations cover identical events, yet tell different stories (again, *Rashomon*). For one it may be a tale of pathos, for another a heroic victory over great odds, for yet another a mystery to be unraveled. Regardless of content, however, each melodrama is a fantasy—a symbolic reality created and transmitted through the newsmaking process—that receives different melodramatic presentations by TV news networks offering diverse fantasies for nightly consumption. To the question, "To what can news be likened if not to truth?," one answer is fantasy, the captivating melodramatic creations of the news media that submerge events in an ocean of possible truth. To see how such storytelling and fantasy construction occur through TV news, we turn to four cases of TV's mediation of the realities.

FANTASIES OF ILLUMINATION IN TV NEWS

There is an oft-told tale about a drunkard who loses his wallet on the street late at night. Not knowing where to find it, he devotes his search to an area located under a streetlight. A passing stranger asks the drunkard what he is doing. "Searching for my wallet," is the reply. "Where did you lose it?," the passerby inquires. "I don't know," comes the answer. "If you don't know, why are you looking here under the lamp?," comes the question. "Because the light is better here!," grumbles the drunkard.

TV news coverage of events is often a drunkard's search. Reports focus on episodes easily pictured by the TV cameras and narrated with melodramatic logic. And TV news not only searches where the light is better, television journalists often see themselves as *the* light. When former NBC correspondent, executive, and presidential press secretary Ron Nessen remarked, "It isn't news until it's on NBC news," he spoke volumes about how TV journalists view their craft.[20] Things simply do not happen (that is, they are not news) until the light of the TV camera focuses on them. Likening the press to light—that is, with the task of clarification and en*light*enment—is not new. Walter Lippmann spoke of it in *Public Opinion* in 1922 well before television. The press, he wrote, "is like the beam of a searchlight that moves restlessly about, bringing one episode and then another out of darkness into vision."[21]

The restless searchlight of TV news frequently spotlights specific types of melodramatic episodes—episodes of celebration, crisis, conquest, crime, and contest.[22] *Celebrations* are news accounts of pomp and ceremony, ritual and performance; they stress the unity of a people's past, present, and future by highlighting custom, traditions, and icons. Coverage of presidential inaugurations, coronations of monarchs, the marriages of princes and princesses, Fourth of July festivities—all exemplify the celebration story. Threats to a people's lives, even the very existence of a way of life, from unexpected, extraordinary events constitute the substance of *crisis* coverage. Famine in Africa, the spread of AIDS, a worldwide stock market crash, or panic over the sales of poisoned pain relievers all produce crisis narratives. *Conquests* are accounts of heroic triumph over immeasurable and insuperable odds: Will the forces of good triumph over all setbacks? The U.S. manned landing on the moon in 1969 was such a story, as was the Allied landing on the coasts of Normandy, France, on June 6, 1944, the D-day conquest of Nazi strongholds. Melodramas of *crime* emphasize evil forces breaking the law, terrorists seizing hostages or assassinating victims, murderers and outlaws running amuck in an otherwise peaceful land. When Iranian terroists held U.S. embassy officials hostage for 444 days in Teheran from 1979 to 1981, TV news spotlighted criminal acts; the news coverage of the Iran-Contra hearings in 1987 focused on a crime of corruption. Finally, *contests* are reports of competition—between presidential contenders in party primaries, between presidential candidates in nationally televised debates, between nations of the Soviet and Western blocs in the Olympics, or between Democrats and Republicans in Congress.

In the remainder of this chapter, we consider the focus of the searchlight of TV news on four episodes—a national celebration, two nuclear crises, a thwarted conquest, and chronic criminality. In Chapter 2 we examine several cases of TV news coverage of contests in the American electoral arena.

A Guiding Light Fantasy: ABC's Coverage of the Liberty Weekend Celebration

> I must go down to the seas again, to the
>   lonely sea and the sky,
> And all I ask is a tall ship and a star to
>   steer her by.

Poet John Masefield (1878-1967) wrote this opening couplet of "Sea Fever" for the popular, not the political, media. But by July 4, 1986, his little rhyme was to take on considerable political content through ABC's coverage of the centennial of a restored Statue of Liberty.* The "star-spangled news package" was dubbed Liberty Weekend. "Never in my experience have so many reporters broadcast and written so much about so little," observed a media critic of the event.[23]

Without imaginative orchestration by a few and the presence of literally a cast of thousands, July 4, 1986, would have been just another holiday weekend. The pretext for celebration was the U.S. Department of Interior's unveiling of a refurbished Statue of Liberty. No matter that it would not in fact be the hundredth anniversary of the statue—that would come October 28, a pe-

---

*"Sea Fever" by John Masefield. From Roy J. Cook, ed., *101 Famous Poems* (Chicago, IL: Regnery, 1958; Chicago, IL: Contemporary Books, 1985), p. 96. Reprinted by permission of Contemporary Books, Inc.

riod of bright fall colors but little red, white, and blue. With Hollywood wizard David Wolper as producer, the cooperation of the news media, and considerable hype, out of such a nothing something was made.

In bidding for exclusive rights to telecast the celebration, ABC anted up $10 million. Betting that viewers would get hooked, ABC sold its audiences to commercial sponsors who paid top price. The network did not lack for full sponsorship in the almost 20 hours of coverage over live days, July 2 through 6. Every dollar invested in exclusive coverage of events—and preferred camera angles for nonexclusive events—yielded $3 for ABC in advertising revenue. Promoted as a presentation of "ABC News," the success of ABC's coverage was a lesson in the crafting of *news as entertainment* formats. "Liberty Weekend Preview," ABC's special shown on Wednesday, July 2, scarcely hinted at what was to come. It garnered a rating of only 10, a share of 20, and a ranking of 35 in weekly primetime program rankings. But consider the overall record for ABC's primetime coverage:

Evening	Rating	Share	Ranking
Wednesday, 7/2	10.0	20	35
Thursday, 7/3	19.9	37	1
Friday, 7/4	18.4	42	2
Saturday, 7/5	7.3	16	48
Sunday, 7/6	15.2	29	11

ABC's coverage on Thursday evening—which featured the lighting of the Statue of Liberty and star appearances by Kenny Rogers, Neil Diamond, Larry Gatlin, Elizabeth Taylor, Frank Sinatra, Shirley MacLaine, Gregory Peck, and others—was the top-ranked weekly program in Nielsen ratings. Both CBS and NBC failed by comparison. These networks covered only the lighting ceremony, President Ronald Reagan's speech, and the swearing in of new citizens by the Chief Justice of the U.S. Supreme Court. In the absence of nonpolitical celebrities, CBS programming received a rating of 7.7, a share of 14, and a ranking of 47; NBC fared better with a rating of 9.3, a share of 17, and a ranking of 39. ABC aired all that and more: Thursday morning a live, one-hour special to hype events to follow that evening, and on Friday morning, July 4, the armada and parade of ships in New York harbor, the latter winning a 13.5 rating and a share of 40.

Because ABC had exclusive coverage rights and hence served as the network of record for "Liberty Weekend," we examine here the network's five days of programming to illustrate how news coverage of celebrations constructs political fantasies. This is not to say that the other networks were not involved in fantasy-making. They were. For example, CBS anchor Dan Rather, open white shirt collar flapping in the wind, the Statue of Liberty basking in the sunset behind him, was ecstatic: "Good evening, and what a *great* day to be an *American*." NBC got into the act by adopting the Statue of Liberty as the logo for its "Nightly News." Yet, ABC's comprehensive programming offers the richest source of political fantasy for "Liberty Weekend."

What Does Liberty Look Like? As a preview to coming attractions, ABC anchor Peter Jennings described what "Liberty Weekend" would be about: an opportunity "to rededicate ourselves to the common values that the Lady, Liberty, represents." Five days later ABC had provided viewers with a panoply of fantastic symbols rendering those abstract, intangible common values visual, touchable, hearable, smellable, and—if we include one fast-food franchise's commemorative ads for its product—tastable. Looking at ABC's coverage, we ask a question that befits a visual medium: What does Liberty look like?

The network wasted no time in addressing the question. Its Wednesday evening, July 2, preview special consisted of four segments, each introduced by anchors Peter Jennings and Barbara Walters live from New York harbor and defining leitmotifs that were to reappear often. The first segment featured a filmed report by correspondent and resident pundit (see Chapter 8) David Brinkley. There were four major symbols of our independence, he said, as visuals appeared of each: the Flag, the National Anthem (a painting of Francis Scott Key appeared), the Washington Monument, and the Statue of Liberty. Three were our own creation, but the fourth was a gift. It was a gift meant to represent Liberty. Its donor (Edouàrd de Laboulaye) could not erect it in France because Emperor Napoleon III (twice wrongly identified in visuals with portraits of Napoleon I) would not permit it. How could sculptor Frederic Bartholdi physically depict Liberty? Said Brinkley, "In that time in Europe patriotic symbols ran heavily to paintings and sculptures of gaudily uniformed soldiers on horseback, half-naked women waving flags," (French painter David's *Liberty Leading the People* was the visual) "and all of this against a background of bronze cannons, smoke, and fire. The message always was that the new order was destroying the old, the new always assumed to be better than what it was replacing. Laboulaye did not want to see this in New York." So, Bartholdi invented a symbol, just as America had invented a form of liberty without destroying an old one. Hence, came the torch, the "light of Liberty," serving as a beacon for all seeking the common value of freedom.

Thus abstract liberty assumed physical form, Liberty's Lamp. Indeed, the official name of the statue is *Liberty Enlightening the World,* a heliotropic metaphor implying that Liberty is the very essence of the visual, namely, light. Or, as says Masefield's line from "Sea Fever," a "star to steer her by." But Liberty is light never achieved without sacrifice. Here entered the second of ABC's segments of its Wednesday evening preview special. Correspondent James Wooten described the *form* "ideas like liberty" take. The form is symbolic. In fact, more than three dozen visual symbols flashed on the TV screen during Wooten's report. From the Acropolis where the "idea" of Liberty was born to waving immigrants at Ellis Island, from the Parthenon to the Lincoln Memorial—all were shown as visualizations of Liberty, "a timeless dream." We "always struggle to give that idea substance," Wooten reported, an "idea whose perfect time seems always yet to come." An idea "so wispy, so flimsy, so fragile," that "our symbols" have only "nearly captured the idea," he said, adding that the Statue is the "second best equivalent," still short of capturing liberty itself. Put differently, the Statue embodies the fantasy of liberty.

It was not the Statue as Liberty that was to be the theme of "Liberty Weekend" but the Statue as light and as dream, metaphor and fantasy, as close as we can come to Liberty. Yet enlightened people can realize fantasies. Hence, ABC's third coverage segment on July 2, introduced by Barbara Walters. Eleven men and one woman received the first Medals of Liberty during the weekend ceremonies. They were "all immigrants," but they were "more than that." They were all achievers who had conquered obstacles to realize success. For Izhak Perelman, for example, it was freedom over physical disability. For Henry Kissinger, it was freedom over place of birth (i.e., the achievement of being the nation's first naturalized citizen to become Secretary of State). Each of the dozen winners was a physical, tangible demonstration of what Liberty looks like, namely, achievement over obstacles, realization of the dream.

"The Lady," as Peter Jennings referred to the statue for five days, is light, dream, success. And the Lady is also commerce and its preservation. Correspondent Hugh Downs provided that message in the fourth segment of ABC's preview coverage. The focus was the poet Masefield's "tall ships," sailing vessels of an earlier era. For Downs the tall ships symbolized Liberty by representing freedom of movement, the wind in their sails being a gust of Liberty. The ships and the sea on which they sailed were a liberation for land-locked peoples, taking them to vast harbors (as vast as that of New York, which all the naval fleets of the world could not fill) and promised islands—Liberty Island and Ellis Island, for example. Tall ships were the vehicles of Liberty and of America. In fact, noted Downs, without tall ships there would have been no America. Tall ships, however, were more than a means of travel for the landlocked. They were essentials of commerce. From the South Street Port, for example, American merchantmen dominated trade. Whalers provided the oil to light (more heliotropic prose) the lamps of Europe. The Yankee clipper "rushed miners to California" as well as made the English tea trade. And there was yet another liberating thing about tall ships. Even after being replaced as vehicles of travel and commerce, they became training ships for the U.S. Navy. Thereby they had another purpose, military preparedness to preserve commerce, the opportunity for success, the pursuit of the dream, and the movement of peoples toward the light that is the essence of Liberty.

Hence, in its preview special ABC's coverage of "Liberty Weekend" defined liberty's "common values." Liberty, as defined by ABC, seemed to consist of light, statues, successful people, ships, seas, islands, and vistas. The

Statue of Liberty symbolized light and dream, and because of its symbolic nature it was the prime icon of Liberty, according to ABC. Medal of Liberty honorees symbolized the realization of light and dream, thereby acting as the first in a long line of political and nonpolitical luminaries who were to symbolize Liberty during the weekend. Add to all this the fantasies of freedom in movement, vistas, commerce, and preparedness, and we now know that Liberty also looks like tall ships!

ABC's Gathering of Fantasies: Statues, Stars, Spectacles, and Ships. The leitmotifs appearing in ABC's preview special reappeared in subsequent coverage as distinct fantasies that, through the values associated with them and their associations with one another, "resembled" Liberty. The first and foremost was the Statue of Liberty itself (Peter Jennings would say "herself"), the symbol of Liberty as light and enlightenment. By associating the Statue (or a picture, design, logo, or other depiction of it) with a wide variety of other symbols, ABC's telecasts conferred a legitimacy on objects seemingly having nothing to do with Liberty. The fantasy construction was in two phases. First, the linking of the Statue of Liberty to two classes of objects, namely, ships and stars. That done, the next phase associated ships and stars with the cherished values that Liberty makes possible.

Tall Ships. Five hours of ABC's "Liberty Weekend" programming featured ships, the sea, and the vast panorama of New York harbor. Had John Masefield written in 1986, "All I ask is a tall ship," ABC would have more than fulfilled his request. With the Statue of Liberty on Liberty Island always in the background of the armada, the association of ships with Liberty could hardly be lost on anyone. And during the four hours of "Operation Sail '86" on the morning of July 4, ships of all kinds paraded by "to pay tribute to the Lady," as Peter Jennings put it. (A less awestruck anchor might have likened the day's events to a Christmas or New Year's Day parade, with ships substituted for floats approaching and passing the ABC reviewing stand.)

What then of the second phase of fantasy building, namely, the association of ships with Liberty's values? ABC began with a cherished sense of history. Through visuals and narration, viewers learned that it was ships that brought immigrants to these shores where they first saw the light of Liberty. But Liberty's light, ABC informed viewers, was not actually the *first* light that arriving immigrants glimpsed. No, that sparkle came from the beacon of a lightship far offshore. Historically, then, statues and ships have much in common: They both light the way to the promised land. ABC emphasized historical mission and discovery in other segments: reports from the former presidential yacht Sequoyah; the "feel of history" on the wooden decks of the USS *Iowa;* reports from aboard the Italian ship *Amerigo Vespucci;* information that the U.S. Coast Guard ship, the *Eagle* (which led the procession of tall ships) was a "prize of World War II"; and even a report that the Staten Island ferry still costs but a quarter to ride.

History teaches lessons. The lesson of ABC's coverage was, essentially, Thomas Jefferson's: "The price of liberty is eternal vigilance" and "a naval force can never endanger our liberties." Liberty is strength, or in Peter Jennings's words, the "power and equality to do as one pleases." No visual so caught the identification of Liberty with military strength as did that of the Statue and the USS *Iowa* side by side in the harbor (with Jennings referring to both as "she"). There were, of course, many other reminders: Viewers heard that the USS *New Jersey* had last fired her guns off the coast of Lebanon; that the USS *Mount Whitney* was the definition of technological preparedness; that the 16-inch guns of the USS *Iowa* could not be fired in the harbor lest too many office windows be shattered (interrupting commerce!); and that from this harbor Americans left to fight World Wars I and II.

If a nation walks softly and carries a big stick, Teddy Roosevelt's phrase repeated by Jennings, then ships translate into peace, friendship, and international cooperation. The harbor panorama of "hundreds of ships from all over the world" was visual proof that free people are a friendly people, that a naval force never endangers their liberties. To underscore the point, French President François Mitterand and his wife joined President and Mrs. Reagan in the tedious four-hour review of "Operation Sail," just as they had at the long unveiling ceremony the previous evening. Liberty, it seems, requires sound presidential kidneys in addition to naval strength.

"Stars to Steer Her By." To link light and achievement and Liberty and success, ABC's coverage celebrated celebrities—that is, stars. Masefield's stars "to steer her by" appear not in telescopes but in *People* magazine. The star-studded production of "Liberty Weekend" was filled with popular celebrities. The unveiling ceremony telecast on July 3 associated no fewer than two dozen celebrities with the *lighting* of the statue, the torch, and the fireworks extravaganza that closed the evening. That does not even count the key designed human experience of the evening: Ronald Reagan, who in his salutes, tributes, and solemnity appeared every bit the character he had portrayed in the patriotic movie *This is the Army* in World War II.

Four ABC telecasts focused solely on the celebration of celebrities (all against the backdrop of the Statue of Liberty, Liberty Island, the Liberty Torch, the Liberty Crown, or the Liberty Logo): the popular music concert on July 4 (capped by a 28-minute synchronized fireworks display lighting up New York harbor and almost dimming Liberty's Lamp by contrast), the classical music concert on July 5, the sports spectacular on July 6, and the closing ceremonies the same evening. The closing linked Liberty to entertainers (Kenny Rogers, Willie Nelson, the Temptations, the Four Tops, Liza Minnelli, and scores of others including 200 Elvis Presley impersonators!), political figures (George Bush), industry leaders (Lee Iacocca), laborers (the workers who restored the Statue of Liberty), and even a jetpack man who flew into the stadium. The evening's festivities closed with a spectacular *light* show wherein at one point the stadium totally darkened; then red, white, and blue flashlights spelled out "America."

Celebrities could represent Liberty, however, only if they were associated with the "common values" Liberty provides. ABC made the connections. One such value is achievement. Hence, actor Gregory Peck revealed how his grandmother crossed the Atlantic in steerage, yet he became a star. The most telling example linking stardom with success through freedom was that of dancer Mikhail Baryshnikov. Early in the evening of the unveiling ceremonies, Barbara Walters introduced a film report on Baryshnikov dubbing him "a success story of the eighties." Later, actress Helen Hayes introduced Baryshnikov who, she said, came to America "to be a success." Baryshnikov then danced "for the first time as an American citizen."

But celebrity is more than success; it is *étoile oblige*. With achievement goes responsibility. Lee Iacocca lectured on the virtues of volunteerism; the Fonz, Henry Winkler, told viewers never to forget our children; actress Elizabeth Taylor said that Liberty is sacrifice, as in World War II; actor Robert DeNiro introduced Chief Justice Warren Burger's swearing in naturalized citizens on Ellis Island with reminiscences of "the family" as a source of freedom, of America's hospitality to the foreign-born. Then, actor Sam Waterson portrayed Henry David Thoreau at Walden Pond urging that Liberty is nature and natural, imposing the obligation to dissent against infringements on Liberty. Or, as Barbara Walters yelled to make herself heard over the raging winds in the harbor, "In essence liberty is the ability to stand up for your own rights." Actor James Whitmore narrated a "Lincoln Portrait," adding Abe and equality to Liberty's common values. Finally, Frank Sinatra sang of "the house I live in . . . that's what America means to me," that is to say a domicile for all who follow the light to these shores.

Spectacles of Fantasy. Thus, through association with the Statue of Liberty those "known for their own well-knownness"[24] were, along with the statue, so celebrated as to take on fantasy status. ABC's coverage linked them to Liberty's values—responsibility, patriotism, sacrifice, the family and children, dissent, equality, and hospitality. And, just as celebrity symbols were transformed into walking embodiments of the Liberty fantasy, so too were ships and naval forces physical reminders of a sense of mission, strength, vigilance, peace, and friendship. No visual so well captured the finished fantasy of the continued pursuit of Liberty's dream and the stars that symbolize its realization than the TV picture of former actor and actress Ronald and Nancy Reagan, standing side by side aboard the carrier USS *John F. Kennedy* on the Fourth of July, the Statue of Liberty behind them, watching as 40,000 fireworks exploded around them and "the Lady."

At the close of its five-day coverage of "Liberty Weekend" ABC provided viewers with a final reprise, as if they needed it, of the major orchestrated events. With an unknown quickly to be known for her unknownness, Sandy Padek from Anderson, Indiana, singing the national anthem, ABC packaged the highlights of its coverage. In a six-minute clip viewers had a final reminder of what Liberty looked like. Liberty looks like the New York harbor; Ronald Reagan; an entertainment stage shaped like Liberty's crown; the Statue of Liberty near the USS *Iowa* and tall ships, unveiled by gradual lighting and surrounded by fireworks; the Chief Justice swearing in new citizens; a color guard; a flag raising; the New York Philharmonic; gymnastics and figure skating; the word "Liberty" spelled out on the floor of the Meadowlands; dancing; workers; bands; gospel singers; Shirley MacLaine; a jetpack man. Then, with the closing words of the anthem the final camera tightened on Liberty's Torch. "There isn't anything left to say, is there?," asked Peter Jennings. Indeed, there was not. Liberty celebrated was liberty idolized and commercialized, perhaps even trivialized.

A "Lights Out" Fantasy: TV Networks' Coverage of Nuclear Crises

Consider two serious events, both labeled as "nuclear nightmares" in TV news broadcasts but separated by seven years. The first began at 4:00 A.M. on the morning of Wednesday, March 28, 1979. Ten miles southeast of Harrisburg, Pennsylvania, sat Three Mile Island (TMI), locale of two nuclear power plants designated TM-1 and TM-2. The TM-2 plant was operating at 97 percent capacity. Suddenly a series of pumps feeding water through the steam generators of the plant, producing electricity and cooling the nuclear fuel core, shut off. Thus began the incident that became "the accident" that resulted in a major news crisis story. In the next month, the three major TV networks devoted almost 6½ hours of all their nightly news programs to coverage of TMI, only 1½ hours less time than they had devoted to coverage of all nuclear energy stories in the previous decade.

The second event occurred at 1:24 A.M. on April 26, 1986. During planned tests at the Chernobyl atomic power station, located in the Ukraine in the Soviet Union, two large explosions tore open reactor No. 4. Two people were killed, a dangerous graphite fire burned for two weeks, radioactive materials polluted the environment, and more than 95,000 people and 17,000 cattle were evacuated from the area. It was the world's worst nuclear accident to date. Again ABC, CBS, and NBC focused their searchlights on the scene, devoting approximately the same amount of time to Chernobyl coverage as they had to TMI.

The two nuclear accidents differed in certain respects, and so did aspects of news coverage. No explosion ripped open the reactor at TMI; there was no loss of lives, no massive release of fissionable materials, and only a precautionary evacuation of small children and pregnant women. The absence of physical and personal signs of damage at TMI, however, did not mean that any less anxiety was provoked by the accident. As a provost at a university located near the TMI plant later pointed out:

> Never before have people been asked to live with such ambiguity. The TMI accident—an accident we cannot see or taste or smell—is an accident that is invisible. I think the fact that it is invisible creates a sense of uncertainty and fright on the part of people that may well go beyond the reality of the accident itself.[25]

News of the accident at TMI broke shortly after the onset of the crisis. "Captain Dave," a traffic reporter for a local radio station picked up an alert from police and fire-fighting units and called his news director. At 8:25 A.M. the station reported the story. Television journalists quickly flocked to the site. First word of the accident at Chernobyl came in terse announcements from Radio Moscow and Soviet television stations two days after the explosion. U.S. television journalists had no access to the site and pieced together reports from filed film footage and secondhand reports.

Yet, differences aside, "coverage of Chernobyl in the U.S. news media was in many ways a replay of TMI."[26] We said earlier that in adapting to the melodramatic imperative different television news networks often use different melodramatic formats to achieve mythic adequacy. Recall Walter Lippmann's statement that news is not a firsthand report of what happens but a report of material after it has been "stylized." Close examination of how the three major U.S. TV networks covered these two nuclear crises reveals that each network—ABC, CBS, and NBC—had a distinctive style of coverage, first used at TMI and then largely repeated seven years later with Chernobyl. In short, stylistic differences persist despite changes in executive and production personnel, news anchors, field correspondents, and technicians at each of the three major networks.[27]

The Managerial Style of CBS Evening News. When faced with confusing happenings—rumors and facts in equal number, and conflicting statements from the same sources—different news organizations look for different "pegs" to hang their story on, different "angles" to pursue in reporting. In effect, on first trying to size up a situation, the journalists of a particular TV network ask questions that set them apart from their competitors. CBS journalists figuratively ask, "Where are the managers?" They want to know who is in charge (that is, who are "reliable" or "official" sources). They probe whether the officials, scientists, technicians, and experts agree. They seek facts, facts verified by copies of "official reports" and statements from "reliable sources." Correspondents relay those facts in a calm, dispassionate, reassuring way. The managerial melodrama evokes a vision of events that are awesome, even threatening. Yet, if the managers are indeed in charge, those events can be understood, coped with, and resolved.

In its 1979 coverage of TMI, CBS correspondents stressed factual information. Stories typically consisted of interviews with energy officials, scientists, and technicians. Correspondents reported from government offices, scientific laboratories, and medical clinics. The picture was, even in the midst of the confusion, one of managers hard at work, a vision of professional competence. Here were responsible members of the community, bringing technological dangers under control. Implicit was a reaffirmation of a faith in trustworthy elites, beneficial technology, and an orderly society. Reality is manageable.

The coverage of Chernobyl by CBS in 1986 also emphasized the role of the management of crisis but with a difference. Here was a situation with two sets of managers: Soviet leaders providing an "official version" of events, and U.S. and foreign officials, scientists, and technicians trying to make sense from afar of what was happening at Chernobyl. Adapting to the imperative of its emphasis on management style, CBS reported the Soviet official version. By retaining its focus on managers, however, it countered the official version with assessments of non-Soviet "experts" (five were so identified in a brief series of reports in one newscast). Hence, managers outside the Soviet Union were coping with crisis (an international management class) for which Soviet managers were accountable. Correspondent reports buried viewers in facts: assessments by experts on the precise probabilities of another such nuclear accident in coming years, estimates of the number of nuclear plants in the United States and the USSR, discrepancies in numbers of persons reported killed at Chernobyl, and so on. As at TMI, CBS emphasized technological concerns but did so by reporting flawed Soviet nuclear technology, which was labeled by CBS anchor Dan Rather as a "design for disaster."

Melodramatic logic requires a tale (the story) and listeners (in the case of TV news, the viewers), but there must also be a teller. In TV news the teller is the network anchor, assisted by correspondents of lesser stature. The news anchor announces and labels each story, reads brief reports, and introduces filmed, packaged, and correspondent reports. The format of TV news, with slight variations, is anchor-to-correspondent-to-anchor. How anchors and correspondents relate to one another defines the tone and style of the newscast.[28]

In the CBS style, the relationship of anchor to correspondent in reporting Chernobyl paralleled that of TMI. In 1979 anchor Walter Cronkite consistently employed alarming lead-ins to correspondent reports, in effect stressing that "Gee whiz! Things are bad." CBS correspondents followed with painstaking factual appraisals that "Yes, things are bad, but don't panic because the experts can manage." A much-reassured Cronkite would close with a comforting, "And that's the way it is." By 1986 the anchor and correspondents had changed at CBS, but the relationship remained the same. Anchor Dan Rather, looking intensely at the camera, introduced reports with alarm. And, as in the Cronkite era, correspondents returned calm, reassuring estimates of the situation that almost put a closing smile on the serious Rather visage.

The Victimage Style of ABC World News Tonight. If CBS news tries to make sense out of critical situations by asking where the managers of those situations are, the initial ABC question is "Where are the victims?" Victimage stories alarm, frighten, threaten, provoke anger, and sadden. Stressing fear and pathos, such stories tug at the heartstrings. Human interest reports emphasizing conflict, suffering, and personal loss are a key element of the victimage style. Even more central is the implicit message that those in charge (that is, the managers of whom CBS may make heroes in crises) are up to no good. The vision evoked is of troubled times brought about by managerial venality or ineptitude. The populace, with all good intentions, had best be on guard in the face of the menace of untrustworthy rulers out to victimize the ruled.

For ABC the accident at TMI was a victimage story. ABC combined metaphors, images, analogies, and verbal/nonverbal messages into an intense melodrama much like the fable of Frankenstein's monster. Where CBS trusted experts, ABC went instead to the townspeople, villagers, and schoolchildren. Human reaction to the event was the story, rather than the event itself. Typical reports pictured an on-the-scene correspondent facing the camera with the nuclear plant's cooling towers in the background. Visuals of empty schoolyards, residents leaving the area, milk cows grazing in the plant's shadow (for a story about possible milk contamination) evoked images of trouble. For ABC there was much to fear—radioactivity, toxic gases, poisoned milk, polluted water, hydrogen explosions, core meltdown, evacuations over clogged highways, and threatening wind currents. Reports of official reassurances carried skeptical overtones. Uncertainty, ambiguity, and fear were the leading motifs of ABC accounts.

As with the competing networks, ABC could not go to the site at Chernobyl and interview local townspeople, nor could they film the inconveniences and dangers the townspeople faced as victims of the worst nuclear disaster in history. This did not deter ABC from relating a tale of victimage, a melodrama of suspicion at Chernobyl. It did so by interweaving four themes. First, in a closed society, Soviet citizens were not being told of the real dangers of what had happened at Chernobyl. Soviet TV, unlike U.S. networks we must assume, focused no light but instead kept people in the dark. The Soviet people "have no sense of what is happening," reported one correspondent. Second, an uncaring Soviet bureaucracy had cut costs in its nuclear program. Hence, Soviet reactors had "no containment" (i.e., housing around reactors to shield against explosion and release of radioactive materials into the atmosphere), and they were graphite reactors that could produce fires impossible to control. Third, with no containment the explosion at No. 4 reactor had emitted fissionable materials into the air. That material, borne on shifting winds, was threatening unsuspecting citizens not only in the Soviet Union but in northern and eastern Europe as well (ABC regularly employed graphics to trace the movement of the menacing winds; competing networks also portrayed the location of radioactive wind by graphics but did not have the winds slowly *moving* east, north, and northwest.) Finally, ABC was not optimistic that the managers would extinguish the fire at No. 4 before disaster; there were "human consequences on an enormous scale" warned anchor Peter Jennings.

A discernible change in crisis coverage from TMI to Chernobyl did occur with a change of news anchors at ABC. In 1979 anchor Frank Reynolds of ABC led with a message of "Good grief! Things are bad and could get worse." ABC correspondents followed with a series of reports showing things indeed getting worse. In contrast anchor Peter Jennings in 1986 employed more restrained lead-ins, essentially replacing "Good grief!" with "Beware." ABC correspondents, however, were no less anxiety-provoking in 1986 than earlier.

Show-and-Tell Style at NBC Nightly News. The NBC stylizing of news addresses the question, "Where is the wizardry?" It combines two thrusts. One stems from the tradition of feature story journalism. Feature stories focus on context and the relationship between news events and larger issues. They narrate in a calming and reassuring style, not threatening and alarming. They show people that a variety of forces, some good and some bad, shape destinies. Features envision affairs neither manageable nor hopeless but people resigned to take what comes and resolved to make the most of it. The second stems from a didactic tradition. Didactic accounts stress explanation and education. They tell how things work, how they are built, how they can be used. The style is of the elementary school teacher breaking down complexities into simplified parts. Mysterious human contrivances and motives can be grasped, diagrammed, memorized. Once the magic is understood, the mystery gone, people survive.

For NBC the TMI story was part feature, part education. NBC devoted a majority of its coverage to features, another quarter to didactic reports. There was a division of emphasis between anchors and correspondents. NBC correspondents used features, lengthy interviews with groups of people—both experts and persons in the street. But people talked less to reporters than to one another. There was minimal editing of videotaped conversations. Talking heads (persons speaking directly to the camera in a rambling, uninterrupted fashion) were typical of NBC features. The didactic reporting by NBC anchors had two key characteristics. First, the anchors employed casual, measured speaking voices paced in low-key tones, punctuated with numerous pauses, and yielding an impression of detachment. Second, anchors strained to make complexities clear, combining professorial calm with colloquial expressions. Anchor John Chancellor took great pains—and much time—to explain visually how a nuclear plant is like a teakettle.

The combination of didactic anchors and feature-oriented correspondents made for an assuring, nonthreatening series of accounts about TMI. "Ah, shucks," say the NBC anchors, "things are bad but maybe not too bad if we learn how things work." To which NBC correspondents chorus, "Ho-hum, yes, things are bad but life goes on." Much the same style appeared in coverage of Chernobyl, even though Tom Brokaw was anchor. Visuals abounded. Whereas competitor networks showed film of the Soviet TV correspondents reading the "terse announcement," NBC added another "show" frill—a camera focused on a shortwave radio as Radio Moscow broadcast the message. And there was again an abundance of graphics. Twice diagrams showed how a nuclear plant works. One evening it was any nuclear plant; another it was specifically of a graphite-cooled nuclear plant. As at TMI, NBC spoke with groups of people and with spokespersons of groups—the Union of Concerned Scientists, the National Resource Council, and so on. And everything was reassuring: Whereas, for example, ABC found menace in the winds of the Ukraine, NBC saw no pattern, hence, no problem.

Three networks, three styles, three visions, three realities spanning two crises, two cultures, and seven years. CBS portrayed a world in which making sense of things means finding the managers; ABC looked to the beleagured masses; and NBC said look and listen for all is not lost. Were there to be another nuclear accident comparable to TMI or, worse, Chernobyl, would these three storylines appear again? One cannot say. But a recent study of Chernobyl quotes one advocate of nuclear power as saying that "within 30 years an accident like Chernobyl or Three Mile Island might be happening every year." So, "we will get used to them, and newspapers will report them on page 37."[29] If so, TV news will not report tham at all! Hence, with no TV searchlight on them, will we know they really happen?

The Light That Failed: CNN Reports a Thwarted Conquest of Space

For a quarter of a century the United States had been engaged in a successful, manned conquest of space. Fifty-six manned space missions without fatality was a record that spoke for itself. Yes, three astronauts had died in a fire aboard a space capsule in a training accident in 1967. Since then, however, Americans had landed on and explored the Moon, worked in space stations, and routinely shuttled back and forth from Earth to outer space. Then, shortly after 11:39 A.M. on January 28, 1986, in the skies above Florida on a crisp, cool day, America's conquest of space was thwarted. One minute and 15 seconds into its flight, in full view of gathered spectators on the ground, the space shuttle *Challenger* exploded off Cape Canaveral. All seven astronauts aboard died. There followed national mourning, a lengthy inquiry by a presidential commission, and an extended delay in the space shuttle program.

A New Kid on the Block. Shortly after the *Challenger* accident, all three major TV news networks began live coverage. In the manner of analyzing a college or professional football game, the networks offered slow-motion replays of the explosion—more than 50 of them over a five-hour period. "This is terrifying and fascinating," intoned the CBS anchor Dan Rather. "Here once again is the stop action," reported NBC's anchor Tom Brokaw. The words of mission control, "*Challenger,* go with throttle up," will remain "etched in memory," observed ABC's anchor Peter Jennings.

When the actual explosion occurred, only the Cable News Network (CNN) was on the air.[30] The Big Three had to play catch-up. CNN became the new kid on the block in 1980 as a 24-hour TV news service available to cable-TV subscribers and users of TV satellite antennas. Although reaching only a little more than a third of the households reached by any of the three major networks, CNN has grown in size and stature as a mediator of political realities. Once derisively called the "Chicken Noodle Network" (in a scramble to fill 24 hours of air time, programming was a potpourri of happenings), CNN gained a reputation for excelling at breaking news stories. Being a news network, CNN by definition has no qualms about interrupting scheduled programming to cover the outcome of elections, national nominating conventions, hurricanes, hostage crises, and so forth. In a four-year period, for example, one of CNN's anchors covered more than a dozen air crashes, noting that correspondents from the major networks have no such opportunity: "We'd have to retrain them in the techniques of dealing with stories that are breaking on the air."[31] For CNN the *Challenger* explosion was a breaking story. Once initial, breaking coverage was over, CNN continued to lead its primetime newscasts with follow-up coverage.[32] What light did CNN throw on the light that failed, that is, the *Challenger* disaster?

CNN's Drama of Mourning. Two communication scholars, Steve Goldzwig and George Dionisopoulos, examined how selected print media (for example, newspapers and news magazines) covered the *Challenger* accident. They noted the mythic quality of *Challenger's* crew and mission, how the astronauts had become "archetypal heroes" and how "the little bird that perched precariously near the huge twin booster rockets was a material embodiment of the spiritual quest for the conquest of the universe through knowledge of space."[33] In epic melodramas, heroes in mythic quests do not die—the Lone Ranger did not die in his quest to bring law and order to the western frontier, Captain James T. Kirk did not die in exploring where "no man has gone before," and, even though killed, Mr. Spock did not *really* die in the movie *Star Trek II: The Wrath of Khan*). Yet, aboard *Challenger* seven heroes did die. When persons die of old age or natural causes, the death is "appropriate"; it is generally accepted and the grief relatively subdued. The "inappropriate" death of heroes, however, produces a deeper, more profound reaction of grief. Goldzwig and Dionisopoulos found that, essentially, print coverage of the *Challenger* explosion and its aftermath constructed a grief fantasy that tried to explain how hero-astronauts could have died in so shocking a way.

In many respects CNN's reporting of the *Challenger* disaster also constructed such a fantasy. It was a melodrama in three parts. First was the live coverage of the explosion and the pronounced state of disbelief that it could occur. Second came a turning point where acceptance of the actual explosion set in, but the question arose "Why?" Finally, as memorial services for the astronauts were completed in the days following the accident, there followed a period of falling action, an acceptance that space exploration would continue in spite of—indeed, in a renewed way because of—the loss.

My God! It Can't Be True. CNN's primetime coverage opened on the evening of January 28, first with a replay of the explosion, then with a statement from the news anchor that combined motifs of mourning, conquest, and light: It was the "worst space accident since man began the search of the stars" and "most Americans and millions of people around the world have joined the mourning for the seven astronauts." The remainder of the newscast emphasized the disbelief aspects of the mourning fantasy, with occasional introductions of the "Why?" theme.

CNN followed the segment by replaying yet again the explosion, but this time there were extended visuals of the reactions of members of the crowd of spectators watching the lift-off. Featured were the reactions of the husband, mother, and father of Christa McAuliffe, the "teacher in space," who had won a nationwide competition to become the first civilian astronaut. Bewilderment was the pictured expression shortly following the explosion. As smoke trails from parts of the falling shuttle appeared, cries of "Oh, no" were heard. An unidentified woman yells, "Oh, my God!" In anguish, as if to deny the explosion's legitimacy, another unidentified woman points skyward and cried "No, they're up there!" Camera shots juxtaposed pictures of an empty sky and grief-stricken spectators holding and comforting one another, then slowly drifting away from the launch area. (This portion of the telecast was replayed in full at the close of the CNN newscast the same evening.)

As CNN's coverage continued, the mourning and conquest themes were joined again and again. CNN anchors spoke of the "grief of a nation," a "loss like a loss in the family," a "sense of loss, tragedy, and disbelief, even by those who had never flown into space," a "feeling like the loss of brothers and sisters," and "everyone feels the loss very personally." A CNN correspondent reported First Lady Nancy Reagan, who had watched the launch live on TV, as saying "Oh, my God, no!" The president spoke of "a national loss," and Congress took a "mournful moment of silence." As Goldzwig and Dionisopoulos had found in their study of print mediation, CNN's mediation dealt with inappropriate grief. These deaths were unbelievable because they were the deaths of heroes of conquest. "The crew knew it was opening the door to the future," reported one correspondent. CNN profiled each of the seven astronauts but devoted the bulk of heroic testimony to Christa McAuliffe. She above all personified the inappropriateness of the tragedy. A three-minute CNN profile closed with how she had "hoped to inspire others to reach out." Later in the newscast another correspondent reported a "personal note" recalling how the teacher-astronaut wanted to "reach out and touch the stars." Another report from Concord, New Hampshire, described the reactions of McAuliffe's students: a "lot of people, lot of grief, lot of shock."

"It All Makes No Sense." Having set up a melodrama of national mourning for fallen heroes, particularly the fallen heroine teacher, CNN coverage introduced a second theme—an attempt to make sense of it all, trying to explain why all this had happened. One reason things did not make sense, aside from the disbelief that heroes and heroines die, was that the nation "had come to take space travel almost for granted," reported the CNN anchor. Given the remarkable record of past success, a "long and rigorous study" would be required to find the cause of the sudden failure.

Although it was on the January 28 newscast, the search for a cause was largely eclipsed by the grief theme until the following evening's news. Now the search became the leading story as "shock was replaced by anger," to quote one correspondent. First, CNN reported the search for parts of the space shuttle in the waters off Canaveral. Second, "20,000 sensors gave no warning" of the impending accident; it would be necessary to "process mounds of data" to discover why. Third, the search might require a probe of the National Aeronautics and Space Administration (NASA) to identify bureaucratic ineptitude as a cause. Perhaps, speculated one correspondent, there might have been "promotion of space administration rather than space exploration" in all this.

The following evening CNN again led the newscast with the search theme. Although "finding answers to Challenger's explosion is like trying to find a needle in a haystack," the effort to "pinpoint" the cause was moving forward. CNN reported the discovery and recovery of a large piece of the spacecraft fuselage, the search for debris, and the work of a review board sifting through the data. In spite of memorial services planned and held across the nation, the grief theme gradually yielded to a quest for cause rather than space. It was then a small step to closure of the *Challenger* mourning: Life goes on.

They Did Not Die in Vain. Toward the end of CNN's second evening of *Challenger* coverage, a correspondent observed that "a space ship blown apart has brought people together." The theme of unity in loss was to take on greater emphasis with each succeeding day in CNN newscasts. It was time to move on from sorrow to rededication. Whereas CNN had reported on the evening of the explosion that the "loss of seven lives puts a cloud" over space exploration, three days later CNN stressed that the space shuttle *Discovery* was being prepared for its next mission (which, in fact, was delayed until October, 1988). With the appointment of a presidential commission to probe the *Challenger* disaster, a CNN correspondent reported that "officials are sure it won't happen again." The commission would probe what "caused the explosion" so that "future conquest of space can go on."

Thus, in a week's primetime coverage of the *Challenger* accident CNN constructed a melodrama of national mourning. Grief, shock, and disbelief were dramatized reactions to the impossible, the explosion, but even the impossible must be explained and grief assuaged by an effort to make sense of the loss. Naming a presidential commission reassured the grief-stricken that a search for cause and cure would be conducted in a deliberate and dispassionate manner. The results of the commission's inquiry would guide a people brought together by national mourning forward to further conquest.

We noted earlier that the likelihood we have not seen the last of such accidents as those at TMI and Chernobyl poses the possibility that should such crises become routine, TV news may hardly take account of them as newsworthy. Could the same occur in the conquest of space? A study for NASA estimates a likely shuttle crash every five years; there is a one in 70 chance that auxiliary power units required to control landings will fail. The three major TV networks and CNN remarked frequently that Americans had, before *Challenger,* taken space flight for granted. Is it possible that, in the face of future likely mishaps in space exploration, space disasters will also be taken for granted? Will losses in space conquest, like future nuclear disasters, also be the sound of a tree falling in a forest with no one to see or hear?

Tales from the Dark Side Fantasies: Terrorist Crimes in TV News

The events that make TV news—celebration of Liberty's rededication, nuclear crises at TMI and Chernobyl, *Challenger*'s thwarted conquest—have mythic adequacy. TV news throws light on them, not so much by explaining the complexities of what has happened but by identifying the events with deeply experienced cultural yearnings: freedom, achievement, and commerce in the case of Liberty; respect for, yet suspicion of, managerial authority with TMI and Chernobyl; hero worship surrounding *Challenger.* American TV news coverage of terrorist activities is also embedded in cultural myth, specifically, a recurrent fear of captivity.

Terrorist acts involve "the use of threatened use of anxiety-inducing, extravagant violence for political ends by any individual or group who is basically autonomous and unconnected with the agencies of state, when such action is intended to influence the attitudes and behavior of a target group."[34] Put simply, terrorists are outlaws, criminals. Crimes of any kind—robbery, murder, rape, and the like—are always newsworthy, as any TV viewer knows. Because of their rarity and unexpected qualities (attacks on authority, violent and melodramatic nature), TV news eagerly covers terrorist crimes. Terrorists know this and frequently commit their crimes specifically to draw the attention of TV cameras.

One form of terrorism has a special appeal to the cameras of American TV journalists. It consists of capturing persons (especially Americans) and holding them hostage for some ransom, booty, or consideration. Tales of captivity, authentic or fictional, have long held a fascination for Americans. Viewers of soap operas are familiar with a standard storyline—namely, the capture of the soap's heroine, who is held hostage for weeks of daily episodes and who finally through escape or rescue resumes her routine agonies of broken hearts, broken marriages, and broken lives.

Our nation had scarcely celebrated a quarter of a century of independence before a tale of political captivity broke. In the early 1800s the Barbary pirates (from Morocco, Algiers, Tripoli, and Tunis) preyed on U.S. ships, captured them, took crews hostage, and exacted tribute for their return. Angered that the United States had paid more than $2 million in tribute, President Thomas Jefferson dispatched a naval squadron to deal with the marauders. Legend has it that his firm action brought the terrorists to heel when Tripoli sued for peace in 1805. As is often the case, however, the mediated political reality (mediated in this instance by legend rather than TV news melodrama) is not altogether accurate. Pirates from the other Barbary states continued to seize vessels and crews and demand booty. It was not until after the War of 1812 that a stronger naval force sailed to the Mediterranean and forced the pirates to fall in line.

This legend from the beginning of the Republic says something about how TV news covers terrorist crimes today, especially why TV news turns its light on such tales from the dark side. Barbary terrorism endured for a long time. Stories of long duration appeal to TV journalists, who are attracted to continuing stories that go on for days, weeks, even months. Over extended periods, the drama can rise and fall in action—much like a soap opera—attracting viewers and building TV ratings as well. The better the ratings, the better the advertising revenue. In November 1979, Iranians seized staff and personnel stationed at the American embassy in Tehran. For the next 444 days, network TV news narrated a story unprecedented in melodramatic proportions: "The seizure of the American embassy was tailor-made for the American networks. Drama, conflict, international tension rising and falling, open and behind-the-scenes negotiations, American hostages, foreign mobs, oil production, hostage families, a stark and simple confrontation between two sides."[35] A former U.S. undersecretary of state commented: "Television played it like a soap opera, and made it the greatest soap opera of the year."[36] For the first 43 days following the seizure, the event was the lead story on all three TV networks' evening newscasts, two-thirds of each dealing with the story. ABC expanded its news coverage with a late-night series, "The Iran Crisis: America Held Hostage" (a title that certainly capitalized on the captivity fantasy alluded to earlier). The series was so successful that after the crisis ABC continued the format as "Nightline."

A captivity story of 444 days is extraordinary, but even shorter hostage crises have mythic adequacy. Armed Shiite terrorists hijacked a TWA airliner on June 14, 1985, forcing the plane to fly to Beirut, to Algiers, and back to Beirut where an American hostage was executed. Again the terrorists forced a flight to Algiers, then again to Beirut. Through it all, 39 Americans were hostage for 17 days while the hijackers demanded the release of 776 prisoners held by Israel. TV network news, in almost five hours of newscast time, covered it all in nightly newscasts, specials, interviews with friends and family members of the captive Americans, and with the terrorists and hostages during press conferences arranged by the Shiites. One of the most vivid scenes was an interview conducted by ABC's Charles Glass (who months later would be taken captive himself, then manage to escape). With pistol-waving hijackers in the background peering from the jetliner cockpit window, Glass talked with the pilot, first officer, and flight engineer. The visual drama was striking, a juxta-position of reassurance (the captives were alive, fatigued, but being treated well) and threat (the brandishing of weapons by grinning criminals).

In such terrorist-provoked crises as that of the TWA airliner, stories about hostage families are at a premium, so much so that network TV crews resort to trickery to interview hostage families. For example, in the TWA case one news team accosted family members in a hotel elevator. The reporter told them, said one family member, of a "new development." And, "if we gave him an interview, he would tell us what the new development was." Another hostage relative quoted the TV journalist as saying, "I'll tell you the latest about your family members if you give us an interview." The relative went on, "And I almost choked him. I couldn't understand how he could do that."[37]

The 444-day Iranian hostage crisis and the 17-day TWA hostage crisis are but two examples of repeated seizures of Americans reported by TV news in the 1980s. The abduction and disappearance of individual citizens, hijackings of airplanes and sailing vessels, threats to U.S. embassies—the list is long. What general assertions can be made about TV coverage? Here are a few:

- The captivity fantasy resonates through most TV reports.
- The terrorists, not TV crews, orchestrate the timing and locale of visuals.
- Personification, that is, telling the story by focusing on one or a few captives, is common.
- In the absence of statements from governing officials, rumors from "sources close to the terrorists" serve as the basis for news reports.
- There is an emphasis on reaction stories—for example, how members of the hostages families are "bearing up under the strain."
- Complex causes underlying terrorist acts receive minimal treatment; the play's the thing.

CONCLUSION: ACQUAINTANCE WITH, NOT KNOWLEDGE ABOUT

Seeing is believing, or so the adage goes. The adage makes no more sense applied to TV news than it does to direct personal experience. Television news offers plausible visions of reality even though they are mediated rather than firsthand accounts. In some ways they are even more believable. Experience, after all, often produces insoluble problems, complex solutions, a sense of confusion. The good, bad, and beautiful overlap; heroes, villains, and fools are not easily sorted out; what seems to make sense today may not do so tomorrow. Not so with TV news. The dictates of the melodramatic imperative call for a clear plot line, sharply delineated characters, simply defined problems, no confusion over causes, and tailor-made solutions.

Seeing is believing in TV news, but it is not knowing. Decades ago sociologist Robert E. Park wrote about the nature of news and of knowledge.[38] Park was a journalist before his teaching career; he had both a practical and theoretical grasp on things. What news does, he said, is give people an "acquaintance with" events. It does not provide a "knowledge about" them. A person is acquainted with something or someone when the thing or person is called to one's attention. It is a superficial relationship, such as being acquainted with the fact that Springfield is the capital of Illinois or with the checkout clerk at the supermarket. The acquaintance may be even more detailed than that, but it scarcely can be likened to an intimate understanding of events or persons. Knowledge, however, does imply a depth of understanding. To know a person is to be far more than a mere acquaintance. Knowledge implies familiarity with details of backgrounds, origins, implications, and consequences. Knowledge is not simply a glimpse but a theoretical grasp as well, a grasp of complexities as well as simplicities, of patterns and contradictions, of alternatives rather than single explanations.

There was no TV news when Park wrote. His distinctions, however, are even more valid today. Television news is an acquaintance medium, not a knowledge source. Nightly network news calls events and persons to viewers' attention and tells a neatly packaged tale about them. One can expect about as much knowledge from TV news as from any twicetold tale. Consider the cases of celebration, crisis, conquest, and crime described in this chapter. The unfolding melodramas captured viewers' interests, gave them a version or versions of what was happening, and a tidy resolution of any inconsistencies. Thereafter, each episode all but vanished from the news. Each had served its melodramatic purposes and having done so was no longer news. Just as one would scarcely claim to have gained knowledge of home construction from the fable of the "Three Little Pigs," one would hardly claim knowledge of what happens from TV news.

Television news provides single pieces of information on a daily basis. It unifies that fragmentary communication, not by building a body of understanding based on a testable theory that explains events, but by weaving bits and pieces into an appealing story. Unlike a scientific explanation that must account for diversified, even contradictory, facts, TV news is selective. What fits the plot line best receives emphasis; what does not, receives less coverage or is ignored. The appeal is not to understanding but to imagination.[39] Recall the quotation from Walter Lippmann with which we opened this discussion of TV news: The press "is like the beam of a searchlight that moves restlessly about, bringing one episode and then another out of the darkness into vision." Now we can grasp what Lippmann then went on to say: "Men cannot do the work of the world by this light alone. They cannot govern society by episodes, incidents, and eruptions."[40]

NOTES

1. Ravi Batra, *The Great Depression of 1990* (New York: Dell, 1988), p. 7.
2. Doris A. Graber, *Mass Media and American Politics* (Washington, DC: *Congressional Quarterly,* 1984), Chap. 8. For media coverage of Black Monday, see John F. Lawrence, "How Street-Smart Is the Press?" *Columbia Journalism Review* 26 (January/February 1988): 23–28.
3. For compilations of such opinion polls, see The Roper Organization, *Public Perception of Television and Other Mass Media* (New York: Television Information Office, 1988); Michael J. Robinson, "Pressing Opinion," *Public Opinion* 9 (September/October 1986): 56–59; and Laurence Parisot, "Attitudes about the Media: A Five-Country Comparison," *Public Opinion* 10 (January/February 1988); 18–19, 60.
4. John P. Robinson and Mark R. Levy, *The Main Source: Learning from Television News* (Beverly Hills, CA: Sage, 1986), p. 232.
5. S. J. Ball-Rokeach and M. L. DeFleur, "A Dependency Model of Mass Media Effects," *Communication Research* 3 (January 1976): 3–21.
6. David L. Altheide and Robert P. Snow, *Media Logic* (Beverly Hills, CA: Sage, 1979) p. 10.
7. Daniel J. Boorstin, *The Image: A Guide to Pseudo-Events in America* (New York: Harper & Row, Colophon Books, 1964), p. 57. See also William S. Maddox and Robert Robins, "How *People Magazine* Covers Political Figures," *Journalism Quarterly* 58 (Spring 1981): 113–115.
8. Shanto Iyengar and Donald R. Kinder, *News That Matters* (Chicago: University of Chicago Press, 1987), p. 4. Emphasis in original.
9. Walter Lippmann, *Public Opinion* (New York: Macmillan, 1922), p. 358.
10. Ibid., p. 347. Emphasis in original.
11. Ibid., p. 340.
12. George Herbert Mead, *Mind, Self, and Society* (Chicago: University of Chicago Press, 1934), p. 257.
13. See Edwin Diamond, "Disco News," *Washington Journalism Review* 1 (September/October 1979): 26–28.
14. Edward Jay Epstein, *News from Nowhere* (New York: Random House, Vintage Books, 1974), pp. 4–5.
15. Walter R. Fisher, "A Motive Theory of Communication," *Quarterly Journal of Speech* 56 (April 1970): 132. See also David M. Berg, "Rhetoric, Reality, and Mass Media," *Quarterly Journal of Speech* 58 (April 1972): 255–263, and Robert Darnton, "Writing News and Telling Stories," *Daedalus* 104 (Spring 1975): 176–194.
16. David L. Eason, "Telling Stories and Making Sense," *Journal of Popular Culture* (Fall 1981): 125–129.
17. John Shelton Lawrence and Bernard Timberg, "News and Mythic Selectivity: Mayaguez, Entebbe, Mogadishu," *Journal of American Culture* 2 (Summer 1979): 328.
18. Robert Rutherford Smith, "Mythic Elements in Television News," *Journal of Communication* 29 (Winter 1979): 82.
19. Ibid.
20. A discussion of other implications of Ron Nessen's statement appears in Dan Nimmo and James E. Combs, *Subliminal Politics* (Englewood Cliffs, NJ: Prentice-Hall, Spectrum Books, 1980), 171ff.

21. Lippmann, *Public Opinion*, 364.
22. Compare the typology used here with that for "media events" in E. Katz and D. Dayan, "Media Events: On the Experience of Not Being There," *Religion* 15 (1985): 305–314; and Gabriel Weimann, "Media Events: The Case of International Terrorism," *Journal of Broadcasting and Electronic Media* 32 (Winter, 1987): 21–39.
23. William Book, "Capital Newsletter: Star-Spangled Coverage," *Columbia Journalism Review* 25 (September/October 1986): 18–21.
24. Boorstin, *The Image*, p. 57.
25. Report of the President's Commission on the Accident at Three Mile Island, "The Need for Change: The Legacy of TMI" (Washington, DC: U.S. Government Printing Office, 1979), p. 81.
26. David M. Rubin, "How the News Media Reported on Three Mile Island and Chernobyl," *Journal of Communication* 37 (Summer 1987): 44. See also Timothy W. Luke, "Chernobyl: The Packaging of a Transnational Ecological Disaster," *Critical Studies in Mass Communication* 4 (December 1987): 351–375.
27. The material reported on TV news coverage of TMI is based on the authors' previous study; see Dan Nimmo and James E. Combs, *Nightly Horrors: Crisis Coverage in Television Network News* (Knoxville, TN: University of Tennessee Press, 1985). Comparative research data on Chernobyl are based on an unpublished study by the authors.
28. S. Sperry, "Television News as Narrative," In R.P. Adler, ed., *Understanding Television* (New York: Praeger, 1981), 295–312.
29. Luke, "Chernobyl," p. 369.
30. Ernest Leiser, "See it Now: The Decline of Network News," *Washington Journalism Review* 10 (January/February, 1988): 49–52.
31. Edward Diamond, Ellen McGrath, and Tatjana Cukvas, "Is CNN Now as Good as Its ABC/CBS/NBC Competitors?," *TV Guide*, March 15, 1986: 7–12.
32. The analysis of CNN's coverage of the *Challenger* accident is based on the authors' study of the content of CNN's "Primenews," January 28–February 3, 1986.
33. Steve Goldzwig and George N. Dionisopoulos, "Explaining It to Ourselves: The Phases of National Mourning in Space Tragedy," *Central States Speech Journal* 37 (Fall 1986): 180–192.
34. Weimann, "Media Events," p. 22.
35. Frederic B. Hill, "Crisis Management with an Eye on the TV Screen," *Washington Journalism Review* 3 (May 1981): 27.
36. George Ball, quoted in *Newsweek* (November 17, 1980): 57.
37. Deni Elliott, "Family Ties: A Case Study of Coverage of Families and Friends During the Hijacking of TWA Flight 847," *Political Communication and Persuasion* 5 (1988): 73.
38. Robert E. Park, "News as a Form of Knowledge," *American Journal of Sociology* 45 (March 1940): 669–686.
39. Robert Petrognani, "Politics as Imagination," *Communication* 5 (April 1980): 239–243.
40. Lippmann, *Public Opinion*, p. 364.

CHAPTER 2

A Man for All Seasons
The Mediated Contests of Presidential Campaigning

The airport fly-in is a staple of contemporary presidential campaigning. A candidate jets from city to city, hopscotching across the country, disembarking just long enough to give a quick interview at the airport, then flies off again for another interview at another airport—all in hopes of making the primetime newscasts in as many locales in a day as possible. There is nothing particularly novel about fly-ins or about much else that makes up presidential campaigning in the media age. Candidates for public office routinely employ a variety of spot advertising, minidocumentaries, lengthy biographical sketches, televised town meetings, call-in radio shows, and assorted electronic devices. Other propaganda pops up in brochures, newspaper advertising, billboards, yard signs, lapel buttons, bumper stickers, even—would you believe?—on toilet paper. Considerable time, money, and artistic talent go to convincing voters that each candidate is a man or woman for all seasons, capable of anything the times, situations, and constituents demand.

As candidates' propagandistic appeals are routine, so also is the coverage of election campaigns by the new media. Thus, for example, studies of recent presidential campaigns repeat what is becoming an old refrain: The news media devote more coverage to the horserace (who is winning, who is losing) than to the substance of the campaign, to the personae of the candidates than to the issues that divide them, to outcomes than to process, and to the day-by-day events of the campaign than to enduring trends.

Comedian Pat Paulsen has campaigned for president in a whimsical way. He satirizes airport fly-ins in a series of staged airport TV interviews. First, in Florida, an interviewer says, "Pat Paulsen has brought his campaign to the

Sunshine State. Pat, welcome to Jacksonville." Paulsen responds, "I'm really happy to be here. Flying over here looking at it, it's so beautiful. I really think that someday I want to settle down here in Jacksonville. The people are so hospitable. Not like people in California. There are a lot of phonies out there, but here in Jacksonville, these are real people." On the same campaign tour Paulsen faces another interviewer in Texas and responds, "I really dig Texas. These are the real people here in Texas, these are real people. They're not like the California people. I really think I want to settle down here in Texas some day." On to New York where Paulsen says in an airport interview, "I'm really excited about being back in New York. It's one of the most exciting towns in the world. This is where I want to settle down some day. Not like California, it's so spread out and the people out there, not like here. These are real people." Finally, candidate Paulsen ends his campaign swing in California, and says in an a farewell airport interview: "I've had it with the other states. It's really been a drag. I'm very happy to be back in California. These are my kind of people. These are real people out here. This is where I live and these are my people. . . . No more traveling. I'm going to stay here in California. I don't intend to go outside California anymore."

The skit ridicules the fly-in and all else that is ritualistic in contemporary contests for the presidency of the United States—staged interviews to fit all situations, sanitized statements to offend nobody, bland, noncontroversial personae. This chapter examines presidential contests, the rituals that constitute them, and how news reporting mediates presidential contests as rituals.

PRESIDENTIAL CAMPAIGN CONTESTS AS RITUAL DRAMAS

Along with stories about celebrations, crises, conquests, and crimes (all discussed in Chapter 1), accounts of campaign contests are a fifth type of happening brought out of the dark by the searchlight of the news media. Contests are regularly scheduled events between people or groups, and they are governed by set rules. Examples are ball games, chess matches, quiz shows, spelling bees, beauty pageants, elections, and even contests between rival bands, cheerleader squads, and pompom wavers. The question of interest is, "Who will win?" The battle between contestants takes on all the elements of drama; witness, for instance, a bowl game for a national college football championship or the college "Final Four" in basketball, the Superbowl, or the World Series. The drama piques the public's interest; they follow accounts of the contest avidly, and ratings of live TV coverage are high.

Much of the drama in a contest stems from the spontaneity of the action and uncertainty of the outcome. It is precisely that spontaneity and uncertainty in contests that create problems for news organizations covering them. The organizations spend vast sums of money in contest coverage in hopes of drawing large audiences. But if one side in the competition is overwhelmingly the superior (that is, the contest is a "blowout") or if all the contestants are relatively mediocre, people retune radio dials, switch TV channels, and turn to the comic pages. As a hedge on their investments, news organizations do two things: They hype and ritualize their coverage.

Hype "can be most usefully defined as the merchandising of a product—be it an object, a person, or an idea—in an artificially engendered atmosphere of hysteria, in order to create a demand for it, or to inflate such demand as already exists."[1] Add event to object, person, or idea, interpret "atmosphere of hysteria" as one of melodrama, and we have a definition that will serve us. Hype is the hard sell—for example, the two-week build-up to the Superbowl, promotion of the season-ending cliff-hanger on "Knots Landing" or "Dallas," or the labeling of primary elections in southern states in 1988 as "Super Tuesday." The aim is to reinforce the possibilities of dramatic uncertainty even in the face of a routine, predictable outcome.

A *ritual* is simply a series of acts that, for the most part, people regularly and faithfully perform time and time again. Attending religious ceremonies, administering the oath of office to public officials, playing the national anthem before sporting events, saluting the flag—all exemplify public rituals. When the elements of a drama repeatedly relate to one another in a ritualistic fashion, we have a ritual drama. Numerous examples come readily to mind. The formulas of romance novels are ritualistic (young, beautiful, lonely girl meets lean, masculine, mysterious man, and the plot unfolds in predictable ways). Also ritualistic are the formulas of daytime soap operas ("All My Children" or "Santa Barbara"), feature comic strips ("Mary Worth," "Apartment 3-G," etc.), and even TV game shows ("Wheel of Fortune" or "Jeopardy").

Oriental theater is a good example of ritual drama that also says something about politics. Oriental drama not only entertains but repeats myths, legends, and stories of why things are as they are, why people and gods do as they do. The dramas sometimes feature people, sometimes puppets. In either case, they are ritualistic, conforming to the audience's demand that the same stories be told over and over in precisely the same ways. One form of ritual drama is the seasonal ritual. Just as the rotation of spring, summer, fall, and winter seasons brings a sense of continuing renewal of nature, dramas of seasonal ritual give a sense that the nation is reborn. The drama brings together the ideals, principles, and aspirations of a people, recalling what they stand for and what they can achieve. The seasonal ritual revives the vitality of a population, reminding them anew of their greatness.

Scholars who have studied ancient civilizations have argued that government might have originated in ritual, that the first kings were skilled in ritualism and magic.[2] There is certainly a ritualistic quality in much of our politics. For example, presidential elections can be likened to seasonal rituals that seek "periodically to renew" America's "vitality and thus ensure its continuance."[3] They consist of dramatic confrontations, each side fantasizing an ideal America either lost but to be regained, or one yet to be found. By renewing the belief that the story will have a happy ending (that is, that the contest can be won and greatness can be found or regained), the seasonal ritual of the presidential campaign plays out its quadrennial scheduling.

In those campaigns most discussion and speeches, writes political scientist Murray Edelman, "consist of the exchange of clichés among people who agree with each other. The talk, therefore, serves to dull the critical faculties rather than to arouse them. Participation of this sort in an emotionally compelling act in which each participant underlines its reality and seriousness for every other is the most potent form of political persuasion."[4] Notice the similarities between Edelman's description of politics and the TV soap opera. In soap operas the characters exchange clichés, often in agreement with one another; the viewer's critical faculties dull; a façade of reality and seriousness prevails; and, yet, it is all emotionally compelling. Presidential campaigns bear another likeness to soap opera in that they seem to be endless. No sooner does election day come than the next contest for the presidency begins, if in fact it did not start during the previous campaign. For example, hours before the Tuesday election day in 1988 Jesse Jackson announced that if his party's nominee, Michael Dukakis lost, Jackson would seek the presidency in 1992; the 1992 presidential campaign begins "on Wednesday," said Jackson.

As a recurring, emotionally compelling, seasonal ritual, the presidential campaign possesses all the requirements of melodrama. No wonder, then, that the news media (especially TV news) adapt coverage of campaign contests to the requirements of the melodramatic imperative. Sensing this, as we shall see later in this chapter, candidates adjust their persuasive appeals to melodramatic requirements. The principal media—TV, radio, newspapers, and newsmagazines—program their contest coverage as a continuing story, running coverage of separate events and piecing them together within the context of a unifying theme, perhaps with catchy gimmicks to remind audiences of the thematic unity. Continuing news of ritualized presidential contests is particularly suited to a dramatic format: introduction, rising action, turning point, falling action, *dénouement*. Each phase of the presidential election coverage, from preprimaries to postelection analysis, is a minidrama using the five-part structure. The overall scenario is roughly preprimary introduction (beginning at least a year before the presidential election), rising action in caucuses and primaries, a turning point with the selection of party candidates, falling action (but with varied levels of intensity) during the general election campaign, and resolution on election day.

The New, Improved Fantasy: Rituals of Candidate Labeling in the Preprimary

Campaigns in the media age place a premium on the projected qualities of newness, freshness, and innovativeness. Advertisers in sales campaigns take products that have been around for decades—be they soft drinks, laundry soaps, pain relievers, or whatever—and label them "new" and "improved" in hopes of sprucing up their images. Much the same holds in politics. Every four years in presidential politics there is a search for the new face, the candidate projected to voters as fresh and innovative: Jimmy Carter was the new face of 1976, shopworn by 1980 when the now forgotten John Anderson was the new face; Gary Hart was the candidate of "new ideas" in 1984 but victim of an old flaw by 1988 (see Chapter 4); new face Michael Dukakis became a loser with George Bush's victory.

In the introductory scenes of the news media melodrama that take place well before the presidential primaries, two things occur—both essentials of the melodramtic imperative. One is that news attaches labels to candidates that characterize them as new or old, as heroes, villains, or fools. Such characterizations inform readers and viewers how to think about the *dramatis personae* of the seasonal ritual. Critic Kenneth Burke has noted that all journalism is a creative and imaginative work that sizes up situations, names their elements, structure, and outstanding ingredients, and "names them in a way that contains an attitude toward them."[5] Here are some all but forgotten news stereotypes, coined before the primaries, of unsuccessful candidates for the Democratic nomination for president: "a tall and witty former professional basketball player" (Morris Udall, 1976), "surviving member of Camelot favored to unseat the incumbent" (Teddy Kennedy, 1980), "ruggedly handsome, Kennedyesque exponent of new ideas" (Gary Hart, 1984), and, "charismatic but unelectable proponent of change" (Jesse Jackson, 1988). How did the news media stereotype the Democratic nominees before the primaries in each of these years? Jimmy Carter (1976) was a "soft-talking, evangelist-sounding peanut farmer, Jimmy Who?"; in 1980 he was "a beleaguered president seeking re-election;" in 1984 Walter Mondale was an "intelligent, experienced politician but not charismatic, fighting an up-hill battle;" and in 1988 Michael Dukakis was a "well-financed, high-tech governor, the rather dull worker of economic recovery."[6]

Such characterizations relate to a second aspect of the melodramatic imperative of campaign news coverage: the unveiling of expectations, when ritualistic coverage labels who are serious contenders, who are not; who is leading, who is trailing; who can win, who will lose. Because a melodrama is a simplification of complexities, the imperative demands that, if there are a large number of candidates entering the contest for a party's nomination, they must be reduced rapidly. Lead and supporting players must be established quickly. Otherwise the plot line is confusing; audiences may leave the theater. The news media use several means to divide serious players from extras: opinion polls, assessments by experienced politicians and observers, the status of each candidate's campaign organization, who is supporting whom, the size of the contenders' financial war chests, even the amount of coverage the media themselves give respective candidates.

The solemn pronouncements emanating from such indicators are sometimes flawed, however. Take opinion polls as an example. For more than half a century (since 1936) pollsters have been trying to get a handle on who might become each major party's candidate by taking the public pulse months in advance of actual nomination. What has been the record? Exclude all incumbent presidents seeking re-election (in polls taken at least one year before the contest they normally are favored for renomination). Since 1936 the Republican record is clear-cut: In 11 cases the frontrunner one year before the campaign survived to become the nominee eight times; in 1940 there was an unexpected nominee (Wendell Willkie); in 1952 and 1976 poll data were too confounded to say precisely who was favored to win the nomination one year before the contest. Democrats are less consistent. There was an unexpected (by polls) nominee in 1952—Adlai Stevenson. Four years later Stevenson, the frontrunner in early polls, again won the nomination. In the 1960, 1968, and 1988 campaigns when a Democratic incumbent was not seeking renomination, polls a year before the primaries yielded such mixed results as to offer little guide to mediating expectations. In 1984 the poll frontrunner, Walter Mondale, received the nomination. But in 1972 and 1976 the withdrawal of Ted Kennedy from consideration as his party's nominee rendered poll projections before the primaries meaningless.[7]

Another indicator—the amount and type of coverage of candidates by TV news in the preprimary period—works at cross-purposes in mediating expectations. Essentially, candidates who receive the most coverage also receive the most negative coverage, at least if 1988 is any indication. From February 1987 to the end of that year nightly network TV news devoted over 11 total hours to coverage of the upcoming 1988 campaign. During that time, more stories were devoted to Gary Hart than to all his Democratic competitors combined. News evaluations of Hart were decidedly negative, however, far more so than those of other candidates. Almost half of all stories about Republican candidates were about George Bush, but the coverage was more negative than that of any other Republican contenders. Who had the most positive coverage? Jesse Jackson, who did not receive the Democratic nomination, and— for the GOP—Robert Dole and Jack Kemp, both of whom lost to George Bush.[8]

Yet, the news focus, be it through polls or TV coverage, does confine attention to relatively few candidates before the primaries. It thereby mediates expectations in a more indirect way than merely predicting who will win, who will lose. Voters pick up a theater program by reading newspapers, magazines, and watching TV. "Here are the major characters, here are the minor," in the melodramatic contest to unfold. Or, "watch this contest, not that one," for that one, because it will not be covered, will not exist.

The Beauty Pageant Ritual: Caucuses and Primaries

Be it "Miss America," "Miss USA," or whatever pageant, there is a ritual to beauty contests. Such pageantry is a time-honored tradition in the United States. Pageants begin with local, then state, contests that select winners and send them forth to the nationally staged-for-TV event. At each successive level, they introduce themselves and shake hands; make short speeches describing their backgrounds, express how "thrilled I am to be here," thank their families and friends for how far they have come, and describe their respective "life visions"; parade in various costumes; display talents for the piano, twirling, dancing, and the like; appear before judges in small discussion groups, hoping to display their knowledge and poise; and submit themselves to interviews, responding with carefully prepared and rehearsed "spontaneity." All does not always go as expected. Outside forces intervene (a ripped evening gown, a sprained ankle), peril besets the contestants, some hopes are dashed and others raised, contradictions develop between what contestants want, what is, and what is to be. The ritual of the beauty pageant thus has its melodramatic features.

It does not demean the importance of what the candidates are doing, or the significance of the caucuses and primaries they take part in, to liken them to beauty pageants as ritual dramas mediated by news coverage. In a carefully orchestrated schedule timed for various caucus and primary states, candidates—like beauty contestants—introduce themselves, offer standardized statements, explain their vision for America, wear costumes appropriate to the setting (hard hats outside factories, billed caps on the farm, Stetsons in the Southwest), display their talents, debate in candidate forums, submit themselves to interviews, and endeavor not to offend. As beauty contestants have their advisers, hairdressers, makeup consultants, speech coaches, and so on, so too do candidates have their campaign managers, speech writers, media consultants, and other personnel. (Think of them as experience brokers—recall our introductory chapter—designing experiences for candidates.) Again, all does not go as hoped, outside forces intervene, fortunes rise and fall, careers advance or perish. And as in the beauty pageant staged for TV, the candidates play continuously to the local, state, and national TV cameras. What one political observer has said of melodramatic coverage of caucuses and primaries applies to beauty contests as well: "The entire melodramatic apparatus of TV news is designed to single out one politician and lift him up to the heights of power and glory. Television loves a winner, a man of the people, the hero of its story."[9]

Although TV coverage of beauty and candidate-nominating contests obeys certain rituals and melodramatic imperatives, there is one key difference in the relationship of the media to the contests themselves. Beauty contests are centrally organized and orchestrated by pageant sponsors who determine which contestants will be featured, and when, in public appearances and before reporters and cameras. Miss Iowa, Miss New Hampshire, Miss Texas, or Miss California is not free to promote her candidacy for Miss America without pageant approval. When presidential candidates travel to Iowa, New Hampshire, Texas, or California, however, they compete for news coverage and for victory, which they hope will carry over to other caucus and primary contests.

Media coverage of presidential contests adds two features not found in beauty contests: alloting news coverage and bestowing "momentum."

Although many candidates are called for news coverage, few are chosen. Candidates vary widely in how much they are covered by journalists, which is not to say that campaign success and amount of coverage are correlated. Rather, in the mediated world of presidential politics there are two parallel contests: the contests of the "visible" candidates, those taken sufficiently seriously by the news media to attract journalists' attention, and the contests of the "invisible," who get little coverage. Consider the 1988 presidential contests. On the eve of decision in the first major contest, the Iowa caucuses, George Bush and Robert Dole were the visible GOP candidates. Combined, they received more than two hours of coverage across ABC, CBS, and NBC newscasts. By contrast, the invisible candidates—that is, the four rivals of Bush and Dole for the nomination—received only slightly more than a half hour's combined coverage across the three networks. On the Democratic side, Richard Gephart and Gary Hart waged the visible campaign (an hour of combined network coverage); the five candidates waging the invisible campaign had less than an hour of combined coverage.

Ritualistic coverage of presidential melodramatic contests has a second aspect. Sometimes it moves candidates from the invisible to the visible campaign. Unlike beauty contestants, candidates compete not only against one another but against a phantom candidate named "Expected." "Expected" is the percentage of the vote—based on estimates of opinion polls—the news media anticipate and report that a candidate will receive. The expected vote serves as a standard for measuring success or failure, victory or defeat. If a candidate gets a higher proportion of the vote than expected, the mediated reality is of "exceeded expectations;" if a lower percentage, the reality was "disappointing." Recognizing this, candidates try to manage media coverage of "Expected," by poor-mouthing their chances, much the way a football coach whose team is contending for a national championship agonizes with reporters over his problems. The goal is to mediate a reality of exceeding expectations in order to seize "momentum" in the unfolding campaign drama.

For underdogs in the invisible campaign, to exceed expectations, then claim momentum, can make the invisible visible. Just as exceeding expectations produces momentum, momentum produces news coverage. As far back as 1976, Jimmy Carter's campaign in Iowa provided a textbook example. Said one of his advisers of the Iowa caucuses, "We knew the thing was going to be covered. Politics is theater. We planned for that."[10] Once Democratic caucus contests were over in Iowa in 1976 more delegates remained uncommitted to any candidate than the number Carter had won. Yet, the fact that "Jimmy Who?" received a plurality of committed candidates became The Story of Iowa. Reported one TV correspondent: "The candidate with that highly prized political momentum tonight is Jimmy Carter."[11]

Since Carter's triumph, however, the mediated "Big Mo" (momentum) has proved fickle. George Bush in 1980 achieved a two-percentage-point victory in Iowa's GOP caucuses, jumped in preference polls, but lost the nomination to Ronald Reagan. In 1984 Gary Hart, by finishing second in Iowa to Walter Mondale, exceeded expectations. Yet he received only 2,000 votes more than George McGovern, who also exceeded expectations. The media focus fell on Hart, not McGovern. Hart challenged Mondale for the nomination but lost. Big Mo's fickle fortune smiled in various ways in 1988. Robert Dole won in GOP Iowa but did not exceed expectations; then he was "disappointing" in New Hampshire. George Bush wrapped up the nomination shortly thereafter. For Democrats the Iowa winner, Richard Gephart, performed *only* as expected; he soon found himself ignored by the news media and shortly left the race. So too did Gary Hart's race after his "disappointing" showings in Iowa; then New Hampshire gave him invisible status. Who then caught the gold ring of Big Mo for the Democrats? Michael Dukakis garnered at least Little Mo from Iowa, but it was Jesse Jackson who, by doing "better than projected" in Iowa, became labeled a "serious" contender. A later victory for Jackson in the Michigan caucuses produced the mediated reality of the Democratic campaign: the visible contest between Dukakis and Jackson who had outlasted the invisible men.

In sum, the mediated realities of the caucus and primary phase of presidential contests combine rituals of the beauty pageant with rituals of media coverage, defining expectations and awarding momentum. There is a pattern to mediated campaigns: (1) Early coverage defines visible and invisible candidacies; (2) early tests of strength between contestants produce clear-cut winners and losers; (3) these outcomes bestow degrees of momentum on candidates designated in news coverage as winners by having exceeded expectations, momentum that may redefine visible and invisible campaigns; and (4) future campaign contests conform to the newly written pageant scenario.

Celebration Rituals: National Nominating Conventions

Although the overall story of presidential campaigns is one of ritual contests portrayed as melodrama, a celebration story is contained within it. That story pertains to mediated realities of national party conventions, mediations that celebrate the two political parties and TV news alike. Before the TV era, the national conventions of the Republican and Democratic parties had clear-cut purposes: nominating candidates for national office, drafting a party platform, mobilizing and rallying support for the party candidates at all levels, and serving as the governing assemblies for each party. These purposes began to change after 1952. That year both parties selected Chicago for the site of their conventions. One reason was highly tangible: The air-conditioning capacity of the amphitheater was the equivalent of a 165-pound block of ice for each delegate, a boon in the summer heat and humidity! A second reason was more important and foretold of things to come. At the time, Chicago was a strategic TV center, a factor that figured prominently in the calculations of planners of what was to be the first truly national video conventions.

As the political parties evolved after 1952, the national teleconventions assumed new roles. Statewide caucuses and primaries are now the focal point of the nominating process, party platforms (although sometimes stirring convention squabbles) are drafted in advance of the convention, candidates and their media consultants mobilize their own bases of support and often do so independently of party efforts, and delegates assembled in conventions ratify the decisions of their party leaders. Delegates are but extras in the carefully orchestrated TV pageant. Today's conventions have other functions: They celebrate the candidacies of nominees hitherto outside the established party order, such as Jimmy Carter in 1976; they project an illusion of national unity among diverse, conflicting interests; and they provide ritualistic expressions of compromise and accommodation.[12] To the degree that the presidential selection process can be likened to beauty pageantry, party conventions are akin to that part of the pageant telecast that is devoted to recognizing the pageant's rich traditions, honoring former pageant winners (former party nominees), and associating the pageant and its commercial sponsors with the nation's sacred values of family, deity, and country.

Contemporary teleconventions are national primetime spectacles that benefit both the political parties and the news media that cover them. For example, they are showcases for local and network TV stations eager to promote their minicams and satellite technologies, as well as their on-air news teams. Party differences aside, both Democrats and Republicans want to put on a show of celebration for a national audience. Success allows each party to celebrate an appealing public image of a caring, compassionate, consistent, competent institution, not a gaggle of self-serving, divisive party hacks. That image translates into votes at the polls, dollars in fund raising, the recruitment of attractive candidates for future contests, and the long term loyalties of politically involved Americans. So, too, do TV news organizations seek a show of celebration. For them, success means to celebrate an image of providing entertaining, yet responsible, accountable, competent journalism. That image translates into larger audiences that can be sold to advertisers for big dollars.

The party celebration and the TV network celebration differ; that is, parties and networks do not agree on what are the mediated convention realities. Yet, parties and networks get to tell their respective stories. The party tells its story through its orchestration of convention events, events televised live and uncut by each party's network of cable TV stations and by the Cable Satellite Public Affairs Network (C–SPAN). What is the party story? It is a podium story; it is the party business, speeches, prepared films, accolades, and celebrations that occur at center stage on the podium. Democrats and Republicans differ in minor details; the former devote more time to floor demonstrations, the latter to keeping to a tight schedule. Both parties select as convention sites mammoth arenas suited to TV exposure—in 1988 the Omni in Atlanta, the

Superdome in New Orleans. Both parties open with a keynote night that is devoted to party oratory, followed by a platform night with speeches devoted to specific issues and to showcasing up-and-coming party stars, a third evening to nomination night, and a closing acceptance celebration. Scarcely are there breaks in the carefully contrived party rituals.

Podium events, floor demonstrations, and party films are decidedly not the mediated realities of TV network coverage of national conventions. Only about 40 percent of the three networks' broadcast time at conventions involves podium events; demonstrations are but a backdrop for banal chitchat between network anchors and correspondents; and party films are rarely aired. Advertising breaks account for a large portion of the major networks' teleconvention airtime. Whereas the convention rites of the two parties differ little, those of the three major TV networks contrast sharply. ABC features discussion between its anchors, correspondents, and analysts. Teleconventions showcase the "ABC Team." At CBS no candidate for either party nomination, no floor correspondent, no convention activity reaps the airtime harvested by anchor Dan Rather. Whether interviewing guests, chatting with analysts and floor correspondents, or just musing, the CBS story is the Dan Rather Story. The NBC coverage consists of featurettes, a mediation of the convention as a fragmented, diverse, pluralist series of happenings that have no boundaries—labeled in the network's 1988 coverage as the "convention without walls."

"Let's You and Him Fight": Debating Rituals

Beginning in 1960, then featured regularly since 1976, has been another key dimension in the seasonal ritual that is the presidential election contest: the televised debates between presidential candidates. They take a variety of forms. During the caucus and primary acts of the ritual melodrama, candidates meet in forums—that is, they come together to respond to questions from interrogators and from one another in front of TV cameras and live audiences. So routine have these become that it is a rare evening during prenominating contests that one cannot find a candidate forum on network or cable TV channels. More highly publicized are the TV debates between party nominees. A key rationale for these debates is that they give voters an opportunity to size up the candidates, their qualities, and their positions on issues and, thus, enable the voters to make a more informed choice than if they had to rely solely on news-mediated or candidate-mediated fare. Watching candidates go at one another ("let's you and him fight"), however, has become a mediating ritual in its own right, one that provides yet another means of fantasy creation and chaining. In fact, presidential debates provide an ideal forum for candidates to espouse their rhetorical visions through ritual.

For one thing, presidential debates are scarcely spontaneous, unrehearsed confrontations. Considerable thought goes into deciding whether to challenge an opposing candidate to debate or whether to accept a challenge. Thus, a predebate debate between candidates' advisers takes place in the news media over whether to debate at all and, if so, how many times. Once that matter is resolved, elaborate negotiations between advisers work out details of attire, rostrum sizes, makeup, lighting and camera angles for TV, the format of the debate, who will participate, location, time, and so on. Indeed, as little as possible is left to spontaneity, so little that a sponsor of the 1988 presidential debates—the League of Women Voters—withdrew sponsorship, protesting the contrived nature of the media events. Moreover, a debate is normally supposed to involve a conflict or argument over a clearly defined proposition. Each side speaks to that proposition for an alloted time, has an opportunity to rebut and interrogate the opposition, and sums up its position. Presidential debates never involve clearly defined propositions. At best, the point at issue is vague. It boils down to "there should be a change." The ins should be replaced by the outs, but there is limited direct exchange over that implicit proposition. Instead, the basic format consists, with variations, of questions asked of each candidate by a panel of journalists, each candidate responding or counterresponding but rarely confronting each other. Although follow-up questions by panelists and candidates, or follow-up comments by the candidates, are part of the debate format, candidates seek to sidestep them. What comes from the candidates' lips are "grooved responses."[13] "Grooved" refers to what one would get if a phonograph needle were placed in a recording groove, that is, a pat, predictable response generally borrowed from the candidate's standard speech made throughout the campaign. In sum, the grooved response is a re-run of the candidate's rhetorical vision.

How informative are presidential debates? A 1988 nationwide poll found that 84 percent of Americans said that their choice for president would be influenced by how the candidates performed in TV debates.[14] That performance, however, is closely akin to that of contestants in the closing moments of a beauty pageant. Consider the similarities: The pageant is presided over by a celebrity emcee, usually a well-known TV star. Presidential debates have celebrity hosts as well. For example, Jim Lehrer, Robert MacNeil, and Judy Woodruff, all well-known TV newscasters—served as moderators in the 1988 debates. Celebrities also constitute the panel of judges at a beauty pageant. They frame the questions to ask contestants, decide when to award points, and provide an aura of serious respectability. In presidential debates celebrity journalists comprise the panel conducting the joint interview of candidates. Their presence signifies that the debates are serious, not frivolous. Pageant contestants devote hours to proper makeup, posture, and stance; so too do presidential candidates preparing for a debate. Beauty pageants are divided into segments—talent competition, evening gown competition, bathing suit competition, and so forth. Presidential debates set aside segments for questions on foreign policy, defense policy, and domestic policy. The studio audience at beauty pageants may applaud favorites but not be unruly. Moderators admonish studio audiences at presidential debates to "restrain" demonstrations of support for candidates. And at beauty pageants the finalists have an opportunity to state their "goals in life," "goals for America," or what they will try to accomplish "during my reign." At presidential debates, each candidate has time for a closing statement, a summing up of the candidate's vision for America and what the candidate plans to accomplish during the presidential reign.

Although the outcome of a beauty contest may be in doubt until the emcee announces the winner, the orchestration of the pageant itself is carefully planned, rehearsed, and timed to the last second. The goal is to produce "good television." In many respects presidential debates are intended to be good television as well. Advisers thoroughly brief candidates on likely questions, frame appropriate answers, even provide one-liners and humorous diverting remarks.[15] They are "handlers" of contenders much as boxing managers handle their fighters. Candidates carefully rehearse their answers and performances with stand-in opponents. They so finely tune their performances that the key problem they face in debates is not with knowing the answers but with guessing the questions to which they will give their memorized responses. The realities of presidential debates imitate their own mediation, mediation through pageantry.

"Waiting for Godot": The Anticlimax of the Election

In any melodrama the unveiling of the mystery proves more absorbing than discovering that the butler did it; rising action seems more intriguing than falling action. In the mediated realities of presidential campaigns, the news protrayal of nomination politics is of such intensity that the general election seems almost an anticlimax. So much so, that waiting for the election to be over is like "waiting for Godot," who never comes. There is small wonder. The Who-Will-Win?, How-Did-He-Win?, Where-Does-He-Stand? stories of the nomination minidrama set the stage, rhetorical visions, and fantasies for much of what is to follow. The preformed stereotypes afford the basis for the What-Is-He-Really-Like?, Who-Is-Ahead?, and the What-Difference-Does-It-Make? stories on the general election campaign.

Falling action is only relatively less intense than rising action, however. Ritualistic though postnomination politics may be, it still can have its exciting moments, or at least they can be seized on as such and dramatized to draw and entertain an audience. The melodramatic imperative dictates a focus on the unusual, the novel, the extraordinary. Frequently, this is the campaign *gaffe*—the error of fact or judgment, the injudicious remark, the off-color joke, or some other *faux pas*. Such items are trivial on reflection, but they are a godsend to journalists striving to convert the daily humdrum of a campaign into appealing fare. This is not to say that such *gaffes* are insignificant or unimportant to many voters. Perhaps they are. Rather, the general election campaign *dénouement* in recent mediated melodrama has stressed two fantasies. One fantasy is that the heroes who emerge from the crowd during the contests are heroes no more, just the last two left standing. They are idols with feet of clay, mere mortals perhaps not qualified to be president. The fantasy of rags to riches yields to a ship of fools. The second fantasy derives from one final requirement of the melodramatic imperative of ritualistic campaign coverage—characterizing the overall plot of the general election, labeling it, and criticizing it. The mediated reality of the last four contests follows:

1976: Two nice, well-meaning, largely unknown and faceless men, average in achievement and vision, seek the presidency (Carter and Ford). What difference does it make? Ho-hum, how dull.

1980: Carter lacks the strengh and vision to make a difference; Reagan's proposals, although tenable, will never clear Congress. What difference does it make? Ho-hum, how dull.

1984: Reagan's not vulnerable; Mondale doesn't play on TV; nice guys finish last. What difference does it make? Ho-hum, how dull.

1988: NBC's "Nightly News'" John Chancellor, *five months before* the election: "Two of the dullest presidential candidates in memory. . . . decent, honorable, and quite boring men." Ho, hum. Need we add, What difference does it make?

Thus entertained for more than a year by the soap opera rituals and pageantry of presidential contests, the audience gets to take part in the play's outcome on election day and thereby provides the final resolution. Half of them leave the theater (do not vote); others half-heartedly wander on stage (vote aimlessly); a minority are avid performers (they care who wins). Paul H. Weaver sums up the overall impact of the news media on those of us who are "captives of melodrama." He writes, "At its best, journalism is a kind of window on the world, one that offers an inevitably limited but useful view of what is going on." But, he goes on, "At something less than its best, journalism is a screen on which deceptive images dance—today's seeming truths, tomorrow's undoubted foolishness." (Recall Plato's anecdote about the prisoners in the cave.) "The problem," Weaver notes, with TV news (and we believe with other media as well) is that, "in its enthusiasm to expand its viewers' sense of the world, it has tended to transform its window into a screen, preventing the people and their representatives from seeing each other unvarnished and unmediated."[16]

THE MAN WHO . . . : HYPE AND HOPE
IN PRESIDENTIAL CONTESTS

Mystery writer Gregory McDonald, creator of the *Fletch* series, one of which became a movie starring Chevy Chase in the title role, wrote a book called *Fletch and the Man Who*. The story concerns Fletch's adventures as press secretary to Governor Caxton Wheeler, candidate for president. The title comes from the widely used ritual of introducing presidential candidates to audiences as "The man who . . ." (will, has, promises, or whatever). The ritual is a variety of the hype we mentioned earlier in this chapter. It typically links the candidate to cherished cultural values—for example, "I give you the man who, like us, knows what it is to work for a living!"

We have noted that some fantasies chain out so widely, become so durable, and are so believable that they become part of a nation's culture. They are myths. One such political myth in America is the presidential myth that endows the office with greatness and power. The person who holds the office is "president of all the people." And regardless of the problems facing a sitting president and the failures of the incumbent in dealing with them, every four years hope springs eternal that a "new face" or the "right man" will restore the office and make it again the nation's salvation as it was with Washington, Jefferson, Lincoln, Wilson, Roosevelt, or any other member of the presidential pantheon.

We said that myths can lend legitimacy to fantasies that conform to them. Myths can also give rise to fantasies. Such is the case of the presidential myth. It inspires among the public the fantasy that it does make a difference who wins, who loses. Among journalists, it yields fantasies that issues should divide candidates, candidates should campaign on issues. But they do not. Hence, there is no real difference, thus giving rise to the "What difference does it make? Ho-hum" coverage of the election *dénouement*. The public and the press are not alone in having fantasies. The presidential myth even inspires fantasies among the candidates about being president—that they are "presidential timber," that they project a "presidential image," that they are "presidential" and will solve the nation's woes. Candidates, of course, are in a position to act out their fantasies. They dramatize their fantasies by creating rhetorical visions. These visions appear over and over again in each candidate's propaganda. Each speech, brochure, position paper, slogan, TV and radio advertisement, and so on is a carefully crafted effort to portray the candidate's rhetorical vision. Such crafting is an artistic enterprise. Hence, campaign propaganda—that is, hype—is an example of *fantastic art,* the use of artistic devices to promote a candidate's rhetorical vision of his presidency. If successful, the candidate's fantasy chains out to become the fantasy of the news media and the voters as well.

Campaign propaganda aims at mediating two closely related, overlapping fantasies. First, propaganda constructs fantasies about the candidate, his qualities, qualifications, program, and destiny. Second, propaganda mediates realities about the nature of the world, the array of forces, dangers, threats, and enemies that must be confronted and vanquished. The linkage of the two fantasies is essential; the destiny of the candidate becomes the destiny of the political world.

An entire industry now exists to construct such fantasies, craft appropriate propagandistic artifacts for them, and espouse each candidate's rhetorical vision. This industry of experience brokers, of "propartists," consists of professional hypesters with a variety of specialties and skills.[17] They are, for instance, organizers, fund-raisers, pollsters, TV producers, filmmakers, advertisers, public relations personnel, press secretaries, hairstylists, and all manner of other consultants. The industry has developed an aesthetic style consistent with the artistry of modern advertising. Three devices in that artistry are particularly key mechanisms: positioning the candidate, fashioning the image, and provoking projected identification.

In commercial advertising *positioning* places a product at a particular point or with a particular stance as a means of distinguishing it from competing products that, in substance, are strikingly similar to the product being huckstered. The attempt is to carve out a share of the market, but it is not the unique traits or qualities inherent in the product that are stressed. Rather, advertisers mold a picture of the product as being distinct because of the people who buy or consume it. Beers are an example. Many are indistinguishable in taste. Yet TV ads alert us that former athletes favor Miller Lite, Bud Light is the beer of partying people—whether the "partying animal" Spuds MacKenzie—and Coors Light is for persons of discriminating taste, such as actor Mark Harmon who appears in the brew's TV ads.

Positioning thus targets a segment of a market—consumers who want to "be like" athletes, partying people, the new generation, or other groups. A product's *image* consists of qualities associated with it, and they include packaging, appearance, design, taste, or other advertised characteristics that marketers think buyers will find appealing. There is an old saying that makes the point: "You don't sell the steak; you sell the sizzle." For instance, when Coca-Cola sought to refashion the product's image, there appeared the "New Coke." Many consumers of the "old Coke" caught up in the marketing campaign clamored for a return of the former product. Marketers obliged. Now there is the "Classic Coke" (the old cola, but with a more sophisticated, traditional image than it had before) and "New Coke. Think about It."

This example says something about mediating realities through images. The process is not one-way. Consumers' impressions of products' qualities derive only in part from advertising hype; how buyers compare advertised preference with their own wants, needs, values, and desires makes a difference. Consumers often project onto objects qualities that as buyers they want to find in them *even when the objects themselves lack those qualities.* This is the process of *projected identification.* Such projection is childlike, as when a child stacks cardboard boxes to form a playhouse; adult insistence will not change the child's view that it is a "house." Think of the TV ad depicting a couple dining in "one of the world's finest restaurants." They sip their coffee with discerning pleasure. Up pops a hypester, intruding on their dinner, to announce that the brew is an "instant" brand. He has interrupted not only their intimacy but their fantasy of projected identification, which is that a fine restaurant would serve only the finest coffee brewed from freshly ground beans.

How does all this relate to politics? Many of the techniques of campaign propaganda derive from commercial marketing schemes. Consider the characters of Frank Bartles and Ed Jaymes. These two homespun, good old boys appeared in TV ads for a wine cooler (they were paid nonprofessional actors). In each ad Frank would tell a little yarn, hyping the wine cooler along the way, as Ed puttered about. Frank would end the pitch with "Thank you for your support." Frank and Ed symbolized the targeted market segment—ordinary, unpretentious people not accustomed to wine. Frank's tale and Ed's actions provided an equally unpretentious image for the cooler. Some gullible viewers sent money to Frank and Ed to help them pay off their nonexistent "mortgage," again projected identification. The producer/creator of the Frank and Ed fantasy, Hal Riney, employs similar techniques for political advertising. In 1984 he produced the "It's Morning in America" theme for Ronald Reagan's campaign. Here too the emphasis was on cherished values, downhome scenes, and homespun people. The group targeted by positioning? People "just like us." The imagery? Family members hugging each other, portrayals of respect for the elderly, trust in the police, and so forth. Projection? An announcer closes with "America today is prouder, stronger, better. Why would we want to return to where we were less than four short years ago?"

In the end, the overarching fantasy formed through the mediation of campaign hype is one of hope. Presidential contestants differ with, criticize, bicker at, and attack one another. But through it all if they are to bind themselves to the presidential myth that it does make a difference who wins, who loses, they must enunciate a rhetorical vision of hope. Granted, once the election is over the hope may be dashed, but the melodramatic imperatives of the campaign demand a rhetoric of hope. In 1960 John Kennedy's message of hope was to "get America moving again"; assassination darkened the vision. In 1964 Lyndon Johnson hoped for a Great Consensus; when he left office there was a seriously divided nation. In 1968 Richard Nixon's hope was to "bring us together"; he later resigned when corruption pulled his administration apart. In 1976 Jimmy Carter hoped to restore trust and provide a "government as good as its people"; those people did not re-elect him. In 1980 Ronald Reagan's vision of hope was a return to an American golden age, a restoration of old values;[18] after eight years the gold seemed tarnished with chronic problems of drugs, terrorism, and budget and trade deficits. Whether the hope for a "kinder and gentler America" espoused by candidate George Bush will mark the nation of President George Bush remains to be seen as the presidential melodrama unfolds.

THIS IS AS REAL AS IT GETS

We realize that there will be readers who will disagree with our assessment of presidential campaigns as seasonal rituals of fantasies, rhetorical visions, pageantries, and melodramas. Surely behind these shadows are real candidates deciding on really important issues that make a substantial difference in who is elected president. Perhaps. We contend that it is more likely that there are several realities to each "real" candidate, several realities to each candidate's stands, and several realities implied in the difference it makes as to who wins and loses. For most of us, that multiplicity of overlapping and contradictory realities is simplified, shrunken to a mediated reality for each presidential campaign. That mediation follows a logic that consists of the constraints placed on candidates, journalists, and voters by the melodramatic imperative and the fantasies and rhetorical visions that parallel it. It is not a choice between a mediated, melodramatic election and a real election. As an oft-repeated ad slogan says, "This is as real as it gets."

Other critics observe that it is "trivially obvious and thoroughly misguided" to regard elections as melodrama. It is obvious, presumably, because elections have always been thought to be, and criticized as, melodramatic. (The horse race metaphor, for example, dates back to the elections of Andrew Jackson.) And it is misguided, presumably, because it fails to take seriously the myth-enhancing rituals of elections; "the real characteristics of elections are the recurring themes, the banal appeals, the dramatic incidents, and the personal images" rather than dispassionate, reasoned discussions of policy alternatives.[19] To such an overall criticism we respond yes and no. Yes, the melodramatic character of elections has long been noted and criticized, but that has not prevented generations of Americans from believing that a given melodrama was the only game in town and being misled accordingly. And, yes, the myth-enhancing features of melodramatic elections are indeed the "real characteristics" of those contests. Granted that elections are not, could not, and perhaps should not be policymaking exercises in America. But if policy choices are not at issue, as they are not, then other choices are: Which fantasies, rhetorical visions, melodramas, and myths are voters to accept? Which political destiny is their destiny? Which candidate envisions it?

Put differently, taking seriously the myth-enhancing rituals in presidential contests means taking into account a feature of ritual that distinguishes it from ceremony, which is that "ceremony simply indicates or recognizes, but ritual transforms."[20] As ceremonies, presidential pageants indicate the candidates, their qualities and positions, choosing between them, and voting. Like getting married for the sake of one's parents or a legal necessity to do so, however, elections as ceremonies have little lasting meaning. Once the ceremony is over the participants go about their business unchanged, unmarked. But ritual transforms. Rituals tap, reflect, and intensify deeply held values, ideals, and desires. Taking part in rituals is an emotional, not just mechanical, experience. Those married through ritual change, are bonded, are made different by the exchange of vows. Similarly, in profound and often unnoticed ways, the rituals of presidential contests change the candidates, journalists, and citizens because ritual mediation teaches us things. The question is: Does it teach us useful things or mind-numbing things?

If we are to begin as citizens to address that question, then perhaps the required skills for citizenship must be more than those taught in civics texts—being interested and motivated to political discussion and activity, acquiring political knowledge, being principled, and reaching choices by rational thinking. Perhaps instead citizens must become critics—drama critics, rhetorical critics, speech critics. They must be able to look beneath surface rituals; they must be able to identify what the melodramas are, how they are portrayed, who the performers are, and what they are trying to do. Thus prepared, citizens can undertake the crucial task of evaluating fantasies, rhetorical visions, and melodramatic rituals. Thereby they might not only demand more of candidates, campaigners, and journalists in the election melodrama but also of their own acting performances as well.

NOTES

1. Steven M.L. Aronson, *Hype* (New York: William Morrow, 1983), p. 23.
2. A.M. Hocart, *Kings and Councillors* (Chicago: University of Chicago Press, 1970); Sir James Frazer, *The Magical Orders of Kings* (London: Dawson of Pall Mall, 1968).
3. Theodor H. Gaster, *Thespis: Ritual, Myth, and Drama in the Ancient Near East* (New York: Henry Schuman, 1950), p. 3.
4. Murray Edelman, *The Symbolic Uses of Politics* (Urbana: University of Illinois Press, 1964), p. 18.
5. As paraphrased by James W. Carey, "The Communications Revolution and the Professional Communicator," in Paul Halmos, ed., *The Sociology of Mass Media Communication* (Staffordshire, England: University of Keele, 1969), p. 36.
6. For other labeling of previous candidates, see James David Barber, ed., *Race for the Presidency* (Englewood Cliffs, NJ: Prentice-Hall, 1978), p. 115.
7. Dan Nimmo, "Handicapping in the Early Campaign: Frontrunners, Dark Horses, and Also Rans in the Polls," *Political Communication Review* 11 (1986): 19–32.
8. "The 1988 Election: The Preseason," *Media Monitor* 2 (Washington, DC: Center for Media and Public Affairs, January 1988).
9. Paul H. Weaver, "Captives of Melodrama," *New York Times Magazine,* August 29, 1976, p. 51.
10. Jules Witcover, *Marathon* (New York: Viking Press, 1977), p. 202.
11. David L. Paletz and Robert M. Entman, *Media Power Politics* (New York: Free Press, 1981), p. 35.
12. James W. Davis, *National Conventions in the Age of Reform* (London: Greenwood Press, 1983).
13. Lloyd Bitzer, *Carter vs. Ford: The Counterfeit Debates of 1976* (Madison: University of Wisconsin Press, 1980).
14. Poll reported by Michael A. Lipton, "Campaign '88 and TV: America Speaks Out," *TV Guide,* January 23, 1988, p. 3.
15. Myles Martel, *Presidential Campaign Debates: Images, Strategies, and Tactics* (White Plains, NY: Longman, 1983).
16. Weaver, "Captives of Melodrama," p. 6.

17. Gary Yanker, *Prop Art* (New York: Darien House, 1972).
18. John Kenneth White, *The New Politics of Old Values* (Hanover, NH: University Press of New England, 1988).
19. W. Lance Bennett, "Myth, Ritual, and Political Control," *Journal of Communication* 30 (August 1980): 178.
20. William P. Harman, "Reflections on What Ritual Does," *The Key Reporter* 52 (Spring 1987): 2.

CHAPTER 3

The Re-Presentation of History in Popular Culture

We are all aware that we live in time, but we can extend our experience of time by using memory of the past and imagination about the future. Thinking about the past or future is often only idle daydreaming but not always. The past and the future are *fantastic references,* imaginary times that help shape our conduct in the present. We all mediate the present by using the past and the future as fantastic references. In the theater of our imaginations, both what we think *did* happen and *will* happen become relevant for what we think *is* happening.

People never know either past or future accurately. Memories of personal pasts are imperfect, limited, distorted, even idealized as much by what one wants to remember as what one can. The future, which has not occurred yet, can scarcely be predicted with perfect fidelity. Many persons look back on their past with nostalgia, making it far happier than it actually was. Many dread the future, making it worse in prospect than it actually turns out. Much of what a person knows of the personal past or future comes from external sources. Parents, friends, associates, and so on aid in filling in the blanks of personal and group history and destiny. Similarly, myths and folklore, as much as factual information, inform and misinform a people about their nation's past and future. Both individuals and nations have a tendency to transform past and future into an unfolding drama of great import that reassures them that their lives have meaning and purpose.[1]

In the past century the mass media, in producing and selling entertainment, have played a major role in shaping and supplementing Americans' visions of past and future. Creators of popular entertainment have always recognized that people are interested in learning about the world beyond their immediate experience. In the late 19th century, for example, people in the eastern part of America, which was already settled and growing, became fascinated with the western frontier. Even though a good bit of the winning of the West involved peaceful settlement by farmers and ranches, there was enough conflict to provide stories for gripping popular drama. The dime novel told readers about gunfighters and gunslingers, cowboys and Indians, sheriffs and outlaws, cowtowns and saloons, cattle drivers and range wars—all shaping visions of a romantic world of violent drama in a spectacular setting. Americans' fantasy lives were thus enriched. The Western became such an indelible part of popular folklore that it will probably be the one great contribution of the United States to world mythology. With the advent of Hollywood (about which we will say more in Chapter 5), the Western film genre acquired such imaginative force that, even today, Americans instantly recognize the figures and stories this genre features. The West, then, is a fantastic reference that serves as an important part of the American mythic past and still mediates realities of the present.[2]

RE-PRESENTATION BY ROMANTIC REPRESENTATION

Novels, films, and assorted other forms of popular entertainment do not necessarily offer an authentic picture of the past but do provide a rich one. Images and narratives from popular culture linger in the mind as the way it was, or perhaps should have been. Consider the Bible. Many Americans have read and believe in the Judeo-Christian narrative of the Bible. Yet, it is safe to say that even among readers of the Scriptures the story of the Bible comes less from the reading than from mediation through popular entertainment. Early Hollywood film directors—Cecil B. DeMille being one of the most notable—invented a formula for turning a biblical story into both a spectacle of faith and a spectacle of sensation. Depictions of sumptuous palaces, evil tyrants, scantily clad dancing girls, contests in the arena, violent battles, and beautiful Christian girls tortured in dungeons were central features of the formula. Certainly they titillated audiences who flocked to biblical movies. Hence did the Bible come alive in both pietist and not so pietist ways. When people think of biblical characters, the Hollywood actors who played them often comes to mind. Screenwriters (as well as writers of popular books) have spun entirely fanciful tales around biblical stories with no basis in the Scriptures (*Ben-Hur*, for example). Jesus has usually been depicted as someone thoroughly Nordic, with blond hair, blue eyes, and fair skin. When the movie *The Last Temptation of Christ* (1988) introduced extra-scriptural elements into the story, it outraged many Christians. Outrage aside, the movies have always interwoven the biblical with the dramatically fictional in order to improve on the text for popular audiences. Biblical movies are not history or theology but entertainment, which has its own rules of presentation. Popular culture—biblical films are but one example, as is the Western—presents the past again, but the re-presentation is more romantic than literal.

Our argument is that people learn politics from mediated pasts and futures that are presented anew in the present. This process is complex and subtle. Certain story lines and conventions, however, are always in demand by audiences—adventure, mystery, romance, nightmare, comedy, and so on. No matter what the content is of the mass media employed for re-presentation, such conventions appear to be essential, as can be demonstrated by a particular type of mass mediation: the *news documentary*.

As noted in Chapter 2, creating news formats to appeal to mass audiences means making news entertaining, timely, and "factual," at least in appearance. The news documentary features a gripping story that appeals to the popular imagination at a particular time, one that conveys the impression that the tale is true. Because the primary purpose of the documentary is to sell the story, however, stubborn, disconfirming facts are not allowed to interfere with the thrust. The documentary form thus combines fact and fiction; more precisely, news documentaries arrange facts to serve the course of the narrative rather than to shape the narrative. In both print and radio news documentaries, the useful fact conforms to the story line. For example, in the 1890s, the Hearst newspapers documented "facts" about Spanish atrocities in Cuba, many of which were untrue or only half-truths. No matter. The loosely substantiated tales appealed to readers' fantasies and may even have produced a climate of opinion conducive to the onset of the Spanish-American War. Similarly, radio and movie newsreel documentaries in the 1930s and 1940s (such as *The March of Time*) often staged events that were shown as news; audiences thought they were hearing or seeing something real.

Documentary formats have evolved into such slick TV present-day news programs as "60 Minutes" and "48 Hours." Naturally, both news and TV critics hotly debate whether news documentaries faithfully re-present past, present, and future. Producers of documentaries often share the entertainment values of those who make biblical epics and Westerns, so it is not surprising to find the documentary formula paralleling one or more of the conventional story lines mentioned earlier. The standard dramatic motif is romantic melodrama, transforming the complexity of history (e.g., the settlement of the West, biblical theological experience, or contemporary social processes) into a struggle of heroes, villains, and fools, all of whom represent some moral or cultural symbol. By so characterizing history and events, news documentaries are in the realm of popular myth and fantasy rather than of critical history or journalistic fact-finding. A story on "60 Minutes," for instance, may be "true" in the sense of reporting actual people involved in a social transaction—say, farmers who invest in a bank that later collapses, the farmers then charging the bank and government with fraud. But as played out on TV, the story incorporates romantic images of a mythic American heartland ravaged by impersonal forces, "little people" pitted against power and wealth, and the pathos of simple, honest, trusting folk driven to desperation.

Producers of documentaries select and tell stories to represent matters important to the everyday lives of audiences (economic security, the fear of being victimized by institutions, the fear of being deprived of hard-earned possessions). Any subject that serves as the basis of a news documentary is probably far more intricate and contradictory in actuality than standard story lines permit. Yet, the dramatic logic of the narrative dictates that for it to appeal to audiences it must obey the canons of romantic melodrama—good versus evil, power versus the people, injustice versus justice, and so on. Audiences do not get, nor may they even want, the "real" story. What they may want, and certainly get, is a real-fiction tailored for audience interest and entertainment. Thereby news documentaries appeal to fantasies about the state of the world and how people might be affected adversely—just like those wretched folks on TV.[3]

DOCUDRAMA FANTASIES: WHAT IS, WAS, OR MIGHT HAVE BEEN

What we have described is a way whereby mass media transform traditions (the Bible), process (the settlement of the West), and events (a clash between banks and farmers) into stories framed by dramatic conventions. Representers of past, present, and future have recently taken fantasy creation one step further with the invention of what is loosely called the *docudrama*. The docudrama is a format that takes a story, real or imagined, and puts it into a documentary form as if the audience were watching the story as it actually happened. The illusion transports audiences to a past, present, or future to witness other persons' private lives; to experience some epic process that occurred in the past or might occur in the future; to see a cautionary tale of possible apocalyptic events in the future; or any other tale that combines the sense of a "documented" historical or futuristic reality. Such a media format can range from the simple and straightforward to the complex and subtle. In any case, audiences are now so familiar with the docudrama that it is easy to accept the documented fantasy as an accurate representation of the real or of the possible. This also makes it easy to accept another fantasy, which is that the mass media have access to what occurred in the past or will occur in the future and that they can portray those events with the same degree of verisimilitude as they inform their audiences about current events. (From what we said about TV news in Chapter 1, the media probably do!)

Such contrived documentation serves audiences in many ways—teaching dry history as rich drama, depicting historical figures as real people, making sweeping events comprehensible in human terms, and prophesying the future.

Millions of children started to "see" history through television in a unique way in the 1950s by watching CBS's "You Are There." CBS news correspondents—the same ones appearing on nightly news programs—purported to "interview" the participants, played by professional actors, in the Boston Tea Party, the Alamo, the charge up San Juan Hill, and other historical events. Today the docudrama format is far more sophisticated, so much so that many schools teach history courses by replaying TV docudramas for students, either to replace or supplement the reading of lifeless history textbooks.

The docudrama format, however, did not begin with TV. One of the most notable examples of docudrama appeared over half a century ago. It serves as a reminder of how docudramas appeal to and construct fantasies. On Halloween eve, October 30, 1938, countless millions of Americans were listening to CBS's "Mercury Theater of the Air" and its radio dramatization of H.G. Wells' classic science fiction tale *The War of the Worlds.* The show's director, the youthful Orson Welles, opened the broadcast with a documentary style that gave many listeners the impression they were listening to something other than fiction. They first heard a program of orchestra music that was quickly interrupted with "special bulletins" from the "Intercontinental Radio Service." A "Professor Ferrell" at an astronomic observatory reported spotting "incandescent gases" spouting from the planet Mars. Eventually the program took the form of a live newscast of a seemingly live invasion from Mars. Listeners heard, and some accepted, the reports as factual. Martian spaceships landed in New Jersey! It must be true, some thought, because they heard it in on-the-spot reports. As this impressively packaged fictional tale in a news format unfolded—telling of the Martian invasion of New York, the destruction of armies, the devastation of cities, the slaughter of populations and panic in the streets—CBS was deluged with nervous phone calls and news of real panic. Welles issues a disclaimer at the end of the program, announcing that it had been but a Halloween trick. Although the relative proportion of Americans fooled by the invasion docudrama was very small, the program demonstrated the capacity of the broadcast media to create the illusion of a news event, of something actually happening and being reported. A study of the reaction to the broadcast speculated that it was the time of the broadcast that caused the mass fantasy. The broadcast followed in the wake of the Munich crisis, during which there had been a great deal of tension about the prospect of war. Perhaps the program triggered latent anxieties in vulnerable people fearing actual invasion. If that was the case, then political and popular fantasy combined to shape the response of the few who did panic.[4]

This is not to suggest that docudramas produce only hysterical reactions. At the right time and place, the power of the media format can produce a variety of reactions, not all of them emotional. For example, in the late 1970s a panoramic TV docudrama, *Holocaust,* transformed the Nazi destruction of European Jewry into a melodramatic and often stereotypical story. Although critical reviews dismissed much of the docudrama as soap opera, the program did humanize an event so vast—the systematic murder of millions as a matter of policy—that many viewers might otherwise have found it incomprehensible. The biggest response to the telecast was in West Germany. The Nazi period and the Holocaust were virtually taboo subjects in German society and schools. When *Holocaust* aired, it attracted large audiences and responses, especially among the young for whom it was the first exposure they had had to a shameful episode in their national past. The response at first was emotional, but eventually there was widespread popular discussion. The atmosphere created by the docudrama contributed to the West German Parliament vote to extend the statute of limitations for prosecuting war criminals involved in the Holocaust. Thus, the stimulation of latent but powerful popular fantasies can have immediate and real political consequences.[5]

The popular depiction of the past, present, or future involves subjects all deemed interesting to potential audiences in a present. The docudrama format itself has evolved into four fairly distinct kinds of stories—the instant history, the historical biography, the historical panorama, and the futuristic projection.

Instant History

There has always been a temptation for the purveyors of popular culture to capitalize on a contemporary newsworthy event by immediately translating it into a popular drama. In the earliest days of the movies, moviemakers made phony film footage purporting to show combat action from the Boer War and World War I. Thereafter, filmmakers were quick to exploit current events for their movie potential. In 1960, for example, when Nazi war criminal Adolph Eichmann was discovered alive in South America and was kidnapped by Israeli agents to stand trial in Israel, Hollywood producers quickly filmed a movie about the Eichmann affair. Television producers learned how to make the conversion from news event to popular melodrama even more quickly. By the 1970s, a type of docudrama emerged on TV that we term *instant history*. A recent spectacular event becomes in the twinkling of an eye a television special. Instant histories yield the illusion that viewers participate in the re-creation of a real event, even though the details of what happened are so clouded that generations of historians may never reconstruct them. Undaunted by such a difficulty, TV's instant historians offer the illusion that people can vicariously witness the event. To satisfy mass audiences, the format includes clearly defined heroism and villainy, peril and conflict, and an outcome consistent with the development of the plot—the hero must triumph, the villain be vanquished, and so on.

In 1976, the United States was suffering from a series of setbacks. After years of fighting in Vietnam, Saigon fell to the North Vietnamese and the United States departed. The Arab oil embargo threatened the U.S. economy and the future of its automotive industry. Arab terrorists were successfully hijacking airplanes and flaunting U.S. inability to stop them. President Gerald Ford sent Marines to rescue an American ship named *Mayaguez,* but what at first appeared to be a successful rescue mission turned out to be botched. There was a popular sense that as a nation and as an international and military power, the United States could no longer cope. If the nation couldn't stop the ragtag North Vietnamese, prevent hijackings, or rescue hostages, then what could we do? No one seemed able to defeat the hostile forces that defied our power.

In that period, a pro-Arab terrorist group hijacked an international flight full of Jewish passengers on their way to Israel and forced the aircraft to the airport in Entebbe, Uganda. The passengers seemed in double peril—from fanatical hijackers who threatened to kill them, and from the unpredictable Ugandan dictator, Idi Amin. Then an Israeli commando unit staged a daring and successful raid, killing the terrorists and spiriting the hostages to Israel and safety. At a time of perceived American bungling and impotence, news of the action at Entebbe created a sensation. How, it was asked, were they able to pull it off when we can't? Televison jumped at the opportunity to provide answers. Immediately, eight projects were in the works, resulting finally in two competing network docudramas. The first to appear had a round-the-clock shooting schedule and premiered nine days after its filming and only a few weeks after the actual event. In effect, "the epic docudrama became a secondary news source for many Americans."[6] In the docudramas on Entebbe, the participants lived up to expectations: The Israelis were heroic and disciplined; the terrorists were fanatical and murderous; the passengers were either pathetic victims or defiant heroes; an Israeli officer died a martyr; and Idi Amin was a mad fool. Rough edges and ambiguities, not to mention the rights and wrongs, of such a situation were ignored, smoothing the way for a satisfying story with a happy ending denied in recent American experience. Such a televised fantasy gave hope that if the Israelis could be so successful, then perhaps America too, by following the example, could rebound in the future.

The Entebbe fantasy was in the tradition of postive spectacles; it evoked the well-worn fantasy of the cavalry charging on the scene, arriving just in time to save the captives and to mete out sweet revenge on the savages. There are, however, other, more negative fantasies evoked by instant histories that also warrant attention. These are mass-mediated realities of chaos rather than control, injustice rather than justice, the triumph of evil rather than good, often events so insane as to defy explanation. In 1978, immediately after the shocking event, there was a macabre fascination with the almost unbelievable mass suicide of 912 members of a religious order, The People's Temple, and their leader, Jim Jones, in the jungle at Jonestown in Guyana, South America. The lurid event was a continuing TV news story, with all three major TV networks devoting coverage to cults, death camps, fanaticism, and demonic leaders—all allegedly exemplified by the mass suicide. News tabloids ran tales of sexual domination, perversion, torture, terror squads, even a photograph of Jones in tinted glasses captioned, "Are these the eyes of a madman?"

In the weeks following the Temple suicides, many observers resorted to a recurring *cult fantasy* to explain the event. In the 1970s, many people were both troubled and intrigued by the emergence of new religious groups with unusual beliefs and often bizarre dress and manner. In many cases, the groups were sequestered from the world. The Moonies, the followers of Hare Krishna, the Children of God, and others were visible on city streets and at airports. People in many quarters regarded them with suspicion as cults capable of evil thoughts and deeds—brainwashing children, ritual sacrifices, crimes of extortion and murder. The Guyana story helped to define for the curious what actually goes on in cults. Jones's Temple, through mediated realities, assumed the characteristics of a satanic cult dominated by a demonic figure who exercised totalitarian power over poor wretches who trusted him but whom he betrayed by brutalizing them, so debasing them that they willingly died at his command. Jones was portrayed as a combination of Rasputin and Stalin. In the CBS instant history docudrama, *Guyana Tragedy: The Story of Jim Jones*, the focus is a charismatic charlatan who descends into megalomania, blasphemy, corruption, and necrophilia. The Jonestown melodrama served as an "immorality play" demonstrating the dangers of cults. *Guyana Tragedy* portrayed poor people with hopes of finding utopia sacrificing their life's earning (and eventually their lives) to follow a crazed leader. It served as a cautionary tale for both adults and children attracted to the strange appeals of cults: what happens when they follow a charismatic leader, join a group or adopt a belief that is different, leave home under the spell of weird strangers, stray from the good things the American Dream promises.

It is, of course, unfair to think that all new religions are evil cults. It is also simplistic to blame a complex social event on the demonic power of a leader, just as it is simplistic to portray cavalry charges as the solution to terrorism. Simplistic or not, the Entebbe and Temple docudramas appealed as tales of fright and reassurance. Entebbe evoked mythical fears of being held captive in the hands of fanatics (see Chapter 2), but it also offered the hope of rescue along with justice done. The Jim Jones tale provided the fright of being possessed by a demonic power, combined with the reassurance that the evil can be thwarted if one but heeds the lesson of Jones's dead victims.

Instant history derives from a human curiosity to know more about events that are the basis of fascinating news accounts without going to all the work, time, and tedium of researching those events by reading the dry and dreary details. Docudramas offer, in the words of radio commentator Paul Harvey, "the rest of the story"—but without all the work. Consider, for example, the case of what *really* was behind the Watergate scandal that finally forced President Richard Nixon to resign in 1974. As a news event, Watergate was one of the most elaborately covered in history. Yet, the whole affair was so mysterious, and the figures in high places so intriguing, that coverage of the event did not end with Nixon's resignation. It continued in TV instant histories based on quickly written memoirs of such Nixon aides as John Erlichmann and John Dean and in a Hollywood film based on coverage by *Washington Post* reporters Bob Woodward and Carl Bernstein.

The Ehrlichmann-based docudrama *Washington: Behind Closed Doors* appeared in 1977, attracting 50 million viewers to witness again why it was that "President Monckton" fell from power. Like all docudramas, it was historically simplistic and selective: The fault lay in the mean and neurotic personality of the president, consistent perhaps with a popular fantasy of Nixon after his fall. In the Dean story (entitled *Blind Ambition*), Nixon and his close aides are duplicitous. But the real evil is inherent in a White House with imperial status, where young men like Dean go astray by yielding to blind ambition to get ahead. Thus, the fault is in the presidential system and the personality flaws it brings out in all those with ambition. In the instant history Hollywood film *All the President's Men,* released in 1976, the evil behind Watergate lies in a system of power emanating from the White House and pervading a repressed and secretive Washington where truth can be disclosed only in whispered conversations in underground parking lots late at night. The popular image of Watergate ranged from family soap opera replete with beautiful but unhappy wives, alcoholism, and disillusionment produced by pressures of work (Dean), to the palace intrigues revolving around pathological personalities (Erlichmann), to the looming specter of hidden power that lurks in every house and street of a paranoid capital (*All the President's Men*). These disparate views of Watergate shared the melodramatic fantasy of the emperor who suddenly has no clothes, of the struggles and strife of courtiers and courtesans, of the pleasurable look at the powerful and haughty brought to poetic justice.[7]

In the 1980s the instant history virtually disappeared from TV. The reasons are difficult to explain. There certainly were political events—the invasion of Grenada in 1983, the bombing of Libya, various terrorist actions, the bombing of the Marine barracks in Lebanon in 1980, the *Challenger* disaster in 1986, the Iran-Contra affair of 1986 and 1987. But no instant history docudramas appeared. One explanation might be that viewers were tired of the instant history formula. There were numerous TV miniseries, but they were usually entirely fictional or about nonpolitical subjects. Another explanation might be that the noteworthy events of the period did not inspire potential audiences with the notion that justice could be done (such as at Entebbe), nor good and evil sorted out (as the Watergate docudramas tried to do). On the other hand, instant history did not completely disappear. A TV drama about the *Achille Lauro* hijacking and the murder of Leon Klinghofer appeared and made good and evil seem clear enough. And a made-for-TV production on Oliver North was in production, although whether he would be cast as hero or villain was unclear.

Perhaps one of the changes in political TV in the 1980s that eliminated the demand for instant histories was that television itself had become a collaborative part of instant history while it was happening. Instant histories of the 1970s were ritual re-enactments of immediate events that gave audiences a fuller look at what happened, framed by largely melodramatic canons of theater. Many such events in the 1980s were themselves transformed into live political theater requiring no ritual re-enactment. For example, a shocking, unhappy event such as the explosion of *Challenger* (see Chapter 2) might have been re-enacted in docudrama; instead, the explosion and events surrounding it were enacted live on TV newscasts. The memorial service for the *Challenger* crew did not re-enact the event, but it did provide satisfying emotional involvement through the live telecast. The televised ceremony constituted a ritual remembrance of the crew, and more than that, a celebration of our identity as a mourning "national family" grieving the loss of life but affirming national purpose and technological power (see Chapter 1).

Finally, the appeal of instant history may have waned because specialists in mediating realities recognize that many viewers now watch public events *as if they were fiction.* For habitual TV viewers—and this must include the vast majority of Americans—television is a daily source of *fantastic spectacles* that transport the viewers to fictional dramas as diverse as game shows, soap operas, sporting events, massive religious revivals, situation comedies, and of course docudramas. News stories structured as media spectacles adhere to the program logic of entertainment television. Both orchestrated (for instance, a presidential "photo opportunity") and unplanned events (a forest fire, a murder) receive coverage that appeals visually, makes few demands on reflective processes, and provides—as we saw in Chapter 2—an acquaintance with, but little knowledge about, what is happening.

Newsworthy fantastic spectacles, then, are thus scarcely distinguishable from the fictional fantasies of other entertainment programming. If skilled political communicators can design and control media events and their coverage, then they provide instant history in the making, not after the fact. A president sharing the grief of the *Challenger* crew families leads a spectacle of public mourning that reinforces a fantasy of a nation united like a family. A president greeting the "rescued" American students of a Grenada medical school promotes the fantasy of a glorious and justified military victory. A follow-up docudrama is unnecessary and redundant; the orchestrated original telling of the story is complete in itself, leaves no mysteries unsolved, and provides a dramatic ending acceptable to all. Thus do innovations in political TV supersede fictional replays, designing mediated realities that reinforce the old adage that truth is stranger than fiction, especially when truth is presented as such.[8]

Historical Biography

A second use of the past for the creation of television fantasy is the historical biography. There the drama focuses on a great historical personage, his or her heroic characteristics and deeds. Such dramas are set in a heroic time, but they are distinguishable from historical panorama, which we discuss in the next section. Although the historical biography is epic in scope, the focus is on the life of the hero at the center of the historic sweep of events. (This docudrama genre also includes portraits of great historical figures who were, at least to some, villains—Huey Long, Joe McCarthy, Eva Peron, and Adolph Hitler.) There are also historical portraits of many noted nonpolitical figures, including athletes meeting tragic death while still young (Lou Gehrig), hell-raising celebrities (Errol Flynn), well-bred prostitutes (the "Mayflower Madam") and the ever-popular mass murderer (Jack the Ripper). However, most historical biographies center on powerful individuals who possess the "right stuff" and who are able to bend history to their will: presidents, famous and successful generals, and committed social reformers. All are usually safely dead and remote enough so that they can be promoted to heroic immortality. A dead politician becomes a statesman when afforded TV docudrama treatment.

The historical biography emerged in the 1970s during a decidedly unheroic time. Presidents of that period—Nixon, Ford, Carter—governing in a climate of perceived national impotence and decline, contributed to a nostalgic popular yearning for a more heroic era. People wanted heroic triumphs rather than petty scandals and squabbles. The venerated heroes, however, were to be made of common democratic clay, not fine aristocratic crystal. Unlike the seemingly remote, often arrogant, leaders of the 1970s—more concerned with their images than their performance—the heroes of TV docudramas were admired precisely because they were devoid of pretension and guided by common sense, like everyday Americans. Here was a re-presentation of leaders as paragons of public greatness and private commonness, with the clear understanding that the leader triumphed because of common goodness. Heroic deeds of presidents, it seems, derive from private traits of character: domesticity, being one of the boys with the manliness to make love to women, often other than their wives. If contemporary politicians seem "imperial," aloof, and sexless, the nostalgic impulse of the 1970s was to celebrate the opposite traits in heroic leaders of bygone days. Hence, for instance, TV biographies provided a President Harry Truman cursing, drinking bourbon and branch water, and playing poker with his cronies; a General Dwight "Ike" Eisenhower smoking heavily, conducting an affair with his pretty English driver; and a President Franklin Roosevelt sipping martinis and consorting with his old flame, Lucy Mercer. The TV biography seemed to suggest that truly great men of the past were so because of their domesticity and their vices, and because they were very like all of us. There is a curious historical double standard at work here. As we shall see in Chapter 4, contemporary politicians such as Edward Kennedy and Gary Hart have seen their presidential ambitions evaporate because of alleged extramarital sexual activity. Yet, similar activity in an Eisenhower or Roosevelt—safely dead and promoted to greatness—makes them all the more endearing. Women, be they wives or mistresses, sense their power; vices are a legitimate portion of their domestic charm.

The historical biography offers us a voyeuristic look at the private lives of past greats, merging their private power and public power, and assuming that the latter flows from the former. Roosevelt, Truman, Eisenhower, and so on are surrounded by loyal and devoted entourages—an extended family sharing birthday parties, poker, and cute pets. Drawing strength from personal and private prowess, as well as devoted followers, the hero or heroine inspires loyalty, always sees the right course, is prescient and persuasive, agonizes over decisions, and remains humble in victory and veneration. Here are common sense, a common touch, and common habits. Thus, viewers watched in docudramas Martin Luther King, Jr., eating "chitlin's" in his kitchen and delivering great speeches; FDR poring over his stamp collection and fighting the Great Depression; Harry Truman interspersing cards and booze with negotiations with Stalin.

The Kennedys remain an eternally popular subject for historical biography. Both John and Robert have been repeatedly profiled in historical biographies on TV, as have other members of the family. Most of the melodramatic conventions applied to other historical figures appear in retelling the heroic triumphs. In *The Missiles of October,* for example, John Kennedy alone sees the right path to force Russian missiles out of Cuba without nuclear war. In another miniseries Robert Kennedy alone fights against the threats to the nation personified by Jimmy Hoffa and J. Edgar Hoover; Kennedy dies at the moment he could have solved the problems of war, racism, and poverty. Both docudramas accord elaborate and charming private lives, including extramarital affairs, to the Kennedys. In the 1987 docudrama *Hoover vs. the Kennedys: The Second Civil War,* political and personal relationships heretofore only rumored are stated as fact: President Kennedy has an affair with Marilyn Monroe; Hoover virtually blackmails the Kennedys with information about their sex lives; the Mafia took part in mysterious ways in the 1960 campaign, in Frank Sinatra's ties to the Kennedys, in the Bay of Pigs debacle, and in the assassination of President Kennedy; Hoover and the FBI cover up evidence of both Kennedy assassinations; and Martin Luther King, Jr., had extramarital affairs monitored by the FBI. How are such themes, which are of questionable authenticity, justified? They make political leaders "more human"! Historical biography often takes so many liberties that they are but fictional fantasies bearing no resemblance to history.[9]

Accurate or not, historical biographies persist on television, expanding to include more remote and gigantic figures in the American past. Both George Washington and Abraham Lincoln have been profiled. Many historians bristle at such depictions, often arguing that there is "a fundamental difference between the histrionic and the historiographic enterprise. . . . In the popular mind, past reality and present fantasy blend more and more into an inseparable mix."[10] One reason for such criticism, aside from the lack of historical authenticity in many docudrama biographies, is the tendency on the part of TV producers to project themes and character qualities of the present into the past. For example, as depicted in CBS's docudrama on George Washington, our first president appeared very much like our fortieth, Ronald Reagan: likeable, stolid, dependable, someone who endured while history's hurricane swirled about him. Gore Vidal's *Lincoln* supported the fantasy that presidential resolve can literally remake the nation in the image of the president, a theme promoted by Reagan supporters during the 1980 presidential campaign.

One of the habits that endeared President Reagan to some and outraged others was his ability to view the past as a romantic melodrama, so revised in his own mind as to make events conform to the conventions of Hollywood. Thus the Soviet Union was "the evil empire" with whom we were locked in a struggle fraught with peril, one the United States was sure to win as the good guys. Such black-and-white thinking can be revised, however. After arms reduction agreements with Soviet leader Mikhail Gorbachev in 1987, Reagan's view of the Russians became sunnier and more hopeful. Similar revisions of thinking and of history appear in historical biographies. Two epics about the Civil War, for example, revised the familiar view of abolitionist John Brown as a murderous fanatic, making him instead an admirable and committed friend of the slaves and martyr in their behalf. President Lyndon Johnson, highly criticized during U.S. involvement in Vietnam, became in a TV docudrama a colorful, lovable, and well-meaning president with a deep desire for social reform and racial justice, not the power-hungry and overbearing paranoiac of previous representations. Perhaps in the future the historical biography will be a popular vehicle for the rehabilitation of presidential reputations. Will there someday be a TV miniseries that depicts the heroic deeds of President Richard Nixon who resigned in disgrace? Don't go away, stay tuned, we'll see.

Historical Panorama

Historical panorama does not focus on one heroic personage but, rather, on several characters in a historical event—war, revolution, imperial ventures— that serves as a backdrop for personal melodrama. This genre undoubtedly received impetus from the perennially favorite movie, *Gone with the Wind,* which uses the Civil War and Reconstruction as a spectacular setting to highlight the personal agonies of Rhett, Scarlett, and Ashley. The familiar relationships of the everyday soap opera are made all the more melodramatic by placing them in the context of historical perils. Identifiable, and often cardboard, characters fight for love and glory not only in relation to each other but also to conquering armies, venal ruling classes, and fanatical revolutionaries. Here is the tradition of popular romance—masculine men and feminine women, heroes and heroines, coping with the sweep of vast historical forces and meeting actual historical figures. History is both fictional and personal, an exciting setting for characters to conquer.[11]

The romance of historical panorama translates nicely into television miniseries through docudrama with didactic undertones. Ordinary people caught up in the maelstrom of history learn that there's no place like home, that family and children are one's proper destiny, that one is more of a victim of history than a participant in it, that survival is the only true glory, but that somehow all works out for the best. These are truly romantic lessons, messages that audiences typically seek and find in historical panoramas. This structure of romance built into historical panoramas was never better illustrated than by one of the most successful of all TV miniseries, *Roots*. First broadcast in 1977, *Roots* traced the life histories of one black family from enslavement in Africa to the present day. *Roots* attracted large audiences; both blacks and whites learned about slavery and black history as they became emotionally involved with a family that was enduring the outrages of slavery and intolerance. Yet for all the degradation of the heroes and heroines of the story, audiences were able to identify with it because of its fantastic assurance of the romantic triumph of values we all hold dear despite the oppressions of history. The panorama of *Roots* placed evil in the past and hope and justice in the present and future. It offered blacks a myth of Eden when Kunta Kinte was torn from his peaceful village in the idyllic setting of Africa. Departed from their African Dream, blacks were then unwillingly caught up in the pageant that eventually made them part of the American Dream, reassuring both black and white alike that oppression and poverty can be overcome by individual heroism and familial perseverance. By depicting various stereotypical white racists—slavers, Klansmen—the miniseries suggested that racism was, and is, the fault of individual villains and not the system itself, thus assuaging any feelings of white guilt.

Roots, noted one observer, was in the tradition of "progressive history . . . [that] viewed history in the simple terms of a conflict between forces of good and evil, freedom and oppression, democracy and aristocracy, and so forth. . . . Its heroes and villains were unambiguous and the program reaffirmed basic American values and ideals."[12] *Roots* was palatable for audiences because it had mythic adequacy, re-presenting an epic of black origins and destiny that made them part of American society. Focusing on a melodrama of the family triumphant, it made the heroes and heroines of Kunta Kinte's family acceptable to white middle-class morality. Here was a family that became "good" Americans by maintaining the values, including the belief in social progress, held by the vast majority of Americans. *Roots* also perpetuated a fantasy that the struggle for black equality has been won, a fiction that many whites accept to allay any lingering guilt over the evils of the past. By contrast, *King*, the televised historical biography of Martin Luther King, Jr., was a dismal ratings failure. Unlike *Roots*, it did not have a happy ending: King's assassination suggested that America's racial problem is not solved. *Roots* was a romantic morality play, a didactic popular entertainment, that combined historical fact with familial fiction in a melodrama that symbolically, if not actually, resolved racial exploitation and inequality.[13]

More recently, televised historical panoramas have refought the Civil War

(*The Blue and the Gray, North and South, Louisiana*), revived the Western cattle drive (*Lonesome Dove*), and followed the rise of immigrant families to power and wealth (*Rich Man, Poor Man*). Perhaps the most popular recent subject for successful historical panoramas has been World War II, our last "good" war. One of the top-rated miniseries of all time was the historical panorama based on the Herman Wouk novels *The Winds of War* and *War and Remembrance*. This 48-hour panoramic docudrama was the saga of the family of U.S. Navy officer Victor "Pug" Henry in the years up to and including World War II. Henry possessed a fantastic knack for being at the right place at the right time—Berlin, Warsaw, Moscow, Pearl Harbor, London, Washington, or elsewhere at precisely the moment when events occured to shape the course of history. He met the great men involved in the titanic struggle—a hyperactive Hitler, a cigar-chomping Churchill, an aristocratic FDR, and a surprisingly avuncular Stalin. All the major battles on land, sea, and air appeared in the historical panorama. And for the first time, a docudrama recreated in graphic detail mass executions in the actual setting, the infamous Nazi death camp at Auschwitz-Birkenau in Poland. This World War II epic revived the fantasy of national heroism and purpose, symbolically returning the United States to its 1945 stature as leader of the free world. The Henry panorama also had the tone of a cautionary tale, evoking a fantasy of evil forces that can never be appeased, only combated.

Historical Projection

The Winds of War and *War and Remembrance* taught lessons of military preparedness in the face of destructive forces, but World War II ushered in the nuclear age. Along with it have come fantasies of the consequences of nuclear warfare. TV producers, ever alert to popular anxieties that might provide appealing dramatizations, are quick to provide docudramas depicting what the world, and specifically the United States, would be like should there be a nuclear holocaust or, alternatively, if the United States were to yield to nuclear threat or blackmail. As a result, we have had docudramas projecting the realities of the destruction of civilization through nuclear war (*The Day After, Threads, World War III, Testament*) and the imminent Soviet invasion and enslavement of the United States (*Red Dawn, Amerika*). Because these were stories of events that might but have not yet happened, we term them *historical projections,* asking the question: What if our fantasies came true?

One of the most controversial of the televised docudramas that projected a nuclear holocaust into the near future was ABC's 1983 production *The Day After*. It depicted the aftermath of a nuclear war on ordinary people in Lawrence, Kansas. Forty-six percent of the nation's TV sets were tuned to ABC. The airing provoked ideological and policy controversy. It apparently changed few minds on nuclear policy (the deployment of Pershing missiles in Europe was at issue at the moment). Both hawks and doves interpreted the docudrama as they wanted to: Hawks could say the way to avoid nuclear annihilation is through ever-expanding military strength; doves could argue that the way to avoid nuclear suicide is to get rid of the weapons. *The Day After,* true to docudrama conventions, reduced perhaps the ultimate political disaster to family melodrama. Because audiences might be interested in what would happen to them in case of nuclear attack, the dramatic focus of the program was to document the fate of common, ordinary citizens. The setting was the mythological and fecund Garden of the American Heartland, where the moral equilibrium of the American family could be expected to have established Eden-like normalcy. The characters were a medley of innocent people of the pluralistic Union—doctors, farmers, students, and so on—who were essentially peaceable and harmonious members of a happy and classless society. The story was structured like a classic horror movie: a peaceable community disturbed by the intrusion of monsters that must be fought and destroyed. Early scenes portrayed images of blissful fecundity—marital love, pregnancy, childbirth, teenage romance. Once the nuclear horror of Death visits, vitality and life vanish from the citizenry. Unable to stop the monster of nuclear fallout by driving a stake through its heart, the story ends with dying survivors wandering through the rubble helpless and hopeless—surely the unhappiest ending ever for a TV program. (There was one hope: Law and order had broken down, squatting and looting were rife, but the U.S. Department of Agriculture's Extension Service survived the catastrophe to give aid!) *The Day After,* then, was a historical projection of an immediate postnuclear future that both catered to and gave shape to many people's expectations of what could happen if the bombs fell. According to opinion polls, the majority of Americans (and large majorities of children and adolescents) believe that there will be a nuclear war in their lifetime. It is no wonder, then, that docudramas such as *The Day After* have widespread appeal regardless of their contrived soap opera qualities.[14]

If *The Day After* purported to portray an America conquered by nuclear holocaust, the docudrama *Amerika* mediated the realities of a nation that had succumbed to a Soviet takeover. In 1987 ABC produced a historical projection of such an event in a $14\frac{1}{2}$-hour miniseries entitled *Amerika*. Set in 1997, it fantasized about Soviet-controlled America years after the bloodless coup. The takeover occurred because, as one character put it, "people stopped caring." The miniseries made recurrent reference to the patriotic ideals of our forefathers, ideals betrayed by a lack of national commitment ("You lost your country," explained a KGB officer, "before we ever got here"). Many Americans portrayed in the docudrama were less than heroic. The series showed quislings and collaborators, high school students willing to inform on one another, women willing to sleep with their captors for favors. Scarcity (Americans lined up in queues), regimentation (students on a march carrying banners of Lincoln and Lenin), elite privilege and arrogance (the Russian administrator of the midwestern "Central Administrative Area" and his American mistress live well), and suppression (dissidents are "reprogrammed" in psychiatric wards) characterized Soviet domination of "Amerika." Large portions of the population lived on drugs and alcohol; blacks and Hispanics formed the bulk of the occupying "United Nations" force; and opposition consisted of a few brave patriots on the run. A generally unflattering portrait of Americans was matched by one that extolled the qualities of the invaders: sophisticated and smart, disgusted by American toadiness and passivity, and committed to values of efficient rule to mitigate total harshness! *Amerika* offered a fantasy of the penetration of evil into the very heartland of the country, playing on xenophobic fears that someday the entire nation could be held captive by an enemy more committed and astute than we. We shall encounter this fantasy of the invading alien again in our discussion of the mediation of political realities in Hollywood movies (Chapter 4) and by televangelists (Chapter 9) and crusaders against conspiracy (Chapter 10).

LONG PAST? NO, YOUR PAST!

In Charles Dickens's fetching tale, *A Christmas Carol,* mean and miserly Ebenezer Scrooge is visited by the Ghosts of Christmas Past, Present, and Future. The Ghost of Christmas Past warns Scrooge to prepare for a journey into the past. Scrooge asks if it is to be the long past. The Ghost responds it is to be Scrooge's past. Throughout the journey Scrooge watches himself as he was in earlier times: as a boy in boarding school, as a young accountant, as a suitor, and so on.

Docudramas try to play the role of the Ghosts of Christmas Past, Present, and Yet to Come in America. But just as Scrooge interprets what he once was in light of what he is when the Ghost takes him on his journey, so do docudramas and their audiences interpret the past in light of the realities of the present. If there is an absence of heroism and triumph in the present, project its presence into the past. If the present seems foreboding, project those anxieties into the past and future. What we know of the past and what we can know of the future derive from what we know in the present projected to past and future. What is it we know in the present? The realities that are mediated for us, the re-presentations of past, present, and future. This chapter has urged that those re-presentations are not representative "as it was," "as it is," "as it will be" renditions but fantastic portrayals to be accepted with caution lest we become what we think we already were and are.

NOTES

1. George Herbert Mead, *The Philosophy of the Present* (Chicago: University of Chicago Press, 1980).
2. See, for instance, Frank Bergon and Zeese Papnikolas, eds., *Looking Far West:*

The Search for the American West in History, Myth, and Literature (New York: New American Library, 1978).

3. Northrop Frye, *The Secular Scripture: A Study of the Structure of Romance* (Cambridge, MA: Harvard University Press, 1976).

4. Hadley Cantril, *The Invasion from Mars* (Princeton, NJ: Princeton University Press, 1940).

5. John Vinocur, "Germans Are Caught Up in 'Holocaust' Telecasts," *New York Times,* January 23, 1979; "39% of German TV Viewers Watch 'Holocaust' Episode," *New York Times,* January 26, 1979.

6. John Shelton Lawrence and Bernard Timberg, "News and Mythic Selectivity: Mayaguez, Entebbe, Mogadishu," *Journal of American Culture* 2 (Summer 1979): 324.

7. Earl F. Bargainnier, "Hissing the Villain, Cheering the Hero: The Social Function of Melodrama," *Studies in Popular Culture* 3 (Spring 1980): 48–56.

8. Daniel Dayan and Elihu Katz, "Television Ceremonial Events," *Society* 22 (May/June 1985): 60–66; Bruce Miroff, "The Presidency and the Public: Leadership as Spectacle," in Michael Nelson, ed., *The Presidency and the Political System* (Washington: Congressional Quarterly, 1988, 2nd ed.): 271–291.

9. Tom Carson, "The Kennedys," *American Film* (November 1988): 40–43; Victor Lasky, "TV Docudramas: 'A License to Lie,'" *Reader's Digest* (April 1986): 92–96; James Combs, "Televised Aesthetics and the Depiction of Heroism: The Case of the TV Historical Biography," *Journal of Popular Film and Television* 8 (June 1980): 9–18; William H. Cohn, "History for the Masses: Television Portrays the Past," *Journal of Popular Culture* 10 (Fall 1976): 280–289; Joseph P. McKerns, "Television Docudramas: The Image as History," *Journalism History* 7 (Spring 1980): 24–25, 40.

10. Richard Nelson Current, "Past Reality, Present Fantasy," *The Christian Science Monitor* (June 28, 1988): 31.

11. Frye, *Secular Scripture.*

12. Lawrence W. Lichty, "Success Story," *Wilson Quarterly* 5 (Winter 1981): 63.

13. Karl E. Meyer, "Rootless Mini-series," *Saturday Review* (January 20, 1979): 52–53; see also Phillip Wander, "On the Meaning of 'Roots,'" *Journal of Communication* 27 (Autumn 1977): 64–69; Kenneth H. Hur and John P. Robinson, "The Social Impact of 'Roots,'" *Journalism Quarterly* 55 (Spring 1978): 19–24; Howard F. Stein, "In Search of Roots: An Epic of Origin and Destiny," *Journal of Popular Culture* 11 (Summer 1977): 11–17.

14. Gregory A. Waller, "Re-placing 'The Day After,'" *Cinema Journal* 26: 3 (Spring 1987): 3–20.

CHAPTER 4

The Fortunes and Misfortunes of Fame

Women and Political Celebrity in Popular Periodicals

In the early days of Hollywood, it was the habit of struggling new movie studios to release silent movies for public viewing without naming in the credits the actors in the film. Soon the studios received inquiries asking, "Who was that actor (or actress) in your recent film? Will we see him (or her) again?" Moviemakers quickly calculated that people liked seeing certain people in their films over and over again. Studios started featuring these actors and actresses as drawing cards. Grudgingly, moviemakers paid these valuable properties more and more money. A few, the movie "stars," became so famous that they commanded fabulous salaries and instant recognition no matter where they went. For example, by some accounts actor Charlie Chaplin was the best-known man in the world. Movie stars hired publicity agents to represent them in contract negotiations, and more important, to publicize them in the mass media in efforts to secure the one major thing they all sought: fame.

Famous people of the past—military generals, athletes, and political leaders, for instance—had achieved their notoriety for what they achieved and accomplished on the battlefield, in the arena, or in office. Movie stars, by contrast, were figures of pure fantasy, famous only through projected images on the silver screen. Movie fans (the term *fan* derives from *fanatic*) admired, recognized, talked about, and idolized male stars, even though no star had ever won a battle, an election, or perhaps a fair maiden's heart. Attractive and popular female stars acquired reputations for all manner of fantastic qualities: paragons of virginal beauty (Lillian Gish), *femmes fatales* (Theda Bara, Greta Garbo), spunky but feminine modern women (Clara Bow, Mary Pickford). Mary Pickford moved through a variety of roles as "America's Sweetheart," demonstrating to women that there were multiple options in the modern era; in the process Pickford became wealthy and famous. By 1920 Hollywood had an established "fame industry" that was the first to mass-mediate "the lifestyles of the rich and famous" stars through fanzines (fan magazines), tours, appearances, stunts, and other means.

Hollywood created personages whose lives, on and off screen, were the subject of *fantastic celebration*. Public personages are larger-than-life figures. People attribute to them qualities or powers that make them key players in the dramatic show of society. People celebrate them, making them into heroes, villains, and fools; fans follow their on-screen and off-screen romances; they gossip about them, daydream about them, and on rare occasions see them, touch them, even get their autographs. The fantastic celebration of Hollywood stars—and later sports stars, radio stars, TV stars, rock stars—gave impetus to the creation of a remarkable contemporary fantasy, celebrity.[1]

THE BIRTH OF CELEBRITY

Like many things in the 20th century, it was during the 1920s that the celebrity became an important personage in mass-mediated realities. Popular magazines featured fewer biographical profiles of idols of production (business executives, bankers, ranchers, and engineers) and more of the idols of consumption (athletes, beauty queens, the stars of Hollywood, Broadway, and Tin Pan Alley). Newspaper sections on "high society" receded before tabloid interest in "cafe society"; gossip columnists such as Walter Winchell and Louella Parsons themselves became celebrities with sufficient popular appeal to influence who else would win fame. The newly born celebrities appealed to the popular imagination for many reasons. Hollywood discovered that many people liked the stars' scandalous behavior; both stars and fanzines obliged with tales of parties, romances, spats, quarrels, and divorces. Both the on-field heroics and off-field foolishness of Babe Ruth made him a much-admired sports idol (see Chapter 6). Not all celebrities were comfortable in the role. Ascetic Charles Lindbergh—first aviator to fly solo across the Atlantic—became a reluctant overnight household word; his very reticence at being a celebrity made him all the more intriguing. Lindbergh was likened to a lone pioneer, a heroic performer in a technological age. To his chagrin, he forever lost his anonymity and thus his privacy. Like Greta Garbo and Howard Hughes, the more he wanted to be alone, the more mysterious and celebrated he became. The popular desire for celebrity makes even recluses famous.[2]

The celebration of celebrity has become a widespread and normal part of everyday life. It has clearly expanded our vicarious fantasy life. Our relationship with the imaginary social world of celebrities is such, one scholar maintains, that it is likely "most Americans probably spend more time in artificial interactions than they do in real ones."[3] This means that Americans spend a good bit of time each day engaging in fantasy relationships with persons they know only by reputation. If this is the case, then celebrities have a great deal of importance in the dream life that is the theater of imagination. Indeed, one student of the phenomenon of celebrity has argued that the "people who existed in this separate reality—the stars and celebrities—were as familiar to us, in some ways, as our friends and neighbors. In many respects we were—and are—more profoundly involved with their fates than we are with those of most of the people we know personally." Political issues, among other things, do not have "real status . . . until they have been taken up, dramatized, in the celebrity world." The politician can "exert genuine influence on the general public" only if he or she becomes a celebrity. Thereby "it is in this surreal world that all significant national questions are personified and thus dramatized."[4]

The presidency of Ronald Reagan illustrated how the power of popular celebrity could readily be transferred to the political realm with ease. In fact, however, rather than celebrities becoming politicians, as in Reagan's case, what more often happens is that politicians become celebrities. The rise of celebrity in Hollywood, Broadway, and other realms of show biz occurred first, but because the logic of celebrity-making could apply to all people who are widely known, eventually it entered formerly "dignified" realms such as politics, business, law, academia, and the ministry where previously a person was not a "star" whose game was fame. Once people dreamed of becoming wealthy; now they dream of becoming famous. Whereas the philosopher Friedrich Nietzsche long ago wrote of the will to power, today he might better write of the will to fame. For example, a businessperson used to be content with building commercial empires; now the goal is to be on the cover of *Time* or *Fortune* or to have a home that is featured in *Architectural Digest*. Then, and only then, do many trendy and ambitious businesspeople know that success has been truly achieved. As another example, scholars were once satisfied to write books for their students and colleagues; now they grow famous writing books for best-seller lists. Political scientists seek fame as pundits (see Chapter 8) on TV news and talk shows; psychologists write pop books and make the talk-show circuit; and many a minister, laboring in virtual anonymity and penury in the parsonage, must at moments envy the rich and famous televangelists (see Chapter 9). Republican politicians formerly sought the company and support of business tycoons, Democratic politicians that of labor leaders; now they seek out the glitterati of Hollywood and New York and hope to be featured in *People* magazine along with them. At the pathological extremes, deranged people express in bizarre ways the need to be seen, known, and celebrated. When John Hinckley, who shot President Ronald Reagan in 1981, was initially interrogated, his first question was, "Is it on TV?"[5] Surely artist Andy Warhol, who said that in the future everyone will be famous for 15 minutes, grasped the essence of celebrity.

The celebrity, then, is a creation of mass mediation who becomes well known through the choices fans make as individuals, choices that converge on the selected star. The celebrity is an ephemeral being, a "human pseudo-event," "known for . . . well-knownness."[6] Celebrities are constantly created and destroyed at the mercurial whim of those persons who seek fantasy relationships with them. Some people fear most being out of power or out of action; *the celebrity fears being out of sight!* The celebrity may work hard to stay in the limelight, but he or she (or *it,* since animals such as "Morris the Cat" or inanimate objects such as "Gumby" are well known) lives in a fantasy world of drama. For fans the celebrity occupies a world that is more exciting, glamorous, and trendy than their own mundane existence—at least in fantasy. The relationship between the celebrity and us is transactional: We need them as objects on which to project a land of dreams, a mythography of the celebrated in dramatic encounter for our benefit. In turn, they need us to sustain the lucrative illusion that the famous are the repository of the true, the good, and the beautiful, as well as the false, the bad, and the ugly. Celebrities indeed live in a surreal world—an irrational dream world—in which they represent values (or the lack of them), personify characters and roles (as good or bad), and enact dramas (for good or ill). People find celebrity endlessly entertaining. Perhaps, as some critics charge, we are absorbed in "Who's Hot? Who's Not?" Is it because our own lives are so boring and vacuous that we compensate by consuming fantasy figures? We cannot say. In any case, the celebrity industry sells the famous, and we are the consumers of fame.

Consider, in this regard, the celebration of royalty. One might think that in a democratic country allegedly committed to equality there would be nothing but contempt for the haughty pretensions of royalty. On the contrary, a glance at popular magazines and tabloids demonstrates popular fascination with the fantasy lives of royal families. The respective royalties of England and Monaco, understanding the uses of celebrity to maintain their status and wealth, cooperate with the celebrity industry to perpetuate mass interest in their public lives. Once reclusive, retaining regal status through privacy and mystery, royal families now exploit celebrity status. American tabloids and periodicals dote on the public and private lives of royalty: relations of family members ("Do Princesses Di and Fergie Get Along?"); royal marriages ("The Royal Contract: Solving the Puzzle of Diana's Marriage"), or Cinderella turned sour ("Happy Anniversary—or Is It?": Charles and Diana . . . face that awful moment when marriage can feel like a bad dream"); the Ugly Duckling who becomes a royal swan ("Fergie: The Tomboy Who Grew Up to Marry Prince Andrew"); and royal intrigue ("Is Caroline Trying to Snatch the Throne of Monaco from Her Brother Albert?"). A cottage industry of journalistic royalty-watchers feeds popular fantasies with the latest palace gossip from London and Monte Carlo.

Even though Americans allegedly have no aristocracy and monarchy, in some ways the advent of, and deference to, celebrity has helped to create a *popular royalty.* The 19th century witnessed creation of an "aristocracy of manufacturers" built on the massive fortunes of the robber barons (the Rockefellers, Vanderbilts, Harrimans, and so on); that aristocracy became respected "old money" as it evolved. Its members were never very popular, however. Even those who became celebrities (Doris Duke, Barbara Hutton, Gloria Vanderbilt) were often despised or pitied as "poor little rich girls." The truly popular royalty in America began in Hollywood, eventually reaching other areas of celebrity—sports, radio, TV, and theater, indeed all the overlapping areas of national entertainment—creating a pageant of well-known stars of the leisure class. These "beautiful people" lived a spectacle of conspicuous play. They were the archetypes of beauty, grace, and fashion, the paragons of the ideal of elegant affluence. They were chosen people of talent who lived in palaces, traveled in limousines, made enormous amounts of money, and were objects of popular adulation and even a kind of worship. They were, in sum, royalty although it was a royalty created out of the fantasy world of Beverly Hills, Park Avenue, Sunset Boulevard, Broadway, the Stork Club, Forest Hills, the Pebble Beach Golf Club, St. Moritz, the Riviera, or whatever place was fashionable at the moment. But it was *our* royalty. Eventually, popular royalty moved easily in the world of old money and other reputed dignified realms and some not so dignified, including politics. The creation of such an ephemeral collage of "royal" personages accustomed Americans to the idea of politics as entertainment, entertainers as politicians, and expectations that both should act in a pseudo-regal manner.

POLITICAL CELEBRITY: FROM 15-MINUTE FAME TO "WHERE ARE THEY NOW?"

In a daily monitoring of the world of celebrities familiar political figures abound. "Entertainment" sections of newspapers report Hollywood stars hosting fund-raisers for political candidates; TV's "Entertainment Tonight" reports celebrity entertainers demonstrating for a political cause. More directly, mass-mediated politics has made politicians celebrities in their own right. Celebrity status is a political resource exploited to advantage or sometimes to disadvantage. Celebrity status is mercurial; it can evaporate as quickly as it appears. A hero can become a villain or fool at any time if popular perceptions shift. For political celebrities enacting a moral drama, for instance, failure to lead an exemplary life that projects high ethical and moral standards can be devastating. Other celebrities, however, such as members of rock bands, thrive on the notoriety they derive from "groupies," drugs, and raucous lyrics. The moral parameters of acceptable celebrity behavior are more limited for politicians. Celebrity status is a vital prerequisite for attaining political power in a mass-mediated society, but by definition such stardom carries with it public scrutiny of one's every action. There is a thin line involving political reputation. The political aspirant must decide which celebrities from the realms of film, sports, rock music, and so on can safely be courted for political gain by exploiting the glamor of the association while avoiding connection in the public's mind with the more negative images of celebrity, such as marital infidelity, drugs, an overlavish lifestyle, and the like.

Popular Royalty: Camelot as Soap Opera

The Kennedy family is certainly the most notable case of political celebrity in this nation during this century. In the 1950s popular magazines, Sunday supplements, and gossip columns focused on the Kennedy clan well before the election of John Kennedy to the presidency. Children of wealthy and politically influential Joseph P. Kennedy, former ambassador to Great Britain, grew up to be celebrities. *Life* and other magazines featured the picture-book wedding of John and Jacqueline Kennedy, the dashing young senator and his beautiful debutante wife. John's sister married a movie star, Peter Lawford. The Kennedy brothers frequented New York cafe society and dated starlets. They moved in international celebrity circles and were the friends of Hollywood stars such as Frank Sinatra. When John ran for president in 1960, the press provided considerable publicity: The Kennedys were "beautiful people" in politics—handsome, wealthy, glamorous, aristocratic but "liberal," moving with confidence and grace in corridors of power and fame. During the Kennedy presidency, the Kennedy family was the subject of endless periodical treatment (see, for example, *Look* magazine throughout the 1960s). Initial press coverage was positive in depicting a unified, happy, and stylish family confident of its position and power. After President Kennedy's death, the family's activities and the political intentions of John's political brothers, Robert and Edward, remained a subject of speculation. Political celebrity had made the Kennedys the first family of popular royalty, an ongoing national soap opera questioning when and if the clan and "Camelot" would be restored to political power. Given the focus and character of the postassassination coverage of the Kennedys, it was not difficult for many Americans to get caught up in the romantic Camelot drama that "once there was a spot," the Kennedy presidency, that had been magical under the reign of the wise young king and his court.

As stated earlier, celebrity implies public scrutiny. The Kennedy image began to tarnish through adverse publicity. The president's admired and attractive widow married Greek tycoon Aristotle Onassis, whose reputation was scarcely spotless. After Robert Kennedy's assassination, younger brother Senator Edward "Ted" Kennedy became the heir apparent, but he was involved in a mysterious midnight car accident on a remote beach in which a beautiful, young, single woman was drowned. Thereafter, sensational tabloid fantasizing about the Chappaquidick Affair, as it was called, plagued the political fortunes of Ted Kennedy and played an important role in his failure to receive his party's nomination for president in 1980. The entire Kennedy family, including their younger generation, remain the subject of media attention. Young Joseph Kennedy serves in Congress, and John F. Kennedy, Jr. (called by *People* magazine "the handsomest man in America") addressed the 1988 Democratic convention. The celebrated Kennedy name retains a certain magic across generations.

However, life in the goldfish bowl as First Family of the National Soap Opera has its downside. Since Chappaquiddick, women's magazines and tabloids have reported every rumor imaginable about the Kennedy men and their relationship with women. Stories emerged, with some basis in fact, that John Kennedy, both before and during his presidency, had short-term girl friends, including one with connections to the Mafia. Even with all the stories about his womanizing, John Kennedy still is consistently ranked in polls as one of the most popular presidents (a status he never enjoyed when president). At one time or another, the popular media have hinted that all three Kennedy brothers were as active sexually as they were politically and yielded to desires of the flesh as well as to those for power. For some persons the fantasy of the Kennedy male potency is a positive sign of a male machismo that is desirable in a president; they equate sexual domination of women with political toughness. For others, it is evidence that the Kennedy men had a low opinion of women and were not committed to female equality but to female exploitation. Both interpretations appear in continuing accounts of the alleged relationship of John and Robert to the late film actress Marilyn Monroe. Since her death (apparently a suicide) in 1962, Marilyn Monroe has remained the classic case of a celebrity who remains celebrated even in death. Such notable writers as Norman Mailer and Gloria Steinem have written books about her. Bookstores are still filled with volumes, calendars, and posters featuring her face and figure. Tabloids compete in providing rumors about how and why she died: that she killed herself over John or Robert Kennedy, that she was murdered by the Mafia in some plot involving the Kennedys, or that she is not dead at all but in hiding!

The fantasy that Marilyn lives illustrates yet another way in which celebrities mediate political realities, even from the grave. There is a recurrent impulse in the popular mind to deny that famous and much revered (or despised) public personages are really dead. This is the recurring *fantasy of celebrity immortality*. Folklorists have traced the extent to which such fantastic rumors, often fueled by the tabloids, persist long after the death of the celebrated figure. Thus, Alexander the Great, Charlemagne, and King Arthur are in their Avalons awaiting the proper moment to return. And articles, books, and films promoted the fantasy of Adolf Hitler's survival long after his death in 1945. Similarly, a decade after the mass suicide of the People's Temple followers, stories circulated in tabloids that Jim Jones had escaped. Given tabloid exploitation of the popular imagination, it is not surprising, then, that the rumor persists that John Kennedy was still alive a quarter-century after his 1963 assassination, although brain-impaired. Rumors placed him variously in Parkland Hospital in Dallas, the upper floor of Bethesda Naval Hospital in Maryland, on an island in Greece, or hidden in the Kennedy family compound at Hyannisport. The King of Camelot lives.[7]

The Kennedy family is the leading contemporary example of a wealthy and politically successful extended family that has benefited and suffered in the limelight of unrelenting publicity that surrounds the cult of celebrity. The Kennedy dynasty is also America's leading example of the popular royalty described earlier. Like the royal families of England and Monaco, the price the Kennedys have had to pay is that they have, in the eyes of the mass media, become public property; privacy yields to the peoples' "right to know" about their most intimate moments. And, as the old saying goes, "intimacy breeds contempt." The Kennedys, like other royal families, are plagued by the whims of admiration and scorn of a fickle public. Admiration comes from living up to the expectations of royalty, scorn from failing to match those elevated expectations. Members of royalty are supposed to sustain the illusion of transcending ordinary human failings and pursuits. The late Duke of Windsor, who abdicated the throne of England in 1935 to marry "the woman I love," wrote in his autobiography that "the role of a successful constitutional monarch consists in no small measure of appearing to be not only above politics but also above life."[8] Although not born to rule in the sense that English royal families are, members of America's popular royalty must seem equally transcendent. Given news media scrutiny, that is not easy.

The difficulties involved in living up to popular expectations as members of popular royalty are illustrated in a comparison of Jacqueline and Joan Kennedy, the wives of President John and Senator Edward. When John became president, his wife was young, beautiful, and fashionable. As a new member of the popular royal family, she lived the recurring *Cinderella fantasy* as a young girl chosen princess, loved by her handsome Prince Charming, and residing in a magnificent palace. The First Lady in the manner of a princess conducted Americans on a nationally televised tour of the White House. She was a fashion trend-setter, envied and admired by young American women as no other First Lady before. After her husband's assassination, she displayed admirable firmness and bearing during and after the state funeral. Her royal bearing fueled the popular fantasy of the "one, brief shining moment" of the Kennedy presidency. She revealed to an interviewer John's love for the Broadway musical *Camelot*. Although her royal image was tarnished after her marriage to Aristotle Onassis, she remains admired—an aging, sophisticated, and slightly tragic eternal First Lady whose prince was taken from her.

But what if Prince Charming is thought to have betrayed his Cinderella? In popular romance, a standard melodramatic formula is for the heroic male to select his princess, then successfully combine love and power in their royal lives in the palace. The story can turn pathetic, though, if the prince is a frog who loves power or other women more than his lady fair. The heroine is a victim, the neglected and abandoned woman betrayed by her prince. At least it can be so perceived if the popular media publicize the marital difficulties within the royal family. If the romantic fantasy of living happily ever after goes unfulfilled, real-world political consequences follow.

This was clear in the political and marital fates of Joan and Ted Kennedy. After the death of his brothers, Edward Kennedy was the heir of the Camelot legacy, but events surrounding Chappaquiddick raised questions about Ted Kennedy's claims to the presidential throne. If he was to remove doubts, he would need to buff up his image as a good husband, loving father, and strong family man. During the 1970s, media portrayals often helped Kennedy's cause: He was "surrogate father of Ethel's eleven children" displaying "physical courage and daring, the ideals of public service, the sense of *noblesse oblige* that attends the rich and fortunate, the incredible mystique of family solidarity and the seriousness of religious observance."[9] But by the mid-1970s, the "troubled marriage of Joan and Ted" rested at Ted's door: If he ran for president the "state of his marriage" would be crucial. Joan was a "nice girl" with "public sympathy," simply "unable to cope with the tough and wordly Kennedys." However, if she refused to "play the role of a happy wife" in a "loveless marriage," this could be politically devastating.[10] The tabloids continued gossip about Ted's alleged philandering; Joan became more and more a pathetic victim in the portrayals of women's magazines.

In 1978, when speculation surfaced that Ted would seek the presidency, Joan told her own story. She revealed that she was an alcoholic, separated from Ted, and trying to rebuild her life. The interviewer noted that as Joan poured out her tale, "innocently, almost pleading for understanding," she was "discovering herself as she talked." The interviewer's mind went back to a childhood phrase: " 'Once upon a time' was the way the tales began, and this one began so easily: 'Once upon a time, there was a beautiful girl with long blond hair and wide blue eyes who met a handsome and very rich prince. . . .' But then the tale would turn tragic, for the next line would be: 'This prince had two older brothers. . . .' Was it possible that her story will, someday, end as fairy stories are supposed to end? Will people ever say, 'And they lived happily ever after?' " The interviewer concluded with admiration "for her courage, her understanding, and her self-reliance. . . . I no longer had any doubt about how the story would end. They would live happily ever after."[11] There were reports that when Kennedy read the article he was furious: It made people ask "What kind of man would do this to his wife?"[12]

What kind of prince, indeed? The negative gossip generated by popular magazines haunted the presidential candidacy of Ted Kennedy in 1980. Although rumors about the royal marriage were rife in tabloids, Joan joined Ted on the campaign trail. *People* in 1979 reported her actively involved in her "husband's daring campaign"; she says, "Yes, I still love him," and makes a "gallant defense" of recurrent tales about his "womanizing." But gallant Joan is still the victim: "Playing enthusiastic candidate's wife, some claim, is

Joan's most skillful acting job since she made TV commercials for Coca-Cola and Revlon 20 years ago."[13] She appeared with him in public and said she would live in the White House with him if elected. She told *McCall's Magazine* that "this campaign has been wonderful for me, the best thing in the world, next to getting sober. It's been terrific for my self-esteem."[14] Joan was no longer victim but a victorious, independent lady. Although Kennedy's campaign failed, a June 1980 woman's supplement in the *Chicago Tribune* opined, "The 'Kennedy Victory' may be Joan's."[15] The once frail and pitiful Joan was by now "as tough and brave and independent as any Kennedy . . . Joan may well deserve the label of the 'bravest Kennedy.'"[16]

Joan Kennedy, then, was in 1980 the heroine of a mass-mediated soap opera with definite political consequences. The popular expectation that political celebrities be good husbands made Ted a villain. If she was transformed in the rhetorical vision of women's magazines from a victim to a brave and independent new person, he was recast as lacking character. The news theater of political celebrity that the Kennedys had used so well to promote their royalty for so long ironically helped to undermine Ted's public image. If his wife was the personal victim, he was the political victim. The 1975 *McCall's Magazine* article was prophetic: The political princess had been betrayed by Prince Charming, and the romantic melodrama was transformed into pathos. The political part of the play had an unhappy ending. The lesson of the Joan Kennedy story is quite clear. We have noted that a political figure exerts genuine influence on the general public in part because of celebrity status, but celebrity must not be notoriety. Cast as a bad husband who disappoints, hurts, and uses his beautiful princess, a politician's influence over public opinion—in the form of votes—wanes. The melodrama of the national soap opera is still a highly moral one: Traditional virtue must triumph in the long run. The domestic melodrama of Joan and Ted Kennedy had no triumphant close; the political melodrama of the royal Kennedy family in 1980 had no happy ending either.

In early 1981, long after the campaign and election, Joan and Ted Kennedy quietly announced they were getting a divorce. Joan emerged with her image as a new woman entact. *People* of February 1981 said she lost her marriage, "but gains control of her life."[17] Armed with her new self-esteem, she became the "winner" of the 1980 election. Yet, the saga is not over for either Joan or Ted. She remains a topic for gossip columns and women's magazines. By the late 1980s, she was permanently cast as the ultimate victim, a lost and pathetic figure in and out of "relationships" and rehabilitation centers but never out of the tabloids. After a car accident and a charge of drunk driving in 1988, a *National Star* headline read, "How Broken Love Affair Drove Joan Kennedy Back to Drinking." The article cited her "heartbreak over a failed romance," her "despondent appearance," how the "look on her face was so sad, so resigned, so tragically lonely." But who was really at fault? A friend confides: "We worried that if the relationship soured, she'd lose it. Joan was love-starved—she'd always talk about loneliness and her fear of growing old alone. Teddy did a number on her."[18] The "number" was done on Ted also. The actual extent of his blame for his wife's troubles is unknown. His failure to supply a romantic *dénouement* of "living happily ever after" in keeping with the expectations of popular royalty relegated him to playing on the stage of the U.S. Senate, not in the great theater of the Oval Office and Camelot.

Celebrity Scorned: The Case of Gary Hart

The impact of Joan's troubles on Ted's political fortunes—and vice versa—reminded other aspiring politicians that they too were subject to the moral logic and public scorn of celebrity. Their political fame, too, and their possible fall therefrom were also dependent on treatment by popular publications. If they failed to rise above life, such politicians clearly saw, the lesson of Ted and Joan was that they too could be politically destroyed. Looking toward 1988, former Colorado Senator Gary Hart was the frontrunner for the Democratic presidential nomination (see Chapter 2) when he announced his candidacy in April 1987. That ended in May. The Miami *Herald* revealed that the married Hart had spent a weekend on a yacht in Bimini and later another evening in a Washington townhouse with a young woman who was not his wife. Hart denied charges of marital infidelity, but the damage was done. The woman, Donna Rice, appeared on the cover of *People,* on the cover of the *National Enquirer* sitting on Hart's lap, and was profiled in *Life.* According to the *Enquirer,* Rice allegedly informed a friend that, while in Bimini, Hart had told her that he was "planning to divorce his wife after he was elected president—then marry Donna and bring her to the White House as his new First Lady." Said Donna, "Gary told me he loved me—and I told him I loved him. . . . I don't love my wife . . . Lee had been a good wife, but he needed a younger one to keep up with [me]." Donna said "she cried with joy. Never in her wildest dreams had she ever thought of being the wife of a president." The revelations forced Hart out of the race and an end to any link between Hart and Rice. "No success as an actress and model can make up for the heartbreak of losing Gary Hart and the chance to live in the White House."[19]

It was not only Gary and Donna who became the focus of media scrutiny. So did Lee Hart, the candidate's wife. As if following the recommendation of the country-western tune "Stand by Your Man," Lee Hart professed belief in Gary's story and campaigned with him, but the same sense of betrayal by her prince began to appear in the popular press as it had with Joan Kennedy. "After sticking with a troubled marriage," noted *People,* "Lee Hart watches a dream die." "I'd have told her to leave the jerk," headlined *Newsweek;* "It was hell," says *Time.* Newsmagazines reveled in Lee Hart's ordeal.[20] However much of an ordeal it was, she remained at her husband's side when he re-entered the race in December 1987 to "let the people decide." Hart participated in the early debates and primaries, but it quickly became clear that the people had decided, and Hart withdrew once again, saying he wanted to spend more time with his family. Gary Hart remained an enigma: For a person who styled himself after John Kennedy, he might be thought to have learned the lesson that popular fantasies of marital fidelity and bliss are a prerequisite to princedom; such a fantasy precludes risky personal behavior. Fame, not infamy, carries a celebrity to the presidency.

FANTASIES OF COURT LIFE

Americans expect a great deal of celebrities. Most people rely on different kinds of celebrities to feed a variety of fantasies: admired rock singers for the social rebellion and sexual freedom they represent; liberal activists and moral leaders for the courage and rectitude we wish we had; and conservative politicians for the political stability we hope they can provide. Hence, there is no inconsistency in idolizing such diverse personae as *U2*, Prince, Jane Fonda, Mother Teresa, Ronald Reagan, Margaret Thatcher, and Oliver North. Polls of people's "most admired" reveal astonishing combinations of celebrated figures. After years of the U.S. public's labeling the Soviet Union the "evil empire," some polls in the United States found Soviet Premier Mikhail Gorbachev more popular than President Reagan![21] So the celebrated *dramatis personae* of fantasies include the famous and infamous, the noted and the notorious, the virtuous and the wicked—anyone who fulfills some vicarious wish that cannot be experienced otherwise.

Celebrities exist in *fantastic settings,* extraordinary places where they enact their celebrated status. The White House was certainly such a fantastic setting for the Kennedys. It has remained so for the First Families that have followed. No item in the private life of the First Family is too trivial to receive notice in Washington gossip columns, women's magazines, books, and TV docudramas dramatizing "backstairs at the White House." The weddings of presidential children have been televised. TV cameras appear at state dinners and other glittering affairs. First Ladies have personal staffs to coordinate appearances, images, and activities of America's surrogate queen—including the First Lady's pet public "project" (highway beautification, a war on drugs, the fight against illiteracy, and so on). Presidents cultivate the public company and support of celebrities. White House gatherings and award ceremonies honor popular singers, athletes, Hollywood stars, literary figures, and other nonpolitical celebrities as much as they do government servants. The White House press office publicizes to the press corps tidbits that help personalize presidential celebrity: Gerald Ford toasted his own English muffins, Jimmy Carter liked to work in denims, Ronald Reagan enjoyed macaroni and cheese, George Bush is fascinated with the remote control of his TV.

With each presidential administration the process of publicizing, humanizing, and personalizing presidential royalty becomes more elaborate. The "performance team" in the Reagan administration (that is, those advisers skilled in the histrionic arts and ways to publicize the presidency in the most appealing fashion) were particularly adept in impression management. In some instances, like experience brokers, they made of the presidency a designed experience for the incumbent. The Reagan team was at ease with the world of the celebrity, and it combined Hollywood and Washington lifestyles as never before.

Consider the molding of an appealing image for First Lady Nancy Reagan. In royal portrayal Mrs. Reagan restored "elegance" to the White House, yet left the impression of being a loyal helpmate and concerned parent in the tradition of the former First Ladies. This royalty-with-the-common-touch character performance did not come about overnight. Her identification with the super rich glitterati and their opulent lifestyle did not play well in the early 1980s as economic recession became worse. The first press judgments were encouraging, though. "Elegant, Opulent, Right-minded," wrote *People;* Mrs. Reagan and her wealthy friends were "world-class party-goers and -givers, and all are movers in California society. . . . We are finally going to see some real style in Washington."[22]

When White House soundings of popular perceptions revealed Nancy's version of the glamorous lady to be less like Cinderella and more like Marie Antoinette, however, the performance team made a conscious effort to recast the *dramatis persona* of the First Lady. First, she performed a self-parodying song at a gathering of the Washington journalistic elite to counter the impression that she was cold and uncaring. To convey the image of a concerned parent as well as social leader, the First Lady's professional staff crafted an antidrug abuse campaign. She toured drug rehabilitation clinics, appeared in White House media events in support of foster grandparents, and was on a TV network situation comedy to speak to a class of actor-children about drug use. The "Just Say NO" program, featuring a televised address to the nation on the subject of drug abuse (with the president and First Lady sitting on a couch holding hands) provided the overriding symbol in the transformation of the royal image. (Skeptics noted that the Reagan administration all the while was cutting federal funds to fight the drug traffic and to promote drug education.)

This mass-mediated campaign shored up the First Lady's image as someone concerned about important social problems. Later, Nancy Reagan again proved controversial when it seemed clear that she was an important political adviser to her husband. Critics accused her of "Nancyism," pushing a malleable husband into such actions as negotiating with the Russians, something he allegedly would not have done on his own. During periods of presidential illness, there were accusations that she was an "incipient Edith Wilson." She, like President Woodrow Wilson's wife after his stroke, would run the nation with a closed set of advisers. That flurry of criticism passed, only to be replaced by more "inside dope" (see Chapter 8) from the popular press. The president's overtures to the Soviet Union bore fruit. (Nancy Reagan's alleged role in promoting the overtures now was forgotten.) The popular press commented favorably on the thaw in the Cold War, only to report that the First Lady was involved in a cold war of her own. It was a war with the fashionable "Gucci Red," Raisa Gorbachev, each of the women trying to outdo the other in fashion excesses, the opulence of formal events, keeping each other waiting at formal occasions, and other such schoolgirl tactics. Tabloids portrayed each as envious of the other's popularity and status as "world-class *grande dame*." "Who does that dame think she is?," Nancy was alleged to have exclaimed of the departed Raisa after a state dinner where Mrs. Gorbachev had impressed President Reagan.

TWINKLE, TWINKLE, LITTLE STAR, HOW I WONDER WHO YOU ARE

As stars glisten in the night skies, they appear to twinkle. One moment they are bright, another dim. Nancy Reagan's changing luminescence in the popular press during her time as First Lady indicates how difficult it is for any celebrity, regardless of the skill of the professional performance team, to achieve a steady glow of popularity. Both Ronald and Nancy Reagan, coming as they did from backgrounds of celebrity in Hollywood films, understood this. Both grasped the necessity of continuously refurbishing their images, not allowing their performances as president or First Lady—no matter how well or badly judged by press or populace—to diminish their starlike, personal appeal. The political philosopher (and dramatist) Niccolo Machiavelli argued more than five centuries ago that whatever good or ill a prince can achieve through governing, he cannot govern at all unless he wins political power and acts to hold on to it. Winning and holding political power in contemporary America requires celebrity status. As we have seen in the cases of Teddy and Joan, Gary and Donna and Lee, Ronnie and Nancy, celebrity is fickle. The populace and popular press can withdraw it as quickly as they grant it. Hence, holding political power today means holding on to celebrity status. Doing that demands celebrity management, that is, orchestrating times, settings, and events to enhance the personal celebrity of a political leader *first,* governing second. As President Ronald Reagan was fond of saying of his administration, "You ain't seen nothin' yet." As popular royalty, their courts, and their performance teams devise even more crafty ways of constructing personal celebrity in the years ahead, we may recall the words of the president who raised celebrity management to new heights, "indeed, we ain't seen nothin' yet!"

NOTES

1. Lary May, *Screening Out the Past* (New York: Oxford University Press, 1980); Daniel Boorstin, *The Image: A Guide to Pseudo-Events in America* (New York: Atheneum, 1972); C. Wright Mills, *The Power Elite* (New York: Oxford University Press, 1956), pp. 71–92; Orrin E. Klapp, *Symbolic Leaders* (New York: Minerva Press, 1964); James Monaco, ed., *Celebrity* (New York: Dell, 1978); Richard Schickel, *Intimate Strangers: The Culture of Celebrity* (Garden City, NY: Doubleday, 1985); Leo Braudy, *The Frenzy of Renown: Fame and Its History* (New York: Oxford University Press, 1986).
2. John W. Ward, "The Meaning of Lindbergh's Flight," *American Quarterly* 10 (1958): 3–16.
3. John L. Caughey, "Artificial Social Relations in Modern America," *American Quarterly* 30 (1978): 73.
4. Richard Schickel, "Fairbanks: His Picture in the Paper," in Monaco, *Celebrity*, pp. 121–127.
5. See the discussion of Hinckley's fantasy of fame in Robert Jewett and John Shelton Lawrence, *The American Monomyth*, 2nd ed. (New York: University Press of America, 1988), pp. 236–242.
6. Boorstin, *The Image*, p. 57.
7. Bruce A. Rosenberg, "Kennedy in Camelot: The Arthurian Legend in America," *Western Folklore* 35 (January 1976): 52–59; Donald M. McKale, *Hitler: The Survival Myth* (New York: Stein & Day, 1981).
8. Edward VIII, Duke of Windsor, *A King's Story* (New York: Putnam, 1951), p. 322.
9. Vivian Cadden, "The Burden of Ted Kennedy," *McCall's Magazine* (February 1974): 48.
10. Penelope McMillan, "The Troubled Marriage of Joan and Ted Kennedy," *McCall's Magazine* (November 1975): 46.
11. Joan Braden, "Joan Kennedy Tells Her Own Story," *McCall's Magazine* (August 1978): 121, 190–193.
12. Eleanor Randolph, "The Kennedys," *Chicago Tribune,* September 10, 1978, Sec. 5, p. 1.
13. "Joan Kennedy," *People* (December 24, 1979): 51.
14. *McCall's Magazine* (June 1980): 48.
15. Ann Blackman, *Chicago Tribune, June 8, 1980, Sec. 12: 5.*
16. Stephen Birmingham, "The Kennedy Women: America's Seven Wonders," *Harper's Bazaar* (October 1980): 29.
17. Gail Jennes, "Joan Kennedy Loses Her Marriage, But Gains Control of Her Life," *People* (February 9, 1981): 37.
18. Rebecca Barnes, "How Broken Love Affair Drove Joan Kennedy Back to Drinking," *National Star,* September 6, 1988, p. 8.
19. Alan Braham Smith, Richard Baker, and John South, "Gary Hart Planned to Divorce His Wife After the Election and Make Me First Lady," *National Enquirer,* June 2, 1987, p. 32–33.
20. M. Green, "After Sticking with a Troubled Marriage, Lee Hart Watches a Dream Die," *People* (May 25, 1987): 38–40; "'I'd Have Told Her to Leave the Jerk,'"

Newsweek (December 28, 1987): 16; "Lee: 'It Was Hell,'" *Time* (December 28, 1987): 19; "Lee Hart's Ordeal," *Newsweek* (May 18, 1987): 31.

21. Steve Daley, "Soviet Leader Met Us on Same Wavelength," *Chicago Tribune,* December 13, 1987, Sec. 1: 25.

22. Kathy MacKay, "Elegant, Opulent, Right Minded: The Friends of Nancy Reagan March on Social Washington," *People* (January 19, 1981): 38.

CHAPTER 5

The Vision from Sunset Boulevard

The Political Fantasies of Hollywood

In 1893, inventive genius Thomas A. Edison wrote a letter describing his new device, "a little instrument which I call a Kinetoscope, with a nickel and slot attachment." He was dubious whether it would be as successful as his other inventions, such as the phonograph: "The zeotropic devices are of too sentimental a value to get the public to invest in." Edison was wrong. Very quickly, Nickelodeons appeared everywhere. A classic capitalist fight soon began for control of the burgeoning new movie industry. Some of the new moviemakers—men with names such as Fox, Warner, Goldwyn, and Mayer—founded fledgling movie studies in a rural town north of Los Angeles named Hollywood. There they made popular entertainment history: The studios produced narrative films that became increasingly complex and spectacular; movie stars burst forth and became the idols of millions; and Hollywood itself became the symbol of leisure, pleasure, and beauty, of fabulous wealth and luxury, a fantasyland that thrived on its ability to conjure up and sell collective fantasies.[1]

DREAMS FOR SALE

Most of us have had the experience of being caught up in a movie. We enter a theater (or put a tape on the VCR) and for a couple of hours we forget ourselves and the outside world of work and care. We travel into the *metareal* (above or beyond the real) world of the movie, sharing in the adventure, mystery, romance, and nightmare that the story portrays and unfolds. At particularly harrowing or moving moments, we must remind ourselves that "it's only a movie." If the movie appeals to us, we deem it a good movie and recommend it to our friends. If the film is a box office hit, we feel vindicated in our good taste; if not, well, other moviegoers simply lack our critical acumen. In any case, the movie was memorable. We remember it, even wish to see it again.

What we are not aware of is the complex fantasy process involved in our enjoying a movie. All of us bring to movie viewing the power of our imaginations, the ability to suspend disbelief for a time and take part, instead, in make believe. We enter the vicarious experience that unfolds on the screen. Moviemakers, motivated by the desire to sell tickets and create a work of popular merit, strive to anticipate and capture the imagination of some segment of a potential viewing audience. They evolve images of the audience they think will want to see a particular move and what the audience would like to see in it. From their beginnings in Hollywood, the moviemakers learned that audiences respond to films that are both familiar and novel, films that tell cultural tales people readily identify, yet that are novel in providing fresh and topical plot lines. For example, moviemakers sensed that people would like Westerns, which at first retold the frontier myth of heroic and violent conquest, then evolved into a genre telling different stories appealing to audiences long after the frontier was no more. The Western became a familiar cultural folktale into which moviemakers, aware of changes in audience interests, could project contemporary currents of thought or concerns. The evolving Western enabled audiences to enjoy both enduring and here-and-now fantasies: Audiences in the era of the Great Depression could see a Western that was a parable of honest folks wronged by scheming capitalists (*Jesse James*); World War II audiences watched Western heroes take on and defeat invading Nazis dressed in cowboy outfits (*Wild Horse Riders*); film audiences during the 1950s watched allusions to Cold War fears (*High Noon*); during the upheavals of the 1960s, audiences viewed in Westerns images of America as an irredeemably violent society (*The Wild Bunch*) or a militaristic imperial power crushing native peoples (*Little Big Man*). Movies are about the cultural myths and stories that we are heir to and that are in the *backs* of our minds; they are also about themes and events in an unfolding present that are *on* our minds.[2]

The metaworld of the movies is a fantasy world, but it is a fantasy world that we, the movie audience, have a crucial role in mediating. In a key sense movies represent vital historical and temporal themes that mark what the culture considers valuable and important at a specific time. Certainly people often learn from the movies—how to dress, how to behave, what to value, whom to admire, what the world is or should be like. The movies learn from us, too, simply because they need to respond to shifting audience fascinations in order to sustain the industry. Moviemakers are sensitive to continuities and changes in the popular mind. When they succeed in representing on screen something important about us, films become cultural artifacts that, like popular art from the past such as Greek plays or Victorian novels, illuminate what it is that we were at a particular time and place. When future historians ask, "What were the Americans of the Twentieth century like?," they can study movies as one record of our fantasies about ourselves and the world. To be able to grasp in the year 2050 the Great Depression of the 1930s will certainly require reading books on the period, examining photographs and newspapers, reading the testimony of recorded oral histories, and so on. Watching movies of that era, however, will offer its own special insight, for these artifacts of the interplay of moviemakers and moviegoers comprise evidence of the popular fantasies that also defined the Great Depression. A 1930s movie such as *Top Hat* with Fred Astaire and Ginger Rogers invites each viewer to reflect on the poor but overworked young man or woman who is barely able to afford admission to a local theater, yet who on watching the elegant and fabulously rich metaworld of the movie can participate in that world in imagination. Empathy with earlier generations of moviegoers reminds us what social functions movie fantasies played when the films first appeared.

It is no accident that Hollywood has been called "the Dream Factory" that offers dreams for sale. Perhaps Hollywood gave too much credence to our illusions and made us believe that the world we live in is (or should be) as it is in the movies. Yet, the dreams on movie screens over the decades are *our* dreams, the cultural myths and immediate fantasies interwoven into film narratives. Movies are not merely mindless escape but a medium of popular learning. When millions of Americans form the movie-attending habit seeking entertainment, they learn and relearn through play. That is, they enjoy the movies for their own sake, not to take lessons away from them directly. Still, they do receive lessons as by-products of the movie experience. People attend movies because the habit is satisfying. Films offer a safe place to indulge in fantasies through vicarious participation in the unfolding spectacle. Thus movies give life to our dreams, and we have the communal experience of sharing the collective representations of our common fantasizing. For those who dream of love, there are movies picturing true romance; for those whose lives are devoid of adventure, the exploits of movie adventurers may serve as a satisfying substitute; those who like to puzzle over perplexing and frightening mysteries seldom experienced in everyday living can view suspense films as a vicarious way of sleuthing. Movies assist us in playing out our dreams and in the process leave their impact on us as well. We are, in that sense, the stuff that movie dreams are made of.

Such a proposition asserts that we would not be who we are without the common and cumulative experience of the movies; they profoundly affect our image of ourselves and the world. The movie experience and the ways we learn through it affect us all, but the process is so diffuse, uneven, subtle, and long-term that we are seldom aware of it. The moviegoing habit is *ritual play,* a structured ceremonial event that we enter with an attitude of quiet expectation (see Chapter 2). We expect the photoplay that is a movie to provide a reliably entertaining experience. Like any ritual, we participate with the unconscious view that it will focus and guide our attention and feelings sufficiently to arouse the fantasy of shared celebration. There is a secular worship in moviegoing: the reverential air audiences bring to the theater; a willingness to let the movie speak to our collective fantasies, rather than to each other (Don't you hate people who talk during a movie?); and a silent talking back to the screen and its god-like images. As with any audience to a ritual (in church at a wedding or funeral, at a parade or school commencement), moviegoers are fantastic participants, sharing, not challenging, the moviegoing ritual. The tradition of mainstream American narrative films has been to establish movies as a ritual form of expression; even the conventions of new genres and the canons of novel direction are but predictable variations on old themes, characters, and stories. In a horror movie, for instance, we know generally what to expect from the genre; we simply don't know what specific variations on suspense, danger, the appearance of the horrible, and the defeat (or nondefeat) of evil the newest form will take.[3]

Movies thus offer insight into the popular imagination, what people imagine about themselves and the changing world they live in. Experienced in the here-and-now, movies help people to be familiar with and conversant about their world. Movies can be a metaphor for that world and its happenings. A metaphor is a likeness or an analogy between objects or ideas. A movie is a metaphor for the present in the sense that it is a symbolic representation of what is occurring at a particular time. War movies are an example of such a ritualized genre: During World War II major war films served as popular metaphors for a war with which most moviegoers had no direct contact. They could, however, imagine the war through the mediated reality of the war movie. Similarly, in the 1980s a spate of movies about the Vietnam War provided a mediated version for a generation of moviegoers born during and after the Vietnam era. War movies are but substitutions, distillations, and condensations of complex and inchoate events (skirmishes, battles, campaigns, planning, and death); they are no more than metaphors, nor are they intended to be. They are *fables,* stories rooted in the mythic folklore and narrative traditions of the culture, applied in ritualized and metaphorical ways to present the present and to re-present the past.

Movies offer audiences entertainment, play, and mythic adequacy. Audience members know this; they come to expect it. They expect movies to be ritual experience that satisfies desires for play; they understand that movies relate to them personally; they respond to metaphorical presentations of realities and readily recognize fables of cultural heritage. When movies represent widespread and socially significant fantasies, they facilitate *fantastic learning* for portions of the movie audience—a learned sense of who and where they are. This reflexive self-conception may differ from person to person, but when many people experience the same mediated reality through movies, there is again collective representation, a shared fantasy of what people thought, felt, and did at a particular time in history.

To be sure, we can never know the number of people who respond to particular movies in common fantastic ways. Because movies mediate reality through fantasies, especially about politics, it would be a mistake to ignore the political importance of films simply because their precise effect on people's everyday lives is difficult to demonstrate and prove. It is our conviction that the widely held fantasies of this nation have been enriched, even defined, by movies in ways we do not fully understand. By examining representative movies from past political periods, we can at least make inferences regarding popular fantasies about power, for *the movies tell us about ourselves in relation to our politics.*

MOVIES AS RITUALS OF POWER

When we go to the movies, we see stories in largely melodramatic and comic formulas, stunning visual imagery, imaginative flights that explore the depths and breadth of our fantasies. Imbedded in movie fare, either overtly or covertly, are also ideas and images about power. In explicit or implicit fashion, movies recurrently address basic questions about power: Who has power? How is it exercised? How should it be exercised? What can it do to us or for us? Who is exercising it at this time? Is it a threat or a promise for our future? The depiction of power is often in a nonpolitical setting in the movies (between a couple or in a family, for example). This does not mean, however, that it does not instruct us as to the nature of power or tell us anything about our fantasies or how power is being exercised in the larger society.

If we look carefully at movies of a particular period, we can detect something about the way that people felt about power during that time—what they wanted out of it, what they hoped and feared about it, and so on. Such movies reveal *rituals of power,* ritual dramas (see Chapter 2) that hint at the conduct and consequences of power. As a metaphor of power, movies teach the uses and abuses of power in fantastic ways. These fables of power either affirm or subvert inherited and current feelings about power. Again, consider movies about World War II. In this nation there was considerable concern regarding if, how, and when America would win the war. Movie rituals of military power preached the political lesson that, just as on the screen, the war was being conducted with honor and courage against an evil and cowardly enemy and for this reason U.S. victory was assured. The movie reality was of American political power in command: The Nazis and the Japanese were doomed by their evil intent to destroy American political values; the source of our political and military power lay in the democratic virtue of our citizens and soldiers. Such fables of exploited long-held myths of national and democratic heritage reassured citizens of the certainty of triumph and, not incidentally, justified whatever sacrifices leaders called on citizens to make. Here was metaphorical affirmation, presented by means of cultural fable, that a stormy and uncertain present would yield to a peaceful and prosperous future.

War is an avowedly political activity; hence, war movies are obviously political fare. What about the content of supposedly nonpolitical films? These no less than war movies teach and preach about power relationships, albeit in implicit ways. Thus, regardless of overt content and themes, movies offer a special kind of political knowledge, a knowledge that is at once an aesthetic, delightful reverie in the movie metaworld and a pragmatic instruction about the way power works in the world outside the theater.

Think again of moviegoers in the Great Depression watching *Top Hat*. The makers of that movie probably intended no ringing political statement. Yet, political communication it was. *Top Hat* portrayed the lifestyle of the rich, who were blamed by many persons for causing the economic collapse and who, according to popular folklore, were still living the high life. Yet the rich depicted in *Top Hat* were not so much venal plutocrats as silly and self-indulgent fools. Foolishness aside, there was an allure in the power bestowed by wealth—access to Art Deco pleasuredomes, freedom from work and drudgery, the privileges of a leisure class. Here were the idle rich who didn't seem to work, had not earned their wealth, and appeared to be irresponsible and aimless. The movie portrayed them as parodies of the American Dream, unproductive economic royalty not part of the real America, sharply contrasted with ordinary folks (maids, for instance). In the end the leading characters of *Top Hat,* sophisticates played by Astaire and Rogers, discovered redemption through romantic love and marriage. Thus triumph innocence and social virtue. *Top Hat* instructed ordinary people, whose power resided in goodness and hard work, not in wealth, that they were the backbone of the nation in trying times, far wiser than the anachronistic rich. There was therefore reason to dance (as Astaire and Rogers did often): The New Deal was restoring power to those who, with apt contempt for the rich, would nonetheless share in a bourgeois prosperity liberated from elite privilege. *Top Hat* implicitly criticized an outmoded concentration of power, leaving audiences amused by, not envious of, frivolous elites. "We may be poor, but we're rich" was a message teaching the moral superiority of the impoverished (servants and manual laborers in the film and in the audience). Astaire's suave, debonair character hardly matched the living conditions of ordinary people in the 1930s. Yet, moviegoers could share his contempt for the pretensions of the parasitic rich and, in the process, his desire for a life of freedom and pleasure far beyond the moviegoers' financial means. Such a film offers a political view: By envisioning the plight of the rich and indulging our own common moral superiority, we may acquiesce in our relatively impoverished social, economic, and political status.

Nonpolitical movies are, therefore, implicitly political. In them the process of constructing and communicating political fantasies is subtle; it involves neither conscious intention on the part of the moviemakers nor conscious connection on the part of the movie audiences. That very subtlety has made movies a key mediator of political realities throughout the decades.

THE POPULIST FANTASY IN THE FILMS OF THE 1930s

With the arrival of sound movies and the Great Depression, which almost coincided, the Hollywood film took on added significance in American life. Movies are far more than a mere escape from the economic devastation of the times, as critics of movies liked to argue. Movies are about the world in which people live, although in a heightened and altered sense. So in Depression Era movies audiences could escape, yet find a way to deal with the threatening world outside the theater. Movies like *Top Hat* offered both solace that supported political quiescence and an explanation as well. Faced with perplexing economic disaster, people asked, "What is going on?" Popular films provided an answer. Fantastic learning from Depression movies didn't give people political truth or a political ideology. It gave them fables of power useful in coping with a difficult real-life situation, however misleading or useless movies turned out to be. The most representative films of the decade—the most memorable, those that evoked the mood of the era—remain as popular evidence of what many people thought, or wanted to think, *was* happening politically. These films today yield visual insights to the most important political fantasies of the 1930s.[4]

The economic crisis of the Depression was an occasion for popular interplay between cultural myth and period fantasy. At stake was nothing less than belief in the efficacy of the American Dream, the core cultural myth that America's search for material and moral prosperity serves individual and collective destiny.[5] The American Dream takes on renewed strength as fantasy in each new age because new problems present new obstacles to the realization of the Dream. Depression Era movies dramatized anxieties about the status of the Dream at a time when its veracity and future were in grave doubt. Movie fantasies were sometimes pessimistic, sometimes hopeful and positive; many captured popular ambivalence about the Dream. All were ritual plays representing a mythic heritage and fantastic life; in retrospect, they were more complex and troubled than a casual moviegoer might have expected.

This was never more evident than in one of the first movie responses to the Depression, the gangster melodrama of the early 1930s. Audiences witnessed in films such as *Little Caesar, The Public Enemy,* and *Scarface* how a poor boy from the urban slums could rise to power and wealth through capitalist enterprise in the best tradition of the Horatio Alger achievement myth. The irony was that in these films the capitalist success ethic was criminal and destructive, promoting individual greed and moral corruption. What precise fantasy moviegoers shared in the Depression we cannot say, but the reality provided by Hollywood mediation was reasonably clear: Acquisitive and high-living gangsters of the movies paralleled captains of industry who had created the speculative prosperity that produced the Great Crash of 1929 (see Chapter 1). Movie criminals, such as those portrayed by actor Jimmy Cagney, operated outside the self-serving rules of the industrial rich. They were outlaws because they were forced into a life of crime. Here was a world in which people seeking to make a decent living faced threats from self-seeking entrepreneurs. The gangster was an inversion of the American Dream, a tragic hero who demonstrated to audiences that to take the honest road was honorable but doomed to failure; to take the dishonest road of the gangster (also an entrepreneur) would produce success but would also corrupt. "We might be poor," audiences could surmise, "but at least we are honest." The gangster's ritual destruction on screen gave audiences a fantasy of social justice; The high and mighty were humbled by corrupt excesses that violated the popular norms of social morality.[6]

The movies of the 1930s often helped audiences in their fantastic search for social scapegoats who could be blamed for the economic ills of the times. Usually this was juxtaposed with the governmental benevolence associated with President Franklin Roosevelt's New Deal, as well as with agencies such as the Federal Bureau of Investigation, which were dramatized as heroes fighting social evils. Cagney himself moved from playing the public enemy in 1931 to G-man in 1935. Hollywood no more than Roosevelt had in mind radical solutions, because both sensed that people didn't want them. Rather, public officials and moviemakers embraced a broad reaffirmation of political populism that exalted the wisdom and perseverance of the common people as opposed to persons who violated the norms of democracy and common sense. The gangster, like his business counterpart in the popular mind, was an uncommon man who was flawed and doomed. Common people would endure, would outlast the criminal element.

So too would common people endure the foolishness of the wealthy. Wealthy families depicted in the "screwball" comedies, such as *It Happened One Night, My Man Godfrey,* and *Philadelphia Story,* were plutocratic but not sinister. The family that Godfrey the butler worked for was idle, useless, and mildly corrupt; by contrast ordinary people—servants, cab drivers, laborers, and even the "forgotten men" of the bread lines—appeared wise and productive. The economic royalists deserved a democratic comeuppance by being depicted as screwballs, a fantasy that vindicated and renewed democratic and capitalist values. Godfrey, the butler, for example, turned out to be a well-born and educated man who had fallen on hard times. He taught his rich employers lessons in popular morality, such as humility, and he married the beautiful daughter, opened a restaurant, and hired the forgotten unemployed. Through such fare, moviegoers could share the fantasy that our common democratic faith overcomes great social divisions, including class inequality.

Many of the movies from the 1930s suggest that people wished to believe in the restoration or completion of the American Dream through the realization of a kind of social solidarity and populist democracy that would overwhelm and defeat the arrogant concentration of power and wealth. Some movies appealed because they evoked nostalgic fantasies about simpler and happier societies in other times and places (*Gone with the Wind, Steamboat Round the Bend, The Wizard of Oz*). Yet even the most socially conscious films avoided proposing a political solution to the Depression that involved major social change. *The Grapes of Wrath,* for instance, blamed remote banks and farm labor camps as exploiters of the Okies, then depicted government agencies as the ultimate hope for the ill-housed, ill-fed, and unemployed. The film revived popular belief in the triumph of democracy and the hope that the yoke of oppressive private power is temporary. With few exceptions (most notably, *You Only Live Once*), social problem films of the time were rituals of hope that promised audiences eventual solutions based on the popular ability to endure adversity and trust social institutions.

Those social institutions could have used some renewed infusion of popular values and desires. Indeed, the movies of that decade tended to say that the Depression had been caused by elite institutions losing touch with the people, and required the institutions to reform by renewing their faith in popular principles. The film director who helped to propagate that fantasy was Frank Capra, especially in his late 1930s films *Mr. Deeds Goes to Town, Mr. Smith Goes to Washington,* and *Meet John Doe.* Capra's films were rituals of popular power renewed, evoking audience fantasies of institutional reform through the revivifying work of a popular hero. Each film told the story of an ordinary individual possessed of the common touch and rooted in the great American heartland. The Capra hero went to the sophisticated big city and its big institutions that were peopled by evil bosses, shyster lawyers, cynical newspaper reporters, tough career women, and scheming politicos—all of whom sneered at and tried to exploit the naive and innocent hero. Eventually his sincere representation of grassroots American values triumphed; he converted the powerful. In Capra's *Mr. Smith Goes to Washington,* for example, a young and naive political innocent (James Stewart playing Jefferson Smith) was appointed to complete a Senate term by a state political machine. Unbeknownst to Smith, the state's political boss, in league with the state's senior senator, believed Smith to be a popular but completely manipulable choice. When Smith unwittingly discovered machine-sponsored graft and tried to expose it, political bosses moved to discredit and destroy him. Even with the state machine and the Senate arrayed against him, he conducted a one-man filibuster on the Senate floor. As one lonely voice pitted against all that power, he was doomed to defeat and disgrace. Then, as Smith eloquently voiced the timeless truths of democratic and Christian values, the senators, reporters, and the country began to listen. In the end, he collapsed, thinking he had failed, but the guilt-ridden senior senator confessed. Smith's vindication also renewed his ideal, the national values to sustain us all through difficult times. Through

Smith, popular power renewed itself in the face of contemptuous machine politics.

Capra's movies spoke to a fantasy that has had recurrent force in American popular thinking and politics. Whenever there is a threat to the community, there is a popular tendency to fantasize that the key to solving the problem of the present and thus save the future rests in the past. If we feel that the American Dream has become denied or inverted, we seek heroes who bring the values and practices of a nostalgic past that we foolishly have forsaken into the present to "remoralize" us and our institutions. This is part of our recurrent *prelapsarian fantasy,* the nostalgic image of a better time or place that can redeem the present. Jefferson Smith was youthful, but he was in touch with the "Old Deal," traditional values and solutions associated with the simple and true democratic folk in the American hinterland. Gangster-businessmen, the idle rich, powerful politicians—all had lost touch with the common heartland of the republic and, hence, had to be destroyed or converted. Like other eras in American politics, fantasies of the 1930s equated the good with simple folk, small towns, and "the West," and the bad with sophisticated people, big cities, and "the East." Dozens of movies played on this theme: The slum kids of *Dead End* grow up to be criminal public enemies and Scarfaces, but the same boys grow up to be moral leaders like Jefferson Smith if given the chance to go out in the country to *Boy's Town.*

If the movies discussed are any guide to the political fantasies of the 1930s, they point to popular beliefs about an unjust and "fallen" world—one that can and should be changed not through socialist revolution or radical reforms but by restoration of the traditional American Dream of a nation in which material and moral prosperity touch everyone who adheres to the national creed. The films of the 1930s presented a belief in the sanctity and solidarity of the American community that was derived from the past and combined with the curative reforms of a benevolent government. The Old Deal met the New Deal. Both, said the fantasies in movies like Capra's *Mr. Smith* were the better for it.[7]

HOLLYWOOD GOES TO, AND RETURNS FROM, WORLD WAR II: THE COMMITMENT FANTASY

The political ethos of the 1940s was dominated by the harsh reality of World War II and its aftermath. Movie melodramas of the 1930s focused on a domestic fantasy that everything would work out all right. After Pearl Harbor, moviemakers and audiences were more interested in the meaning of the war. The war movies were rituals of power that reassured citizens that the war was worth fighting as a struggle between right and wrong, American fighting men and women were gallant, Americans at home were stalwart and supportive, allies were tough and resolute, and enemies were evil and not easily defeated. There was propaganda in the war movies, but it was propaganda Americans wanted, packaged in a ritual format that omitted thoughts of American cowardice and viciousness, or fears that victory was not inevitable. The movies convinced citizens that power derived from the depth of commitment, assuring victory and final realization of the peace and prosperity inherent in the American Dream. Indeed, cinema suggested that winning the war and peace would spread the promise of America abroad as well as vindicate it at home. Jefferson Smith went to Washington to retell us who we were during a domestic crisis; now heroes would represent what we stood for in London and Moscow, Normandy and Guadalcanal, and eventually Berlin and Tokyo.

Many Hollywood films of the war years were fantasies of commitment. Indeed, war films often tried to shame or frighten Americans into commitment. A few films depicted the heroism of gallant allies, shaming the United States into joining the war on their side. One such was *Mrs. Miniver,* a 1941 film that showed the suffering and will to resist on the part of the ordinary English people during the Blitz. Another (*Back to Bataan*) scared Americans by picturing the villainy of the enemy and the evils of Japanese occupation. *Hitler's Children* described Nazis crimes against their own people, turning Germans into obedient robots coveting world domination. Nations formerly held suspect or in contempt by Americans became, in Hollywood films of the 1940s, virtuous allies. Most notably, the Russians of the movies were brave soldiers and peace-loving peasants; dictator Josef Stalin, in *Mission to Moscow,* was stalwart, wise, and avuncular. Americans, great and small, who had committed themselves to fighting a war to bring about lasting peace in the past were extolled. *Wilson* retold the story of the president who had fought the "war to end all wars"; *Sergeant York* told again of the simple and religious mountaineer who overcame his pacifist beliefs to become a hero in World War I. Such ritualistic depictions demonstrated that Americans were more committed than her enemies; the outcome of the war on the battlefield would be as certain as that on the movie screen.[8]

The most notable and enduring wartime fantasy of commitment from Hollywood is *Casablanca,* released early in the war (November 1942) at a time when many Americans were still uncertain about why the United States was fighting Nazi Germany. The movie is set at the fateful time of December 1941 in Morocco, one of the territories of Vichy France, with which the United States had diplomatic relations despite Vichy's being a puppet of the German Reich. President Roosevelt viewed the film on December 31, 1942, and soon thereafter severed relations with Vichy! Not long after, Roosevelt secretly traveled to North Africa to confer with Churchill and the new leader of the Free French, General de Gaulle, in the actual city of Casablanca. The film (thrown together so haphazardly that the key actors came to the studio to shoot the last scene not knowing the outcome) won an Academy Award for best picture of the year.

Casablanca's story revolves around the uncommitted Rick Blaine, a mysterious and bitter American who has been disillusioned by both politics and love. He is no innocent like Jefferson Smith; he is more like a 1930s big-city mobster for whom the American Dream has gone sour. Blaine is a sophisticated blend of American and European, symbolizing the new international status and foreign involvement of Americans. He is as well a political hero, with antifascist credentials from the 1930s when he fought in Spain and ran guns to Ethiopia. The clientele of the Cafe Americain over which Rick presides is an international potpourri, mostly refugees trying to escape the Nazis. Here are the French, resentful of Nazi occupation, and a microcosm of the Grand Alliance of the anti-Nazi resistance (Russians, Norwegians, German Jews). Into this casino of bitterness, intrigue, and corruption walks a Czech refugee (Victor Lazlo) and his wife Ilse Lund, who just happens to be Rick's lost love from Paris. Lazlo, a resistance leader, has a clear goal—to destroy fascism. The Nazis on their part express their commitment to world conquest. Everyone, it seems, is committed. But Rick, cynical and embittered, is not: The problems of the world, he says, are not his department; the only cause he is interested in is himself. He alone refuses to commit, which he could do by helping Lazlo escape certain Nazi imprisonment. Spurning appeals to accept his responsibility as an American for Europe's struggle, he says only, "I'm a saloonkeeper."

Rick, however, is more than a saloonkeeper. In many respects he is a symbol, one representing prewar America. His internal anguish over whether to reunite with Ilse by helping Lazlo escape or by arranging for Lazlo's imprisonment reflects America's agonizing in 1939–1940 over whether to commit to a war in defense of European democracy. Seeking solace in drink after seeing the lovely and beloved European Ilse, Rick ponders the fate of America, conjuring up the fantasy of his country (to which, mysteriously, he cannot return). America, he concludes, is "asleep," oblivious to the international Nazi menace. In the end Rick Blaine and America as well decide to do the right thing. He puts the Lazlos on the plane to Lisbon and freedom. Lazlo, reminding Americans of their commitment, welcomes Rick "back to the fight . . . this time I know our side will win." The Lazlos fly off to continue their fight, and Rick walks into the mist to join a Free French garrison in central Africa.

By his act of commitment, Rick now has become a patriot, will join in the Grand Alliance, and be able to live with himself and return in victory to America. The political fantasy of *Casablanca* is one of individual commitments that add up to a national commitment against fascism. America must fight, however reluctantly, just as Rick Blaine renounces romantic love for love of country and the antifascist cause. The individual, Rick's lesson says, must suppress personal desires for the big job of defeating the Nazis. In so doing, Rick restores America to an honored place as the hope of the world (the Promised Land all the refugees hope to get to) that turns the tide against European-bred evil. Rick Blaine is a fantastic figure who blends the union of purpose of the two continents and asserts once again American leadership in the war effort. He exemplifies the necessity for personal sacrifice. *Casablanca* permitted wartime audiences to solidify their own commitment by identification with the character of Blaine. The ritual of power gave the story an acceptable outcome—even if Rick did bid farewell to the teary-eyed Ilse—and reassured American audiences that their dreams about themselves would be fulfilled in the now inevitable victory over the last evil: They would be as tough and resolute as Rick Blaine.

THE ALIEN FANTASY IN THE 1950s

Movie rituals of power are creations and product of a fantasy industry. Hollywood merchandises fantasy for the entertainment of audiences. What happens in the ritualistic *reel* world does not necessarily correspond or predict what happens in the *real* world. However, the former may affect popular imaginations about, and expectations of, the latter. The movies helped sustain the fantasy throughout World War II that "this time our side will win." All the Rick Blaines could march home to a domestic world prepared for them by social optimists like Jefferson Smith. In fact, they came home to a world much more problematic and troubled, as is reflected in the Oscar-winning *The Best Years of Our Lives* of 1946, which treats the postwar problems of three returning soldiers. In the film are creeping doubts about the promise of prosperity in the face of unemployment and whether the war commitment was worth the sacrifice. The wartime alliance quickly crumbled. Territorial and ideological demands of the Soviet Union indicated that the American Dream, heralded as the hope of the future during the war, was not shared by all. Movie themes showed the new mood. Anticommunist movies (*I Married a Communist* and *I Was a Communist for the FBI*) addressed emerging fears of domestic subversion by an alien conspiracy directed from Moscow. Whether the fears were real or imagined, such movies gave cinematic credence to the threat. More subtly, the "dark movies" (*film noir*) of the late 1940s depicted a bleak world of sinister motives and forces, of disillusioned and alienated and often doomed antiheroes. Such a grim social vision (see films such as *The Big Sleep* and *Out of the Past*) signified a popular mood that was pessimistic and resigned about the postwar "best years," including politics.

　　The 1950s evolved into the Eisenhower normalcy of relative calm (by Korean War and World War II standards). Movies continued to perpetuate the alien fantasy, however, either the fear that some alien force would conquer all—converting citizens to something "un-American"—or that social change would produce something alien to traditional American concepts of self and society. The alien fantasy took conservative political form in the search for an enemy within—communist spies and traitors in government and institutions, including the movie industry. The alien fantasy also took liberal political form—namely, criticism of the banality and conformity of the newly prospering American suburban middle class. Conservatives worried that communist subversion or "creeping socialism" would undermine freedom and individuality; liberals worried that the fear of communism would engender paranoia and orthodoxy and thus render Americans into totalitarian robots akin to the fantasized Soviets. In the conservative fantasy, Americans would be subverted by foreign enemies; in the liberal fantasy, Americans would become their own worst enemies and subvert themselves.

Films of the 1950s exploited and fed the persistent dark fantasy of a malevolent communist threat armed with the atomic bomb and evil intent that would invade and annihilate or enslave America. The box office failure of heavy-handed anticommunist movies did not deny the potency of the alien fantasy, only an unwillingness to accept its most overtly political version.

Without any conscious design, Hollywood then created a genre of movies that encouraged people to indulge their fears in an entertaining, subtle fashion. The message was: The alien threat is real, so be ever alert. A cluster of popular science fiction films (*Invaders from Mars, Them!, It Came from Another World, Earth vs. the Flying Saucers,* and so on) exemplified the genre. Through sci-fi movies audiences played out political fantasies (subconsciously, in most cases), displacing their fears of political annihilation or dehumanization onto a seemingly nonpolitical setting. Such *fantastic displacement* is a process of projecting mass fantasies into a "safe" context that covertly mediates hopes or fears by offering resolutions in dramatically predictable ways.

The most noteworthy of sci-fi films is *Invasion of the Body Snatchers* (1956). The movie is a ritual of power set in a metaphorical small and idyllic American town. It is a fable of how this tranquil Eden is suddenly captured by a powerful and subtle alien force. In the story, a young doctor, Miles Bennell (a man with the domestic roots of a Jefferson Smith but the sophistication of a Rick Blaine), discovers that local residents inexplicably don't seem to be acting normally. Dr. Bennell diagnoses the affliction: People are being enslaved by alien space seedpods that germinate, grow, and duplicate human bodies, then replace each local resident. The new beings take over the town, claiming to be of a higher order and intellect than humans but without emotion ("There is no need for love and emotion," one explains. "Love, ambition, desire, faith—without them, life is so simple"). The aliens plan to take over the entire world, turning humanity into obedient and passive vegetables. In the end, Bennell is alone in his humanity, pursued by the entire new community of podpeople. He escapes and tries to warn of "the malignant disease spreading out all over the country." He shouts to passing motorists, "They're here . . . you're next!" A psychiatrist, to whom the police take Bennell, thinks him crazy until Bennell accidentally discovers evidence proving his claims. The film closes with a call to the FBI "before it's too late." But at this point can trust be placed even in the FBI?

Invasion of the Body Snatchers invites dual interpretation. First is the fantasy of the conservative parable on the communist menace. An alien communist force invades a peaceful American community and subverts its way of life, dehumanizing and regimenting. The new town order has all the worst features of Soviet Russia—loss of identity, zealous controls on behavior, the right and obligation to betray or annihilate those who refuse to comply. Too, *Body Snatchers* played on a nagging fantasy that maybe somehow communists *were* superior and might indeed subvert and conquer a complacent nation through cunning, deceit, commitment, and amorality. Like the imagined Russians and Chinese of the 1950s, the podpeople offer the comforts of mindless obedience to authority but no freedom to feel (no more love, no more beauty, no more pain). The other political interpretation of the movie is of a liberal persuasion—that is, fear of what Americans were becoming as a people, fear born not of external threat but of self-subversion. In the 1950s warnings of political paranoia, deteriorating into madness, were common. The fear of communism in this interpretation was simply a fantastic projection of what was happening at home—a nation turning itself into banal and puerile conformists afraid of any thought and individuality that might disrupt a comforting, distracting, diverting mass consensus. In either interpretation, American individualist Miles Bennell must yield by death and/or conversion. Neither the democratic preachments of Jefferson Smith nor the courageous individual choice of Rick Blaine would be welcome in a world that makes no place for heroes.

Films of the 1950s such as *Invasion of the Body Snatchers* suggested that underneath the placid façade of the postwar world were lingering doubts about where the pursuit of the American Dream was heading. *Body Snatchers* captures in sharp relief the vague sense that something indefinable was wrong, that the threat (unlike Smith's Depression and Blaine's fascism) was insidious, puzzling, and frightening. Smith and Blaine could take their fight to an identifiable enemy, but in the 1950s no one knew for sure who the enemy was. Was there an alien, as some fantasized, or were *we* the aliens? Bennell can't fight the aliens, so in a way he becomes an alien too, fleeing the community in order to save his precious humanity. The metaphorical tale of *Invasion of the Body Snatchers* was a powerful one for 1950s audiences because for them there was no place to flee, although they sensed that there was something to flee from. But what? Was it *Them,* alien invaders from another world? A popular political cartoon character of the time, Pogo Possum, said, "We have met the enemy and he is us." So then was it "Us"? *Invasion of the Body Snatchers* raised the terrifying fantasy that from the stultifying political and social conformity of the time there was no exit.[9]

CHANGE AND HOPE IN THE 1960s

The perceived undercurrent of trouble in the affluent paradise created in the 1950s surfaced in the explosive and eventful decade of the 1960s. It was an era of change and hope, reaction and despair, fear and vision. The 1960s were full of contradiction: political leaders slain by unknown assassins, the promise of a Great Society and the hostility of urban riots, hi-tech transportation that allowed us to walk on the Moon and to die in the Vietnam War, the rise of the student movement and the Wallace movement, the advent of the counter-culture and the "silent majority." With social consensus seeming to vanish, the decade witnessed fantasies that there *was* an exit—be it social reform, a nostalgic return to some happier and more predictable time, or even the achievement of transcendent destiny. More than any previous political time, the decade's fantasies made it to the movie screen.

The first years of the 1960s witnessed the 1,000 days of the John F. Kennedy presidency. The shock of his assassination signaled the begining of the violent and rebellious 1960s. Subsequent years created the Camelot myth and a fantasy that none of the worst features of the 1960s would have hap-pened had Kennedy lived. The nostalgia for the Kennedy era is a *fantasy of prelapsarian moment,* a period celebrated as a last and lost age of innocence before years of war, scandal, and political disruption. Movies produced in later decades still emphasize the prelapsarian qualities of the 1960s. Examples are *American Graffiti, Dirty Dancing, Tin Men, Eddie and the Cruisers, Little Shop of Horrors, Hairspray,* and *Stand by Me.*

After Kennedy, the "Swinging Sixties" took shape, and the political per-spectives implicit in the cultural rebellion of the moment entered the realm of movie fantasy. In 1964, two movies gripped the imagination of many young people who would soon witness the changes of the decade: the civil rights movement, the counterculture, the student protests, the sexual revolution. The Beatles' film *A Hard Day's Night* legitimated the babyboom generation as a fun-loving people with a new *ethos* and a novel perspective on life. *Dr. Strangelove* hinted that the war mentality that had emerged from fear of com-munism had itself become insane, dooming all to certain death at the hands of military leaders running amok. Many youthful rebels shared the idealism of Jefferson Smith and the sense of alienation of Miles Bennell, but unlike Rick Blaine, they didn't believe the war of their time to be worth fighting. Some of the most memorable 1960s movies told stories of powerful, widely accepted, yet evil social authority. Freedom was resistance or flight. As the Beatles demonstrated, youthful and zestful freedom was possible, but it re-quired rebellion against the Strangeloves of social authority.

In representative youth culture films of the 1960s, the ritual of power changes from that of earlier decades. Youthful heroes are virtually powerless to affect their fate unless they rebel, and even then they may be doomed. Movies of the 1960s often abandoned the ritual happy or just ending. In *The Graduate* (1967), for example, the hero, a newly graduated college student, Benjamin Braddock, wants his life to be different from that of his parent's generation. No pursuit of money, consumption, or status in a "plastic" society for him. He searches elsewhere. To that end he rescues his girlfriend Elaine Robinson from wedding a man of her parents' choice. They flee authority and respectability rather than bow to convention. In *Bonnie and Clyde* (1967), the youthful rebels are criminals but charming and free; they ultimately die at the hands of a society portrayed as being more violent than they. In *Easy Rider* (1969), two bikers roam America, smoking marijuana and enjoying sex, but they are constantly attacked by "respectable" elements of society and finally murdered. In these films, the podpeople are firmly in control, perpetuating a system of plastic values that demands podlike conformity even though evils such as war, racism, and poverty flow from such values. This movie fantasy is about the ritual of *resisting* power, social power that demands the abandonment of individual freedom and destroys those who would be free. By implication, political power, from policeman to president, is hostile to the young and free. The American Dream had become nightmare.

For many Americans in the 1960s, the most telling evidence that American political power had gone mad was the Vietnam War. With enormous problems at home, such as racial conflict and poverty, that endless and extremely violent (nightly on TV) war seemed a bloody waste. Movies perpetuated the fantasy that America was a violent society. *The Wild Bunch, A Fistful of Dollars, Joe,* and *Straw Dogs* showed irredeemably violent worlds of murderous intent. Innocent victims of violence often suffered at the hands of malevolent aggressors. Yet, few movies dealt with the Vietnam violence. John Wayne's *The Green Berets* did, placing the tale in Western format, with special U.S. forces fighting barbarians on a frontier, thus legitimating defensive violence. Yet another movie used the Western motif to stress the theme of violence in the 1960s. *Little Big Man* (1970) portrayed American Indian society as natural, tolerant, and sensual; white society by contrast was shown as corrupt, vindictive, and greedy. Every institution of white society (family, church, law, business, town government) was an agency of repression or exploitation; every hero was either a fraud or an egotist, including General George Custer. The U.S. Cavalry committed atrocities and massacres against the Indians, seemingly bent on killing all those of different race and creed. The Indians saw themselves as civilized human beings, and the whites as soulless savages. The Vietnam analogy was clear, appealing to the fantasy that the dark side of American character revealed in Vietnam was something endemic to the political culture.

With such themes running as a current through the decade, in retrospect it is no wonder that people also entertained fantasies of transcendence. Americans might well transcend the petty meanness of the 1960s and rise above it all. Politics as usual had failed. Americans must instead seek answers in the transcendent hope for universal peace and brotherhood, ecological balance, and cosmic piety. This earnest longing took many forms, not the least of which was Stanley Kubrick's 1968 film, *2001: A Space Odyssey,* which offered a fantasy of transcendent hope in the cosmic view that the conquest of space would yield contact with our own mystical destiny. It was a ritual of the triumph of a transcendent power that would bring to earth reconciliation through benevolent technology legitimated by higher truths. The film was a fantasy that many people in the late 1960s desperately wanted to believe during the seemingly irreconcilable strife of the era.[10]

DOUBT AND DRIFT IN THE 1970s

The decade of the 1970s occurred in the wake of, and in many ways was a reaction to, the changes and movements of the momentous 1960s. In a sense, it was a transitional period between two more clearly defined political eras, and is hard to define because it had a fragmentary character that gave it little political focus. The country's social turmoil of the 1960s made the 1970s appear apolitical and reactionary by comparison. The decade was apolitical in that many people sought individual, private solace. The era earned the labels of the "Me Decade," and "the culture of narcissism." A graffito of the mid-1970s proclaimed bitterly, "Benjamin Braddock [of The Graduate] went into plastics."

The social hopes and commitments of previous movie heroes seemed to dissipate in the confusion and even cynicism of the decade. People sought private hope in religious revival, New Age and human potential beliefs, "relationships," or making money. In reaction to the liberalism and radicalism of the 1960s, a new political conservatism emerged that tried to balance assertions of authoritarianism with libertarianism. Especially after the Watergate scandal and the fall of Saigon, for many people it was a time of "the big chill," with hope replaced by hopelessness, enthusiasm by apathy, movement by what Jimmy Carter called malaise. The American Dream drifted, and no political leader or force seemed able to capture the public imagination. There were doubts about America's mission and virtue, and fears that it might be a declining and decaying political power. Movies such as All That Jazz, The Shootist, and Heaven Can Wait were fantasies about dying and death. Others were about the indestructibility of evil (The Exorcist, Halloween, Friday the 13th) and recurring disaster (Jaws, The Towering Inferno, Earthquake). Movie heroes of the 1970s were powerless to defeat personal, supernatural, or natural forces.

Political power is difficult to identify in the 1970s movies. Sometimes power is highly concentrated in secret places that are malevolent; other films portray power as incapable of coping with the forces that beset the people. The growth of extraordinary executive power during the Nixon administration, and the subsequent Watergate scandal and Nixon's resignation, gave impetus to the fantasy of powerful and conspiratorial forces ruling without popular consent. Movies responded with ritual dramas of hidden power, imagining American government as a conspiracy of shadowy forces. The Conversation (1974) depicted a paranoid world of electronic surveillance and corporate power plays by secretive and unfathomable forces at the top of society. All the President's Men (1976) presented a somber nation's capital with dark secrets revealed in whispered conversations in underground parking lots, and government itself as a tissue of mysteries and lies. In *Chinatown* (1974), power resided in an evil and Byzantine network of corruption beyond the ability of anyone to understand and control, for "nobody knows what's going on." In the disaster movies, power is open but incompetent, incapable of coping with threats to the community; officials by their evasions, incompetence, and corruption—be they the city fathers of a resort town attacked by sharks, the architects of the world's tallest building that catches on fire, or presidents of the United States—produce chaos.

The 1970s fantasy of political decay and powerlessness was vivid in the movie *Taxi Driver* (1976). The taxi driver, Travis Bickle, inhabits the mean streets of New York, a symbol of urban decadence and corruption. For him society is a hypocritical "open sewer" in which he knows not how to act. He is totally alienated from any community. His sense of social powerlessness is driving him mad, and he decides to devote himself to the mission of killing a pretentious candidate for president, demonstrating to the world that "here was a man who would not take it anymore." Unable to kill the candidate, he massacres instead criminals and, ironically, becomes a hero. At the end, he returns to driving a taxi in an urban underworld as insane as he; he is at one with his environment. Government and politics remain a remote sham, irrelevant to life on the streets. *Taxi Driver* is a ritual of powerlessness, in which the hero inhabits a world so far from the corridors of power that the two worlds touch at their mutual peril. Travis Bickle is not called to reform the Senate, lead the fight against fascism, warn the community of alien danger, or even run off with Elaine Robinson. He is left to wander alone in a nightmarish landscape of social hopelessness unaffected by power at the top or powerlessness on the bottom of a decaying and immoral world. This was the mediated political reality of the 1970s: Nobody knew what was going on, and like Travis, nobody knew what to do.[11]

RENEWAL AND REFLECTION IN THE 1980s

The pessimistic fantasies of the 1970s were difficult to deal with; it was no wonder that more heroic and optimistic images made their way to the movie screen. The most important trend of the late 1970s that anticipated the politics of the 1980s was the reappearance of the superhero performing mighty deeds and reasserting power over the world. Figures such as Luke Skywalker, Indiana Jones, and Superman implied a fantasy of a decisive and uncomplicated political hero who represented traditional American values and aspirations. People wanted, both in politics and the movies, a ritual of power that reasserted the patriotic fantasy of victory over, and punishment of, enemies, a reassurance that cultural heroism can renew faith in values that allegedly worked in the past but that had been abandoned. There was a strong nostalgic impulse in electing Ronald Reagan as president. Through him were united the fantasies of Hollywood and Washington with the wish that the American story would have a happy and victorious ending, as in *Mr. Smith Goes to Washington.*

Reagan's agenda included the reassertion of American power in the world and inspired Hollywood military fantasies, some positive and some negative. If movies are any guide to the political fantasies of an era, they surely reveal that our visions of military adventures ranged from the bellicose to the fearful. Clint Eastwood's *Heartbreak Ridge* was a traditional ritual of military power, expressed through the experience of a small unit whipped into shape by a tough sergeant who then leads them in a baptism of fire in Grenada. *Rambo: First Blood,* Part II, provided a fantasy of revenge on America's enemies in the Vietnam War, their Soviet counterparts, and even the Washington Establishment that was supposedly responsible for U.S. defeat; it centered on the rescue of Americans missing in action (MIAs) held in Vietnam. The MIA fantasy was durable in the 1980s as evidenced by *Uncommon Valor, Missing in Action,* and other such films. Perhaps the domestic equivalent was the fear of children being kidnapped, as dramatized in *Adam, Missing,* and most nightmarishly, *Aliens.* As indicated in Chapter 1, the hostage fantasy recurs in news stories as well as in movie melodrama. A few 1980s movies (*Firefox, Rocky IV, Red Dawn*) revisited the podlike villains of the 1950s. Movies also provided fantasies about World War III that were provoked not by the Russians but by U.S. aggressiveness and willingness to fight a nuclear war. In *War Games,* for example, a computer hacker who accidentally breaks into the computer network of the North American Air Defense Command (NORAD) provokes a narrowly averted nuclear disaster; moviegoers are left to wonder if the computer's lesson will really prevail: "The only winning move is not to play."

Movies of the 1980s have also offered visions of what it would be like after a postnuclear war (*Testament*) and indeed of postcivilization reversions to barbarism (*The Road Warrior*) or "postmodern" urban ruins (*Blade Runner, Brazil, Robo Cop, Running Man*). If Rambo reduced the Vietnam War to a cartoon conflict, other films reminded us that war is an inglorious existential nightmare (*Platoon, Full Metal Jacket*), serving for some as cautionary tales warning us against similar involvement in Central America (*Under Fire, Salvador*). The movies' most ambivalent and conflicting fantasies about conflict tell us that, unlike in the 1940s, there is no single mediated reality of war.[12]

In some respects fantasies of the 1930s reappeared in the 1980s. A few films in the 1980s dealt with inequalities in wealth (*Down and Out in Beverly Hills*), with the rich portrayed as silly and vacuous (not unlike *My Man Godfrey* in the 1930s). Others dealt with the fate of ordinary people displaced by adverse economic change (*Country*) and the dubious ethics and power of big business (*Wall Street, The Secret of My Success*). Reminiscent of the 1930s, some of these movies suggested that only those persons who are free of moral constraints and consumed by greed will succeed, but others suggested a distinction between good and bad capitalism, even that people can achieve not only wealth but justice (*Trading Places*). Portrayed in decidedly negative fashion in movies has been the overly discussed fantasy of the "Yuppies" (the young, upwardly mobile, urban professionals) in *The Money Pit, Lost in America, Something Wild, After Hours,* and *Desperately Seeking Susan.*

A recurrent theme in movies of the 1980s involves a nostalgic fantasy of an America that never existed but that Hollywood once envisioned—white, classless, peaceful, moral, and wholesome. This Hollywood version of America last existed in the prelapsarian 1950s world of the TV Beaver Cleaver and Ozzie Nelson families. Perhaps it could be captured again, and as in the 1950s, if not in real America at least in reel America. *Back to the Future* (1985) exemplifies the theme. For young Marty McFly, the present of the 1980s is threatening and disheartening. He lives in a dingy and rundown town and is a member of an unsuccessful and unhappy family. But "history is going to change," he vows, and as if by magic, he finds himself returning to 1955. By altering his parents' personal history (including the willingness to use violence against aggression), he returns to the 1980s to find his family transformed into a wealthy, confident, and happy group living in a plush home. Even though the town is still decayed, with abandoned stores and homeless street people, the erosion of political reality is not as important as the reintegration of private happiness through family ties and consumption that takes precedence over public responsibility. Marty McFly returns to a present that is still fallen from the grace of the 1950s, but history has been manipulated to deny that the fall took place, restoring the romantic illusion that nothing has changed in the interim even though the evidence is all around us. Such a film is a ritual of private power reasserted as a substitute for the erosion of political and economic power. *Back to the Future* ends with not only the recent past defeated, but also the future; our hero has set off to the future to free his children—who have not yet been born in the present—from trouble.[13]

LOOKING FORWARD

As America moves through the 1990s and approaches the end of a century, we will again face ambiguities in the exercise of power. It is likely that power will be no less troubling and threatening than in the past. As a people, we will continue to use fantasy to try to understand and even control power, hoping for outcomes of the conflicts of power that we find desirable. We will seek heroes in both politics and popular culture to guide us through the emerging political uncertainties of the time. They will both resemble and be different from the Jefferson Smiths and Rick Blaines and Elaine and Benjamin Braddocks of the movie past. Sitting in the dark of movie theaters and letting our fantasies soar, we will nevertheless recognize them as they conduct once again the rituals of power that give us important clues to the unfolding political ethos of that age. In the most subtle way, Hollywood and Washington will be forever united.

NOTES

1. There is a burgeoning literature that states the relationship between popular film and American culture and politics. See, variously, Robert Sklar, *Movie-Made America: A Social History of the American Movies* (New York: Random House, 1975); Michael Wood, *America in the Movies* (New York: Basic Books, 1975); Garth Jowett, *Film: The Democratic Art* (Boston: Little, Brown, 1976); I.C. Jarvie, *Movies and Society* (New York: Basic Books, 1970); Andrew Tudor, *Image and Influence* (New York: St. Martin's Press, 1974); Sari Thomas, ed., *Film/Culture* (Methuen, NJ: Scarecrow Press, 1982); Paul Monaco, *Ribbons in Time: Movies and Society since 1945* (Bloomington: Indiana University Press, 1987); Robert B. Ray, *A Certain Tendency of the Hollywood Cinema, 1930-1980* (Princeton, NJ: Princeton University Press, 1985); Bill Nichols, *Ideology and the Image* (Bloomington: Indiana University Press, 1981); Lary May, *Screening Out the Past* (New York: Oxford University Press, 1980); John E. O'Connor and Martin A. Jackson, eds., *American History/American Film* (New York: Frederick Ungar, 1979); Peter C. Rollins, ed., *Hollywood as Historian* (Lexington: University of Kentucky Press, 1983); Terry Christensen, *Reel Politics* (New York, Basil Blackwell, 1987); Michael A. Genovese, *Politics and the Cinema* (Lexington, MA: Ginn, 1986); Michael Paul Rogin, *Ronald Reagan, the Movie* (Berkeley: University of California Press, 1987. Fiction writers have also addressed the powerful fantasies of the movies: Robert Coover, *A Night at the Movies* (New York: Simon & Schuster, 1987); Christopher Durang, *A History of the American Film* (New York: Avon Bard, 1978); David Thomson, *Suspects* (New York: Knopf, 1985).
2. John H. Lenihan, *Showdown. Confronting Modern America in the Western Film* (Urbana: University of Illinois Press, 1985).
3. Vivian Sobchack, "Genre Film: Myth, Ritual, and Sociodrama," in Thomas, *Film/Culture,* pp. 147-165); Dudley Andres, "Film and Society: Public Rituals and Private Space," *East-West Film Journal* 1 (Winter 1986): 7-22; Jean Collet, "Cinema and the Sacrifice of Narcissus," *Cross Currents* 20/17 (Summer/Fall 1987): 159-167. The social significance of ritual fantasy is suggested by Orrin Klapp, *Collective Search for Identity* (New York: Holt, Rinehart, and Winston, 1969). For television, see Gregor T. Goethals, *The TV Ritual* (Boston: Beacon Press, 1981); a valuable collection is Ray B. Browne, ed., *Rituals and Ceremonies in Popular Culture* (Bowling Green, OH: Bowling Green State University Popular Press, 1980).
4. Roger Dooley, *From Scarface to Scarlett: American Films in the 1930s* (New York: Harvest/NBJ Book, 1981), pp. 425-420; Arlene Croce, *The Fred Astaire and Ginger Rogers Book* (New York: Outerbridge and Lazard, 1972).
5. Walter R. Fisher, "Reaffirmation and Subversion of the American Dream," *Quarterly Journal of Speech* 59 (April 1973): 160-167.
6. Andrew Bergman, *We're in the Money: Depression America and Its Films* (New York: Harper & Row, 1971), pp. 3-17.

7. Peter Roffman and Jim Purdy, *The Hollywood Social Problem Film* (Bloomington: Indiana University Press, 1981); Nick Roddick, *A New Deal in Entertainment* (London: British Film Institute, 1983); Charles Maland, *American Visions* (New York: Arno Press, 1977); Nick Browne, "The Politics of Narrative Form: Capra's *Mr. Smith Goes to Washington,*" *Wide Angle* 3:3 (1981): 4–11; Glen Alan Phelps, "The 'Populist' Films of Frank Capra," *American Studies* 13:3 (1979): 377–392.

8. Bernard F. Dick, *The Star-Spangled Screen: The American World War II Film* (Lexington: University of Kentucky Press, 1986); Colin Shindler, *Hollywood Goes to War* (London: Routledge and Kegan Paul, 1979); Robert Fyne, "From Hollywood to Moscow," *Literature/Film Quarterly* 13 (1985): 194–199; David D. Lee, "Appalachia on Film: The Making of *Sergeant York,*" *Southern Quarterly* (Spring-Summer, 1981), 201–221.

9. Patrick Lucanio, *Them or Us: Archetypal Interpretations of Fifties Alien Invasion Films* (Bloomington: Indiana University Press, 1987); Michael Rogin, "Kiss Me Deadly: Communism, Motherhood, and Cold War Movies," *Representations* 6 (Spring 1984): 1–36; Stuart Kaminsky, "On *Invasion of the Body Snatchers,*" *Cinefantastique* 2:3 (Winter 1973): 16–23; Glen M. Johnson, "'We'd Fight . . . We Had To': *The Body Snatchers* as Novel and Film," *Journal of Popular Culture* 31 (Summer 1979): 5–16.

10. On the 1960s, see Leonard Quarte and Albert Auster, *American Film and Society Since 1945* (New York: Praeger, 1984); William L. O'Neill, *Coming Apart* (New York: Quadrangle Books, 1971); Jerome Agel, ed., *The Making of Kubrick's 2001* (New York: Signet, 1970); Jeff Greenfield, "Retrospective: *Easy Rider,*" *Esquire* (July 1981): 90–91.

11. Colin L. Westerbeck, Jr., "Beauties and the Beast: *Seven Beauties* and *Taxi Driver,*" *Sight and Sound* 45 (Summer 1976): 134–139; Robert Phillip Kolker, *A Cinema of Loneliness* (New York: Oxford University Press, 1980); Seth Cagin and Phillip Dray, *Hollywood Films of the Seventies* (New York: Harper & Row, 1984).

12. Michael Ryan and Douglas Kellner, *Camera Politics* (Bloomington: University of Indiana Press, 1988); Richard Schickel, "No Method to His Madness," *Film Comment* (June 1987): 11–19; "Rocky and Rambo," *Newsweek* (December 23, 1985): 68–62; Harvey R. Greensburg, "Dangerous Recuperations: *Red Dawn, Rambo,* and the New Decaturism," *Journal of Popular Film and Television* 15:2 (Summer 1987): 60–70; Jo Hoberman, "American Dearest," *American Film* (May 1988): 39–45, 54–55.

13. Phillip J. Landon, "'Back to the Future' with Rambo and Reagan." Paper presented at the national conference of the Popular Culture Association, 1987.

CHAPTER 6

Fantasies of the Arena
Popular Sports and Politics

An enduring legend of American sports is the story of how a small Catholic liberal arts college in Indiana named Notre Dame went from obscurity to international renown through success in football. Notre Dame was America's first Cinderella team. It developed a national following of working-class Catholic immigrants. These ethnic Americans worked in mills, mines, and factories. They were unable to send their children to Harvard, Yale, Princeton, or even to the U.S. Military Academy at West Point. So they cheered instead for the little college whose football team members carried the names of Poles, Italians, and Irish and who handily defeated the elite schools. The "Fighting Irish" of Notre Dame quickly became the stuff of sports fantasy; kids all over the country dreamed of playing football on that team. Not everyone, however, cheered Notre Dame's success. Success also bred contempt; millions of Americans were happy on Saturday afternoons to see Notre Dame lose. In any case, football put Notre Dame on the map, and the fame and wealth that followed converted the small, obscure college into a large and thriving university of which the football team remains justly proud.

Much of the Notre Dame legend began during the tenure of a dynamic and histrionically gifted coach, Knute Rockne. During the 1920s and 1930s, his teams made Notre Dame a household word. His ability to inspire players and fans contributed to the Notre Dame mystique; friend and foe of the team expected gridiron miracles. Rockne died in an airplane crash in 1931 and quickly joined the pantheon of sports immortals. Sports journalists of the time viewed athletics as more than contests between mortals; this school of sports writing thought instead of a mythic struggle fought for glory. Rockne, recalled his assistant coach "Hunk" Anderson, "was a spellbinder who could make the players believe that the opponents were the plague destined to wipe out our civilization, and only a Notre Dame victory could prevent the catastrophe."[1]

One Rockne legend that circulated in sports circles concerned a Notre Dame running back, George Gipp. Gipp died in his senior year at Notre Dame (1920) of peneumonia, partially induced by Rockne's yieding to crowd pressure to send the sick Gipp into a game during bad weather even though the Fighting Irish were leading by a comfortable margin. Allegedly—only Rockne heard it—on his deathbed Gipp said to Rockne something to the effect (it took various forms) that someday when the going got tough for a Notre Dame team, Rockne should tell them to go out and win one, or score one, for "The Gipper" (a nickname never used in Gipp's lifetime). George Gipp was a talented but undisciplined athlete. He was also an amateur bootlegger and pool hustler ("a Rembrandt with a cue stick," recalled Anderson) whose winnings kept him in residence at a plush South Bend hotel. Gipp regularly broke training, bet on Notre Dame games, played pro football on the side, and had dark and enigmatic moods. In death, however, both Rockne and sports journalists, playing to the heroic fantasies of sports fans, exalted Gipp as a model of the noble young athlete who in death becomes an inspiration for all. Rockne apparently used the story more than once during pep talks designed to revive lagging team spirit. In 1928, Rockne told the Gipp tale to sportswriter Grantland Rice, one of the pioneers of sports journalism, the night before playing Army with a weak Notre Dame team. Rockne told the "win one for the Gipper" fable to his team the next day (witnesses divide as to whether it was before the game started or at halftime), undoubtedly helping Notre Dame narrowly defeat Army. Rice included the story in his postgame syndicated column, and the Gipper became an indelible part of sport legend.[2]

All this would have remained a relatively minor incident in the history of team motivation and tear-jerking sportswriting were it not for the fact that a young radio sportscaster in Iowa named Ronald Reagan was inspired by the story. He used it on his radio show in the early 1930s. He proposed the Rockne-Gipp story as a screenplay when he first reached Hollywood; and he won the role of George Gipp in the movie *Knute Rockne—All American* (1940). As president, Reagan identified himself with "the Gipper," using the "win one for the Gipper" line in seeking the passage of legislation, getting votes on the campaign trail, and urging American athletes to victory at the 1984 Olympics. During his presidency, he twice traveled to the Notre Dame campus, obviously enjoying the association and reveling in his identification with a sports legend.

Like Rockne, Reagan was famous for uplifting pep talks that played fast and loose with the facts but appealed to collective fantasies of heroic deeds that teach moral lessons. In the movie, Rockne's (played by actor Pat O'Brien) halftime speech goes like this:

Well, boys, I haven't a thing to say. You've played a great game—all of you—a great game. I guess we just can't expect to win 'em all. I'm gonna tell you something I've kept to myself for years. None of you ever knew George Gipp. It was long before your time. But you all know what a tradition he is at Notre Dame. And the last thing he said to me, "Rock," he said, "sometime when the team is up against it, and the breaks are beating the boys, tell them to go out there with all they've got and win just one for the Gipper. I don't know where I'll be then, Rock," he said, "but I'll know about it, and I'll be happy."[3]

In his 1981 speech at Notre Dame, Reagan drew lessons from the movie:

As a coach, (Rockne) did more than teach our young men how to play a game. He believed truly that the noblest work of man was building the character of men. . . . (Rockne) told the story at halftime to a team that was losing and one of the only teams he had ever coached that was torn by dissension and jealousy and factionalism. The seniors on that team were about to close out their football careers without learning or experiencing any of the real values that a game has to impart. . . . Rockne told the story and so inspired them that they rose above their personal animosities. For someone they had never known they joined together in a common cause and attained the unattainable. . . . (I)s there anything wrong with young people having an experience, feeling something so deeply, thinking of someone else to the point that they can give so completely of themselves? There will come times in the lives of all of us when we'll be faced with causes bigger than ourselves, and they won't be on the playing field.[4]

Even though college football is only a game, and a movie such as *Knute Rockne—All American* a maudlin and deliberately erroneous version of events, the entire folktale of the Gipp and Notre Dame was so important to the president of the United States that he returned to the campus in 1988 to take part in ceremonies honoring Rockne and Gipp. In his farewell address to the 1988 Republican convention, he urged the party to "go out there and make it one more for the Gipper."[5]

THE SPORTS VISION OF THE AMERICAN DREAM

Americans are used to the idea that we learn something from sports and that political figures are going to talk about sports for a wide variety of political reasons. Even though something like Reagan's identification with a famous sports institution and legend was politically expedient, we expect politicians to make reference to sports, pay homage to sports, and understand the didactic uses of sports and politics. Time was when voters expected candidates to refer to their war background; now voters find virtue in a background of sports achievement. Political orators employ sports metaphors, associating political fantasies with the analogy drawn from popular fantasies of the playing field. Phrases about social causes "bigger than ourselves" take on added meaning when inspired by heroic action in the sports arena. Political campaigns are "a race to the finish line"; a nominee needs to "hit one out of the park" in a major speech; candidates win political struggles by "playing hardball"; an official vows to have an economy that is a "level playing field"; an opponent is defeated by a "knockout punch" or by being "blindsided"; a political underdog pledges to win by "pulling it out in the fourth quarter" or with a "Hail Mary play at the buzzer." The U.S. military constructs elaborate models of warfare from game theory, as if war were a game with all the characteristics of sports. Military leaders consider sports as good training for the military—a latter-day version of Wellington's view that the battle of Waterloo was won on the playing fields of Eton. In his acceptance speech at the Democratic convention in 1988, Michael Dukakis evoked his Greek heritage by reference to the pledge the ancient Athenians took on the occasion of the marathon. Republican George Bush countered, saying he had lived the American Dream—including going to high school football games on Friday nights.

As Reagan intuitively understood, a game is not just a game. When sports teams or individual athletes fail, we are concerned about what that communicates to the rest of society. When the owners of a sports franchise move the team to another city, when well-known athletes take bribes or drugs, or when a coach or player abandons team loyalty in favor of the offer of big money, people worry. Somehow such behavior damages social morality. The playing field is an Edenic fantasy offering the sports spectator vicarious pleasure in the agonistic struggle of godlike athletes in a spectacle of power. Because many people believe that the drama of sports is a pristine ritual enacting fantasies of pure competition and poetic justice, considerable effort goes into sustaining and enhancing the illusion that athletics is beyond reproach.

Consider one example. The history of baseball ("the American pastime") is filled with unsavory, all-too-human behavior—holdouts, league-jumping, strikes, franchise shifts, lockouts, payoffs, exclusions, to name but a few common occurrences in the sport's past. Yet, as baseball grew to be a highly lucrative business for owners and a profession for players, Americans' love of the national game produced a child-like innocence extolling the "boys of summer." In 1919 some of those boys on the pennant-winning Chicago White Sox conspired to throw the World Series to the Cincinnati Reds after taking bribes from gamblers. The scandal shocked the country. It inspired sermons, editorials, and calls to ban professional baseball. Organized baseball responded to the crisis by banning the eight Black Sox players from baseball for life, and hiring a tough old judge, Kenesaw Mountain Landis, as commissioner to enforce standards of conduct consistent with fantasies of what the sport should be. The importance of the Black Sox scandal (which was the source of the story for the 1988 movie *Eight Men Out*) for the moral tone of the nation was symbolized by a single incident: Outside a courtroom, a small boy ran up to one of the accused baseball stars, "Shoeless Joe" Jackson, tearfully pleading, "Say it ain't so, Joe."[6]

In a sense, we have been saying it ain't so ever since, maintaining the fantasy that sports are immune to corruption, that athletes live in a sanctified state of grace. The irony is that our desire to believe that there is something special about sports has transformed both professional and amateur athletics into big business, tainted all the more by the lure of big money, the temptations of the flesh, and the display of ego and childish temperament. By one estimate, sports is a nearly $50 billion industry, making it the twenty-fifth largest in the country. Americans spend $16.2 billion annually on participatory and leisure sports. Sporting goods produces revenues of $15.1 billion. TV networks pay more than $1 billion annually for rights to sporting events; the advent of cable TV has made the bidding all the more fierce. Successful athletes not only command enormous salaries (in baseball, the average salary is now $325,000 a year), they profit from endorsements, appearances, and side ventures. (Chicago Bulls basketball star Michael Jordan signed a seven-year endorsement deal with Nike shoes for an estimated $19 million.) Some sports greats receive $6 an autograph! The line between amateur and professional sports is uncertain. Olympic athletes ("amateurs") profit from endorsements, hiring agents to promote their "amateur" careers.[7] We are a long way from the simple locker-room truths of the mythical Knute Rockne and the boyish "Send me in, Coach" enthusiasm of the equally mythical George Gipp.

Yet Americans idolize sports and athletes in the face of all the commercialism. Why? Perhaps because through the mediation of sports they learn, or think they learn, something about themselves and their nation. For example, the noted French-born Columbia University professor and observer of America, Jacques Barzun, once wrote, "Whoever wants to know the heart and mind of America had better learn baseball."[8] Baseball, after all, is uniquely American, a Lockean game with elaborate rules reminiscent of the U.S. Constitution; a game with a busy urban infield of traffic and conflict surrounded by a pastoral green outfield; a game that tries to balance individual achievement with the necessity of social cooperation; a game whose rules enforce the principle that all players are created equal and compete fairly. Not who you are but how you perform puts a premium on pragmatic results.

Professional basketball has a reputation for being "streetwise," exhibiting the survival skills of the threatening streets of urban America, with intense, swift, cooperative action in an enclosed and contested space. Even board games and games of chance tell us a great deal about political cultures. Americans play poker, a fast-paced competitive game of capital acquisition with pluralistic and shifting results produced by the interplay of player, skill, and luck, emphasizing the idea of individual life as being largely a gamble. Russians prefer chess, a slow-paced and careful game (often played as a team wherein the individual is a subordinate to the team effort), in which planning and forethought eliminate as much of the chance element as possible. Chess emphasizes that patient skill and tenacity lead to eventual victory (a tie is often acceptable) through secretive, deceptive, and smart moves that avoid undue risk. We may only speculate how much the assumptions and conduct of such popular national games affect approaches to politics and negotiations between nations.

SPORTS AND MEDIATED HEROIC FANTASIES

It is a common fact, often unrecognized, that very few people are good athletes. In home and school, children learn that the sporting life is a good thing, that excellence in sports is highly prized. Kids engage in sports during recess and after school, but few make the varsity team. Fewer still excel sufficiently to enter college or professional athletics. Approximately 20 million children of assorted ages participate in organized sports; a skilled high school athlete has one chance in 12,000 to become a professional athlete. In baseball alone, about one in every 1,500 American 18-year-old males demonstrates sufficient ability to play at the lowest professional level. Only about 500 players play major league baseball in a given season. Of the thousands that have played in the major leagues in baseball history, only 200 have been inducted into the Hall of Fame.[9] Thus, for the vast majority of people sports celebrity is beyond hope. Unable to become sports heroes themselves, the vast bulk of Americans are content to laud the few who can.

The social base of sports derives from heroic fantasies that develop in childhood, go unfulfilled, but survive as projections onto admired athletes. Sports heroes serve as role models to be imitated, even mimicked. Watch Little League or adult slow-pitch softball players; notice how much they use gestures and chatter that they associate with baseball superstars. For some, the dream that "maybe I could have been a major leaguer" or "I could have been a contender" persists throughout life. One form of merchandised designed experience (recall the discussion in the "Introduction"), or "fantasy leisure," is the adult baseball camp. There middle-aged men pay for a simulated training exercise with major league stars serving as celebrity camp counselors while campers enact the fantasy of playing for a major league team.[10]

Most people, however, play out their fantasies of sports heroism vicariously, watching and reading about sports. They are spectators, not gladiators. Sports communicators—sportswriters, announcers, promoters, and so on—feed the fantasies. They construct spectacular sport melodramas: contests between the virtuous and the villainous, building suspense and hinting that evil might triumph, allowing for the intervention of fortune through heroic deeds and untimely errors, and reporting the "thrill of victory and the agony of defeat" (as ABC's "Wide World of Sports" labels it). Sports journalism favors soap opera—petty rivalries of players, bickering owners, pouting superstars, fights and fines, salary disputes and team jumping, romances and legal troubles, even premature deaths. Paralleling soap opera coverage is epic coverage, heroic battles of titans over gigantic stakes (observe any NFL film of past Super Bowls). In this version, sports heroism is unsullied, the athlete a godlike exemplar of the heroic ideal representing leadership, clean living, moral purity, willingness to work and sacrifice, team sprit, religious piety, and patriotism.

This heroic ideal developed in popular literature, especially in the fictional exploits of Frank Merriwell and other exemplars of the Protestant ethic of hard work, pluck, and ambition to succeed. These classic sports heroes were too good to be true, but real-life sports figures, such as Christy Mathewson, Lou Gehrig, and for that matter Knute Rockne (born in Norway), embodied the classic ideal. Immigrant children overcame class barriers and ethnic prejudice to rise to fame and fortune. Baseball, for instance, held out the hope of upward mobility for waves of urban immigrants who started at the bottom of the social ladder—first Germans and Irish (with names like Wagner and Ewing, Bresnahan and McGinnity), then Italians and Poles (DiMaggio and Lazzeri, Kurowski and Musial), blacks and Latinos (Robinson and Doby, Carrasquel and Marichal).[11]

Thus, success in the arena fed not only fantasies of heroes as role models but also the fantasies of social success for those heroic enough to claim it. And gifted athletes could claim it because there is another feature of the sports myth in America, namely, that sports builds character and instills values essential to personal and national success. In the *Knute Rockne* movie Rockne defends the "elaborate spectacle of sport" before an academic investigating committee. Football, he argues, is an "absolute necessity to the nation's best interests." So that America will never lose its "most precious traits of daring and courage" coaches devote their lives to making "men tough," rejecting the "flaccid philosophy" that mere classroom learning alone can protect a nation that is "getting soft." Since "the finest work of man is building the character of man," sports is vital in teaching toughness and tolerance, serving as a moral equivalent of war for "red-blooded" young men with the "natural spirit of combat" in a safe social outlet. This heroic spirit echoes Theodore Roosevelt's espousal of "the strenuous life," which argues for Americans to live the life of individual strength, seeking hard and dangerous endeavors, to achieve the goal of national greatness. Roosevelt and others of his era promoted a cult of toughness and praised the patriotic and martial attitude derived from athletic competition.

Rockne's fear that a nation without football grows soft thus takes on political significance: A nation that is soft cannot compete in international political contests. Thus, physical fitness, competitive achievement, and a potent masculine attitude are essential for the successful exercise of political power, especially military power. President John Kennedy created the President's Council on Youth Fitness to organize in public schools sports and physical fitness programs that were often compulsory to reverse the feared decline of fitness, strength, and by extension, the character of American youth. "Our growing softness, our increasing lack of physical fitness, is a menace to our security," Kennedy said. The belief that national security in an age of advanced military technology remains dependent on "character" learned through athletics is the *Eton fantasy*. Its critics find the fantasy blatantly chauvinistic and sexist: equating sports with warfare, viewing conquest as the only possible solution to conflict, and exalting the virtue of toughness but demeaning the virtue of intelligence.[12]

In any case, politicians, military leaders, and members of the coaching fraternity extol the merits of sports as a political resource. Early in this century, U.S. presidents began a ritual: Each president would throw out the first ball on the opening day of the baseball season. Their exploitation of sports now extends to other rituals: receiving contingents of victorious athletes at the White House, claiming to be ardent fans of all sports, calling locker rooms to offer congratulations to triumphant teams and athletes, tossing the coin to begin the Super Bowl as President Reagan did or—as President Nixon did for the Washington Redskins—devising a play to be used in a game! Presidential candidates seek endorsements and support of famous athletes on the campaign trail. Both Herbert Hoover and Al Smith sought the endorsement of Babe Ruth in 1928; in 1976, Gerald Ford, who pointed with pride to his football achievements at the University of Michigan, featured Joe Garagiola, former catcher and TV sportscaster, reading a list of "athletes for Ford" (including Jack Nicklaus) in a radio commercial. The ploy doesn't always work: Both Al Smith, whom Ruth backed, and Ford, whom Nicklaus backed, lost. In 1988, Michael Dukakis hitched his star to the Boston Red Sox (they lost and so did he) while George Bush campaigned with baseball Hall of Famer Ted Williams and frequently reminded voters he had played first base at Yale.

Given the popular fascination with heroism in the arena and the political relevance of sports, it is no wonder that achievement in athletics often leads to political office. U.S. Senator Bill Bradley of New Jersey played a decade for the New York Knicks of the National Basketball Association. In his first campaign, along with his other qualifications, he claimed that sports taught him competitiveness and teamwork, exposed him to "many layers of national life," and gave him "a unique perspective of our problems, particularly since I was a white man in a predominantly black world." A TV spot featured Bradley tossing a piece of crumpled paper into a wastebasket from 10 feet (give him two points!). Former Representative Jack Kemp was elected in the House district where he had once played for the NFL Buffalo Bills. As a conservative, he compared the virtues of a competitive economy with athletic competition and claimed that football had trained him for leadership. His economic adviser, Jude Wanninski, said of him, "He wasn't just a football player. He was a quarterback. That's different. He plotted out offensive strategies. He was an expert in counterforce theory long before his involvement in supply-side economics." When Kemp ran for president in 1988, his campaign biography concentrated on his football exploits, and his campaign video began with pictures of Kemp in his football uniform and switched to Kemp in a blue suit walking onto a football field with a football in his hands, while the voice-over intoned, "Since he left the football field, Jack has had even greater success." During his 1988 campaign, Kemp repeated often: "You can't be a quarterback and be a pessimist. If you are a quarterback calling a play, you've got to believe in it, make your team believe in it."

Sports sociologists have concluded that there is little evidence to support the notion that participation in organized sports builds character, or teaches moral development, leadership, or other valued traits.[13] No matter. So long as the fantasy of sports heroism persists, evidence to the contrary notwithstanding, there will be a close relationship between political and athletic achievement. Bradley and Kemp may be but the first of what could become a host of superstar sports politicians seeking high national office. Jim Bunning, once a major league pitching star, is now a state legislator; Steve Garvey, long-time major league first baseman, contemplates entering politics; and Roger Staubach, former Dallas Cowboy quarterback, is a Republican notable in Texas. In politics as in sports, victory may go to the swift.

SPORTS: SCHOOL FOR POLITICAL VIRTUE OR SCANDAL?

Athletic heroes are living proof of the good and bad of the sports experience. The playing field, according to fantasy, is a classroom where players and spectators learn eternal truths relevant to everyday life. The rhetoric of the sports banquet speech, the newspaper sports column, or the oration by the sports-minded politician—each identifies sports with achievement in commerce, politics, and other endeavors. This belief that athletics teach lessons of how to live and how to succeed constitutes a *didactic fantasy*. As with the legend of George Gipp, the stories in the sports lesson books are often apocryphal.

Ronald Reagan's use of sports tales to teach eternal truths for everyday living typified the apocryphal character of his lessons. As president, Reagan liked to draw on his own limited athletic experience to teach good citizenship to his fellow Americans. For example, he reminisced about football back at Dixon High School. At a crucial stage of a game, young Ron committed a foul. The officials didn't see the infraction and would not uphold the protest of the opposing team. An official asked Reagan if he had fouled. The expedient thing would have been to lie, but "truth-telling had been whaled into me, also a lot of sports ethics," said the president in relating the tale. "I told the truth, the penalty was ruled, and Dixon lost the game." As in Parson Weems's fable about George Washington's cutting down the cherry tree, Reagan could not tell a lie. The lesson that Reagan, and by extension everyone, should learn is how you play the game: Being truthful in the face of pressures to win displays moral character, precisely what one would want in a president. Reagan's mediated reality, however, is not strictly accurate. The game, like Washington's felling of the cherry tree, did not happen; no game with the outcome Reagan remembers occurred while he was playing for Dixon High School.[14] Yet, accuracy in spinning sports legends is not the point. The apocryphal sports story offers a "higher truth" about ethics. The story may not be literally true, but that does not diminish the value of the lesson, which is, ironically, that one should always tell the truth!

For both those who think sports offer didactic preparation for life and those who believe that sports serve perverted social purposes, something does get overlooked—namely, that people might engage in sports competition purely for the fun of it. Among both sports advocates and critics, there is a residual Puritan streak that says, in effect, that at bottom sports are frivolous. To be taken seriously, sports must be more than fun, athletic contests must be instructive. Consonant with the work ethic is the widespread sports fantasy that the athletic arena (and the political arena) exists not as an end in itself to be enjoyed for itself but to teach, inspire, and promote established social values.

Consider two sports fantasies: (1) the notion that sports teach patriotism and piety, and (2) that sports promote democratic sportsmanship. Polls indicate that Americans believe "sports are valuable because they help youngsters to become good citizens." Once justified on the grounds that athletic competition "makes men out of boys," now the ideal is to make boys good citizens. And of what does good citizenship consist? For many an advocate of organized sports, good citizenship means love of country and love of God. Athletic competition allegedly teaches both. One would therefore expect athletes to be more devoted to nation and to religion than those who have not been tested in the arena or on the playing field. Presumedly, competition, hard work, sacrifice, suffering, and team loyalty lead to patriotism. In fact, there is scant evidence that athletes are any more or less patriotic than nonathletes. The fantasy persists nonetheless—as polls suggest—often with chauvinistic and militaristic overtones. Similarly, there is little confirmation that participation in organized sports increases religious faith or piety, but there remains a fantasy that sport is this nation's "civil religion." Norm Evans, former Miami Dolphins lineman and activist in the Fellowship of Christian Athletes, said: "I guarantee you that Christ would be the toughest guy who ever played this game. . . . Jesus was a real man, all right . . . aggressive and a tremendous competitor. . . . I have no doubt he could play in the National Football League. . . . He would be a star." Thus, sports occupy a sacred niche; only godly figures can achieve superhuman stardom in that hallowed arena. Belief in God and His Son might lead the unathletic to heaven, but only the truly Elect become All-Pro in the National Football League (NFL).[15]

Do sports also teach democratic sportsmanship? Before the high-dollared days of professionalism, a sportsman was a gentleman committed to excellence in some form of competition, bound by ethical rules that excluded cheap tactics or dirty tricks. The sportsman played fair, fought hard, treated opponents and referees with respect, enjoyed the contest, and accepted victory with magnanimity and defeat with grace. A classic book on the democratic way of life opines that "democracy is sportsmanship."[16] Even today Americans profess to admire a good sport. Thus, politicans who act like poor losers or arrogant winners invite public scorn. Americans have a phrase for it. The political candidate, winner or loser, who "acts bush" violates a norm of sportsmanship common to athletics and politics.

In a competitive society that values success, however, rewards go to athletes and social competitors for winning—achieving the most home runs, the most car sales, being the most beautiful, garnering the most votes. The success ethic is the ethic of the winner, and the winners' code bears scant relationship to the good sportsmanship code of a bygone age. Speakers at banquets honoring home teams and their heroes talk of good sportsmanship; they seldom mention lessons learned in how to cheat and lie, or that playing by the rules is for suckers. Consider lessons contained in memorable quotes from notable, successful coaches: "Winning isn't everything, it's the only thing," Vince Lombardi (famous NFL coach) was misquoted (he said "Trying to win . . ."). "Nice guys finish last," said Leo Durocher, baseball manager. (He too was misquoted; looking at an opposing team he actually said, "[They're] nice guys. [They'll] finish last.") "Only winners are truly alive," said George Allen, NFL coach and friend of Presidents Nixon and Reagan. "Winning is living. Every time you win, you're reborn. When you lose, you die a little."

Are the codes of good sportsmanship and of winning compatible? Not so long as winning is the primary, indeed, only point of the contest. The code of the sportsman appears in the rhyme, "For when the great scorer comes to write against your name, he'll write not that you won or lost but how you played the game." The winning code is something else: "He'll write that if you did not win, how well you shifted the blame." The stakes are too high to be unduly bound by sporting rules of conduct, since all's fair in love, war, and politics. Stealing game plans (candidates' debate briefing books in presidential politics), holding and kicking in the clinches or throwing at hitters (negative advertising in political campaigns), being a little meaner than your opponents (following the three rules of campaigning—that is, ATTACK, ATTACK, and ATTACK) is a matter of nasty necessity.

This vision of life as a "King of the Hill" game is a form of *popular Machiavellianism,* the ambivalent view that both sports and politics are not areas of action where the ordinary rules of morality can apply, given the imperative of winning. It is precisely this ambivalence that produces another set of fantasies about sports (and politics) that is less positive than those contained in the view that athletics teach sound values of patriotism, piety, and democratic sportsmanship. Avid sports fans may be more authoritarian, nationalistic, and conservative in their political orientation than the rest of the population.[17] But not everyone is a fan, let alone avid. Some are critics.

For sports critics the emphasis on winning symbolizes much that's wrong with the moral tone of the country. Many critics dislike the violence of sports, which they believe teaches aggression and virtually underwrites the tendencies in American society to resort to violence and war. For them, the regimentation of sports such as football teaches militarism—the art of conquering territory through concerted violence that defeats the enemy. Computer war games at the mall arcade, say critics, ready people to pull the trigger and annihilate rather than negotiate. Furthermore, sports teach imperialism by emphasizing domination of defeated people ("We're number one!"). The emphasis on competition makes for a more individualistic and less cooperative society, and it supports the great inequalities of wealth and power that capitalist and political competition engenders.[18] Of course, sports boosters see none of these criticisms as being valid. Or, if they do see them as valid, they view that validity not as corrupting but as being positive side-benefits of athletic competition.

However, sports critics on many fronts continue to chip away at the fantasies of the arena. We can readily illustrate how much the image of sports was transformed in but a few years. For example, in his 1952 novelette, *The Old Man and the Sea,* Ernest Hemingway evoked baseball star Joe DiMaggio as a symbol of perfection: "I must be worthy of the great DiMaggio who does all things perfectly," Hemingway had his Old Man say.[19] By the 1960s, however, songwriters Simon and Garfunkel could ask in a popular lyric, "Where did you go, Joe Dimaggio?" In the face of franchise shifts by greedy owners, exhorbitant salary demands by players, players' strikes, and cases of player dependence on drugs and other substances, many sports fans have become as disillusioned as Simon and Garfunkel. Those charged with keeping the flame of the fantasy of sports heroism alive have not helped matters. For example, in 1988, a survey of coaches in major colleges found that most of them thought their coaching peers knowingly cheat to win games; nine in ten said that they themselves felt "a great deal" or "much" pressure to win. Adding to fan disenchantment has been an awakening to the narcissistic egos of many sports celebrities. Public displays of self-promotion, arrogance, rudeness, and bad manners—not to mention simple greed—transformed images of heroic figures into (at best) indulged, spoiled brats or (at worst) villains.

With the advent of the feminist movement, organized sports faced criticism from another front. The charge was that sports were largely male-dominated, relegating women to the passive role of spectators, or at best, cheerleaders shaking their pom-poms. Ever so gradually, female athletics have produced opportunities for achievement undreamed of in earlier decades in professional golf, tennis, track and field, gymnastics, and a wide variety of other sports. What is at issue, however, is whether a revision of one of the oldest tenets of the sport credo, namely, that sports are a male-dominated world, will also produce long-term revisions in other aspects of the overarching fantasy of the arena. Or will both males and females accept a slightly revised vision of sports: Sports build character of both males and females, produce heroines as well as heros, teach piety and patriotism to all citizens regardless of gender, and place the rewards of winning well above how the game was played.

A final criticism of sports fantasy derives from the view that sports, in the end, teach not participation but passivity. Sports are mass-mediated spectacles involving a few highly talented and highly paid athletes, male and female, at levels of competition that most Americans can only dream about. The implicit message from the playing field is that the vast majority of lesser mortals are passive spectators, expected to take part in the Big Game vicariously. Sports spectacles teach habits of watching, not acting. Not only is such a habit bad for our health, it is also bad for our politics. There is, of course, a carryover to politics. Political events as mass-mediated realities also are vast spectacles that are played out with pomp and ceremony, contrived conflict, and colorful pageantry. Be they campaigns for the presidency, summit meetings between world leaders, congressional inquiries into major scandals—all these events invite viewing as spectators, not participants. The logic of spectacles that TV sports teach so well turns on the mass expectation that what we watch should be dramatically satisfying, yet evoke no response other than vicarious approval or disapproval, cheering or booing in the privacy of the TV den. By extension, politics as a spectator sport relegates most of us to seats in the grandstands, excluding us from access to the playing field. Sports and politics are both arenas of play offered for amusement, justified by their advocates as vital, yet with no seeming consequences for our lives beyond the claim itself. Rather than instructing us in democratic values, as Hollywood's Coach Rockne argued, or threatening those values as sports critics suggest, the elaborate spectacle of sports may serve us not at all.[20]

SPORTS AS A DRAMATIC SETTING OF POLITICS

There is a more directly dramatic way in which sports stimulate political fantasies among mass audiences. This is when the athletic contest, or at least the way it is mediated, assumes political significance because of conduct on the playing field. Sports events often occur in explosive political surroundings. The pageantry of sports and the political spectacle become one, or at least become so intermingled that the conduct of the Big Game and the rituals surrounding it acquire political overtones.

Even though the Olympic Games are intended and billed to be nonpolitical, a glance at their history demonstrates clearly how international sport not only mediates political reality but becomes political itself. The "Nazi Olympics" staged in Munich in 1936 are a prime example. Nazi dictator Adolf Hitler hoped that the Olympics would showcase the superior athletic ability of white "Aryan" competitors from Germany over allegedly inferior races and nations, a central tenet of Nazi racial ideology. Such fantasies of racial superiority could be sustained only if the "master race" indeed defeated "inferiors." It did not happen. Black American track and field stars Jesse Owens and Ralph Metcalf consistently outran the German runners, a point of considerable personal and sporting embarrassment not only to Hitler but also to his political claims.

In some cases, rituals surrounding a sports event evoke political dramatization. During the Vietnam era, televised football games were politically charged with the increase of patriotic ritual and pageantry before the contest and at halftime ceremonies. In 1970, ABC–TV refused to carry an antiwar halftime show by a college band on grounds that it was a "political demonstration." However, the network did broadcast a halftime show at an Army-Navy game that featured Green Berets who had just conducted an unsuccessful raid attempting to rescue prisoners of war held in North Vietnam, and a speech by a military general condemning antiwar activity in the United States. Political statements at athletic events, when not sanctioned by authorities, quickly become controversial. Thus, after black athletes raised clenched, black-gloved fists in symbolic protest of racial injustice in America during televised medal-awarding ceremonies at the 1968 Olympics, criticism quickly transformed the victorious hero-athletes into villainous troublemakers. Ritual dissent threatens the credibility of fantasies of national affirmation, but ritual affirmation confirms patriotic feelings. For instance, there was a virtual love feast for released American hostages returning from Iran at the 1981 Super Bowl—yellow ribbons everywhere, on everyone, and a gigantic ribbon around the New Orleans Superdome itself.[21]

A nation playing host to a spectacular event such as the Olympic Games finds it difficult to resist the temptation to use the spectacle as a propaganda event. The Soviet Union sought to use the 1980 Moscow Olympics for propagandistic purposes, attempting to structure the conduct of the games to ensure victories by Soviet athletes as evidence of the superiority of the Soviet social and political system. The attempt suffered a setback when the Soviet Union invaded Afghanistan, and in protest, the United States led a western boycott of the games (including not televising them). In the wake of political tension, the 1980 winter Olympics—not held in the Soviet Union—took place as scheduled. The underdog American hockey team, to everyone's surprise, defeated the vaunted Soviet team. The game had all the elements of political melodrama—tension and danger, clear heroes and villains, a David and Goliath scenario, a political moral, and an ending on the playing field that the nation could cheer. There was spontaneous celebration across America, made even sweeter when the American hockey team went on to win the gold medal. Greeted at the White House by President Carter, the team then toured the nation and was later the subject of a television docudrama (see Chapter 3). Neither the U.S. triumph in the winter games nor the U.S. boycott of the summer games forced the Soviets out of Afghanistan, but the substitute victory yielded its own symbolic satisfactions. Such is *fantastic substitution,* whereby a mass-mediated nonpolitical fantasy alleviates anxiety, however temporarily, by helping people project unresolved political tensions onto a substitute object, in this case a sports melodrama.[22]

Host to the 1985 Olympic Games, the United States also exploited them as a propaganda event. During the early 1980s, tensions between the United States and the Soviet Union mounted, and after the Russians shot down a Korean airliner in 1983 there were moves to bar Soviet athletes from participating in the Los Angeles Olympics. In May 1984, the Soviet Union announced it would not participate in the games because of "anti-Soviet hysteria" in the United States, and most Soviet allies followed suit. The upshot was to make the games into an event dominated by the host country. The Reagan administration, corporate sponsors, and the TV network that broadcast the games made the 1984 Olympics into an pro-American spectacle. The mass-mediated fantasy was of American resurgence in the world. Telecasts featured American victories, corporate power, and political consensus behind Reagan. Critics labeled the event as "the capitalist games" because almost all pretense of amateurism vanished, and corporate sponsorship and advertising dominated. Foreign teams complained that ABC's coverage of the Olympics was overwhelmingly of U.S. athletes and victories; the achievements of athletes from other nations might as well not have happened because they did not appear on TV. It was a lament and criticism repeated four years later in NBC's coverage of the 1988 summer Olympics from Seoul, Korea.[23]

Sporting spectacles need not always derive from or contribute to political tensions. Sometimes they symbolize the reduction of political conflict. In 1989, as the USSR and the United States endeavored to grow more cordial in their relations, the thaw in the Cold War was symbolized through a sporting event. The two nations scheduled a football game between two U.S. college teams—the University of Southern California and the University of Illinois. And what title did they give to the game to be played in Dynamo Stadium in Moscow? Appropriately enough, perhaps, it was the "Glastnost Bowl"!

Finally, the sports arena serves as a dramatic setting for experiments in social and political change. One of the things most noteworthy about professional baseball for decades was who was *not* on the diamond: Players were all white. After World War II, there was sentiment on the part of many Americans to remove the formal and informal racial barriers that had marked the nation for decades. A pioneering effort to do so took place not in the political arena but on the playing field, in one of the most conservative of all American institutions, baseball. In 1947, the Brooklyn Dodgers promoted a black player named Jackie Robinson into the National League. There was considerable opposition: Critics thought it would ruin baseball, fans would boycott games, white players would refuse to compete, even racial conflict would result. No small part of the opposition to Robinson's entry into the major leagues stemmed from something else—a clear prejudice that blacks should play with "their own kind" because they were simply inferior to white players. The gritty and proud Robinson endured racial slurs, threats, spikings, beanballs, ostracism, even threats to strike, but opposition was for naught. Robinson proved to be an excellent player. He was named Rookie of the Year for 1947, and in 1949, Most Valuable Player. Other successful black players followed, and a major racial barrier fell.

Robinson's sporting example carried its social and political implications: If baseball, why not schools, other places of employment, public facilities? If Robinson, why not me? There is a direct line between Robinson's successful 1947 season with Brooklyn and many of the protests, successful and not successful, that comprised the civil rights movement. From Jackie Robinson to Martin Luther King, Jr., to Jesse Jackson. Perhaps not only the "heart and mind" of America are revealed through baseball; sometimes so is its future.[24]

THE POWER AND THE GLORY OF POPULAR SPORTS

The mass-mediated world of popular sports, in the ways we have specified, informs our political realities. Our visions of politics frequently flow from what we learn about ourselves, our nation, and our leaders as spectators in the arena of popular sports. We have said that in large measure there is considerable overlap between popular sports and politics. The two enterprises possess a common thrust; both appeal to popular penchants for drama, spectacle, and pageantry—but let us not get carried away with the similarities. They have much in common, but popular sports are not politics nor should popular politics become sports. As spectators supporting our favorite teams and players, we have society's approval, even blessing, for doing what is not accepted in other settings—cheering, waving wildly, booing, hissing, threatening death and mayhem upon offending opponents and upon officials. We can't go so far in politics. Yes, we can applaud and we can complain, but whereas we yell "Kill the umpire" within earshot of incompetent authority, venting our frustrations at presidential mediocrity, corrupt officials, or uncaring tax collectors is not so easy. They must be removed and replaced by means more peaceful—and more effective—than simply making it so by yelling. To be sure, the mass-mediated arenas of sports and politics, at least during those moments when things are going well, appeal to our romantic fantasies. Good wins over evil, poetic justice triumphs, our morals are vindicated, and we celebrate. And in sporting contests when none of these things happens—when Casey at the bat strikes out, and there is no joy in Mudville—we do have something to fall back on. We wait 'till next year.

In politics there is no next year, only the daily here-and-now. There is no playing field that goes dark when the lights go out, no crowd that vanishes when the game ends and the concessions stands close. No, in politics—unless we are content to live solely in a world of mass-mediated fantasies—we not only enter and stay in the arena, we actually play. Popular sports indulge our romantic fantasies, but romantic fantasies do not alter a world of political power. In politics only at our own peril can we title our national autobiography, *I Never Played the Game*.[25]

NOTES

1. Heartley W. "Hunk" Anderson, with Emil Klosinski, *Notre Dame, Chicago Bears, and Hunk: Football Memoirs in Highlight* (Oviedo, FL: Florida Sun-Gator Publishing Co., 1976), p. 96.
2. Gary Wills, *Reagan's America: Innocents at Home* (Garden City, NY: Doubleday, 1987), pp. 120–124.
3. Film, *Knute Rockne—All American* (Warner Brothers, 1940).
4. Ronald Reagan, quoted in Wills, *Reagan's America*, 122–123.
5. Ronald Reagan, Address to the Republican National Convention, August 15, 1988, New Orleans, LA.
6. Eliot Asinof, *Eight Men Out: The Black Sox and the 1919 World Series* (New York: Holt, Rinehart and Winston, 1983).
7. Eldon Snyder and Elmer Spreitzer, *The Social Aspect of Sport*, 2nd ed. (Englewood Cliffs, NJ: Prentice-Hall, 1983); Wilbert M. Leonard II, *A Sociological Perspective of Sport* (Minneapolis, MN: Burgess Publishers, 1984); see also *Sport Inc., Times Mirror Magazine*.
8. Jacques Barzun, *God's Country and Mine* (Boston: Little, Brown, 1954), pp. 159–160.
9. Michael Novak, *The Joy of Sports* (New York: Basic Books, 1976). Less effusive and more critical is Richar Lipsky, *How We Play the Game* (Boston: Beacon Press, 1980).
10. Gerald A. Brandmeyer and Louella K. Alexander, "I Caught the Dream: The Adult Baseball Camp as Fantasy Leisure," *Journal of Leisure Research* 18 (1986): 26–39.
11. See, for example, Stephen Hardy, *How Boston Played: Sport, Recreation, and Community, 1865–1915* (Boston: Northeastern University Press, 1983).
12. Donald J. Mrozek, *Sport and American Mentality, 1880–1910* (Knoxville: University of Tennessee Press, 1983).
13. John W. Loy, Barry McPherson, and Gerald Kenyon, *Sport and Social Systems* (Reading, MA: Addison-Wesley, 1978); Jay J. Coakley, *Sport in Society: Issues and Controversies* (St. Louis, MO: Times Mirror/Mosby College Publishers, 1986).
14. Wills, *Reagan's America*, p. 128.
15. Norm Evans, quoted in Robert Lipsyte, *Sportsworld: An American Dreamland* (Chicago: Quadrangle Books, 1980), p. 104.
16. T.V. Smith and Edward C. Lindeman, *The Democratic Way of Life* (New York: New American Library, 1963), pp. 81, 83, 88.
17. Robert H. Prisuta, "Televised Sports and Political Values," *Journal of Communication* 29 (Winter 1979): 94–102.

18. Associated Press, News Release, August 22, 1988.

19. Ernest Hemingway, *The Old Man and the Sea* (New York: Scribner's, 1952), p. 75.

20. The classic statement of the bread-and-circuses argument is Lewis Mumford, "Sports and the 'Bitch-Goddess,'" in Marcia Stubbs and Sylvan Barnet, eds., *The Little Brown Reader* (Boston: Little, Brown, 1977), pp. 238–241.

21. See the articles in Gerald Redmund, ed., *Politics and the Olympic Games,* Part III (Champaign, IL: Human Kinetics Publishers, 1986).

22. This notion is adapted from Harold Lasswell's theorem in *Power and Personality* (New York: Viking, 1962), p. 38.

23. Dale P. Toohey, "The Politics of the 1984 Los Angeles Olympics," in Redmund, *Politics and the Olympic Games,* pp. 161–170.

24. Jules Tygiel, *Baseball's Great Experiment: Jackie Robinson and His Legacy* (New York: Oxford University Press, 1983).

25. Howard Cosell, *I Never Played the Game* (New York: Morrow, 1985).

PART II

Group-Mediated Politics

The mediation of political realities through mass communication makes it possible for entire communities to share the fantasies created and spread by news, entertainment programming, popular films, celebrity magazines, sports, and other media. Precisely what proportion of persons exposed to the fantasy content of mass media respond to it, and how, current research does not permit us to say. Yet, the potential is there, in part because people do not have the opportunity to deal directly with the things they view and hear in the entertainment and news media. If they had that opportunity, say, through personal or group experiences, they could live in a real world experienced firsthand, not a world of mediated fantasies. But would they? We address that question in Part II. We look first at how, even among group members dealing directly with tangible problems, there is a strong tendency to construct and share fantastic political worlds. Then we examine how this process operates in various areas—among public officials, journalists, political insiders, selected religious groups, and highly publicized political movements.

As with mass-mediated politics, our discussion derives from studies of communication within political groups and speculations about group communication. Consequently, we offer the same disclaimer plus an invitation to readers that is contained in Part I. The following chapters suggest propositions about how group experience mediates political realities and thereby frequently builds fantastic worlds. We urge readers to reflect on these propositions and examine them further, something they can do in their own group life. In that way, they participate in the research scholar's version of the American Dream—that is, the quest for a tested body of knowledge explaining how and why the members of the human family behave as they do.

CHAPTER 7

Elite Political Fantasies
Groupthink Sources of Massthink

The year was 1918. Before the fighting stopped, the United States suffered more than 320,000 casualties since entering World War I the year before, more than a third of them being deaths. Americans celebrated the armistice of November 11 that ended "The Great War." Now the carnage would cease. Yet a carnage of another form did not. In 1918–1919 an epidemic of influenza, the "Spanish flu," killed 548,000 Americans, four times the number who died in World War I, and 20 million worldwide. More than seven decades have now passed. The "war to end all wars" that ended in 1918 did not end war. Americans have since died in World War II and the Korean and Vietnam Wars, not to mention other conflicts. Nor was the 1918 Spanish flu the last to take its toll on Americans. Periodic outbreaks, even epidemics with exotic names, still produce flu-related deaths—"Asian flu," "Hong Kong flu," "Russian flu," and so on. So common is influenza that every fall and winter TV ads remind us that "the cold and flu season is here" and we had best prepare ourselves by stocking up with the latest patent remedy and getting flu shots.

Presumably, governing officials learned lessons from World War I that prepared them, sometimes well and sometimes ill, for future military conflicts. So too officials thought that the great influenza epidemic of 1918 taught something—that to be forewarned is to be forearmed. Hence, when in 1976 warning signals appeared that another major epidemic might be in the offing, policymakers harking back to acquired presumptions about the causes and consequences of the 1918 catastrophe prepared to act.[1] The result was a case of elite political fantasy that ultimately became a mass fantasy.

The 1918 flu pandemic (i.e., worldwide epidemic) had a noteworthy aspect beyond devastating human populations. It also attacked pigs and decimated them just as readily. In January 1976, 13 army recruits in boot camp became ill and one died. The diagnosis was influenza from a virus commonly found in hogs, one not detected in humans since 1930 but possibly similar to the 1918 virus. Was this *déjà vu* and another disaster on its way? Would the new flu, dubbed "swine flu," wreak havoc? In both 1957 and 1968 there had been flu epidemics in the United States. By the time officials acted to curtail them, they had done their damage—but nothing on the order of 1918—and were over. In the face of the possibility that the 1976 swine flu might be a repeat of the Spanish flu, officials acted to prevent an outbreak. Granted that in the month since the army recruits had been diagnosed there had been no new cases, it would be better to err on the side of caution. Caution in this instance would be a program of mass immunization against swine flu. The director of the Center for Disease Control prepared a plan; appropriate officials throughout the federal hierarchy concurred (including President Gerald Ford advised by an *ad hoc* panel of experts); Congress approved. Once a vaccine was developed, produced, and tested, mass inoculations would begin around July 4, continue through Thanksgiving, and by then Americans would be protected for the upcoming flu season. Public information programs in newspapers and newsmagazines, on radio and TV, would alert people to the flu danger and the inoculation program. What officials believed would become beliefs for everyone.

However, the shared belief, or fantasy, among official elites that a swine flu epidemic similar in cause and consequence to that of 1918 was possible and could be prevented carried with it implied beliefs as well. One was that without prevention swine flu would run rampant. Yet, elsewhere in the world where prevention had been neither planned nor executed, swine flu did not occur. Another was that an acceptable vaccine could be readily developed, produced, tested, and mass-distributed. Unfortunately, tests of the vaccine were not promising. Children did not respond well, hence, child inoculations ceased. Then, manufacturers who feared lawsuits if the vaccine proved harmful refused to produce it. Now all immunization ceased. President Ford sought and ultimately received congressional approval for the federal government to assume the risks of litigation stemming from immunizations. It was not until mid-October, one month before they were to end, that flu shots began. Again there were problems. Two men in a nursing home suffered heart attacks following inoculation. There followed another suspension of inoculations. By the time they were renewed, TV publicity given to the heart attack story had eroded public confidence in the program. Then came discovery of potentially harmful neurological side effects from the vaccine. Another inoculation suspension ensued. Not until January 1977 did evidence indicate that the likelihood of harmful side effects was negligible. It did not matter. The mass inoculation program never resumed.

Swine flu epidemic or swine flu fantasy? In the year after the 1976 outbreak of influenza among 13 army recruits there was no case *worldwide* of swine flu that could not be traced to close contact with pigs. Yet during that year policymaking elites had devised an elaborate but flawed and expensive plan to combat swine flu. Why? They presumed a similarity between what actually had occurred in 1918 and what could happen in 1976. It is out of such taken-for-granted presumptions that elite fantasies grow; it is by sharing those presumptions with wider audiences that fantasies spread to the mass. This chapter examines how that happens.

WHOLES GREATER THAN THE SUM OF THEIR PARTS

When people gather to make decisions in small, face-to-face groups, interesting things happen, whether they congregate to make political decisions, as do public officials, or commonplace decisions in everyday life, as we all do. There is a reason why the groups form; presumably people want to accomplish something. Group members have a task to perform. Take political groups. They exist to deliberate on threats from disease, swine flu, or AIDS; to decide to build a new weapons system; to recommend tax reductions or increases, to ration paperclips; or whatever. And they have a prior goal, which is to build a consensus, cohesion, and solidarity among group members that will permit the group to exist and act as a group, not merely as a collection of individuals. Normally, that cohesiveness emerges as an unconscious by-product as people go about the social amenities of getting acquainted, exchanging pleasantries, asking and receiving advice, becoming colleagues, friends, and so forth. Soon, two overlapping sets of things begin to happen among group members: They socialize and promote group solidarity at the same time that they confront the task that brought them together.

Sociologist Robert F. Bales experimented with small, face-to-face groups and observed closely how members acted as they went about their work.[2] He classified their exchanges into two categories. One consisted of all the things that dealt specifically with the group's task, for example, members asking and giving information, opinions, and suggestions regarding how the group should deal with a problem. The second consisted of the social relationships between group members, for example, being friendly or antagonistic, joking and laughing, or being tense and withdrawn, complimenting or criticizing one another. One thing Bales concluded from his research was that if the group was to remain in being and, thus, perform its task, it must have means of releasing hostilities and disagreements, of continuously re-establishing friendly relations among group members. The desire to promote social harmony and keep the group intact may become an end in itself; indeed, camaraderie may replace the performance of the group's task as the rationale for the group's existence.

In the name of group solidarity, disagreements, criticism, information that strains social relations, and other matters vital to the group's task are swept under the rug. "Don't rock the boat" is the motto.

This tendency of task groups to develop into social groups engages the interest of scholars who study group behavior. Jerry Harvey is one. Harvey examines how people manage their affairs in organizational settings. He argues that "the fundamental problem in contemporary organizations broadly defined to include families, and churches, and businesses, and government, and academic institutions is the inability to cope with the fact that we agree with one another, and not the inability to cope with the fact we're in conflict."[3] This thesis runs against the grain of conventional belief. If we could just agree, we often hear, and just settle our disputes, the world would be a better place. Harvey argues, however, that people's disagreements are, to use his term, "phony." We pretend to disagree on little things, matters that occupy much of our attention in order to *avoid* disagreement on larger, more divisive issues that shake the very foundations of our group life. We shift back and forth, but we never stand up for fear of rocking the boat to the point of capsizing it.

Consider an example from everyday life. We have a student not doing well in a college course, say, in biology. Assume the course ends with a standardized exam. Assume, also, that a few of the student's friends discover a way to steal that exam, work out the answers and, thus, assure themselves of high marks on the final exam and in the course. Now our student may have all kinds of reasons for opposing such a scheme—moral convictions, fear of being caught, and so forth—but the call of group loyalty is higher. So instead of voicing reservations about the wisdom of the plan that brought the group together in the first place, she confines herself to arguing about when or how the exam is to be pilfered, or to how to look up the answers once the group has possession of it. Add one other assumption: that one of the student's friends also thinks the whole idea of stealing the exam is silly, even hazardous. He too keeps quiet, preferring instead to quibble over details. Conceivably no one might want to steal the exam, yet everyone conforms to the group's decision and goes along. Such things do happen. As Harvey says, people often find agreement harder to handle than disagreement.

Another student of group behavior, psychologist Irving Janis, has provided a label for and analysis of what happens when groups make decisions that reflect the tendencies of individuals to suppress their reservations about a course of action in order to preserve group unity. He calls it *groupthink*. Groupthink, he writes, "refers to a deterioration of mental efficiency, reality testing, and moral judgment that results from in-group pressures."[4] When people gather to do a job, make a decision, or otherwise act in concert, pressures develop to persuade group members to think alike. These pressures are usually subtle, not blatant. Also, cohesive groups expect members to conform to informal standards of friendly social behavior. Subtle or not, such pressures can subvert the original purpose for the group's existence. Instead of hard-headed appraisals of the problems, resources, information, and courses of action before the group, the stress is on amiable relations, warm feeling, and a cozy atmosphere. Members think as "we," talk of "our job." As the saying goes, "Reasonable men (and women) can disagree," but only within limits that do not threaten "us." Loyalty to the group becomes the highest form of loyalty; this requires members to resist raising controversial issues, criticizing weak arguments, or challenging faulty information. A member who persists in dissent is ignored, even rejected. Characteristics of groupthink dominate—some of the group hold contradictory beliefs but do not admit it, shut out information that does not conform to group solidarity, selectively forget and remember what and how the group decided as it did in the past, and preserve unity.

One feature of group life, then, that leads to groupthink is the pressure to solve problems in conformity with the dictates of group solidarity and loyalty rather than with specifics of the group's task. Janis maintains that this produces a series of defects as follows:

- Groups do not survey a full range of options open to them but seek solutions from a limited number of alternatives.
- Group members reach decisions, then fail to reexamine them in the face of drawbacks. Once a course of action has been rejected, the group neglects to reconsider it even though it may have advantages over the chosen option.
- Information from nongroup experts that runs counter to the group's thinking is avoided.
- Group members display selective bias in responding to the assessments by nongroup members, quickly assuming an "us" versus "them" posture.
- Groups ignore the likelihood that it is impossible to carry out the socially satisfying option.

Thus, when people form groups, tender-minded social considerations often override tough-minded efforts to solve the problems that brought the group together in the first place. That aspect alone suggests that groupthink influences group-mediated realities. There is more, however: There is a distinct fantasy component of groupthink. Groupthink is a fantasy-constructing rather than reality-testing process; groupthink is fantasythink.

In his study of small groups Bales developed an elaborate scheme for coding the task and social acts of group members toward one another. For example, if a group member gave another help, that reflected the social behavior of showing solidarity; if one asked another to repeat what had been said, that was coded as asking for orientation, a task behavior. One social act of importance Bales coded as "shows tension release." If a person joked with others, laughed, showed satisfaction, smiled, and so on, that eased the tension in the group and put members at rest. He later changed "shows tension release" to "dramatized." Bales concluded that group well-being, even survival, depended on releasing tensions. Hence, groups must show tension release, often through members giving dramatic performances that build group cohesion.

It was precisely this point of Bales's analysis that Ernest G. Bormann relied on in fashioning his fantasy-chaining ideas (see our "Introduction"): "Some, but not all, of the communication coded as 'dramatizes' would chain out through the group. When it did, that is, when group members got excited, interrupted each other, lost their self-consciousness, the meeting would become lively, animated, even boisterous."[5] Although not all scholars agree with Bormann, he and his colleagues believe that people, in short, get caught up in group dramas; any group is no longer a mere collection of individuals but assumes a life of its own.[6] Dramatic (i.e., social) performance supplants task performance as the first priority of the group. Thereby, groupthink acts as a source of group fantasies that, when communicated to wider audiences, provide the basis of massthink.

FROM THE HORSE'S MOUTH: FANTASIC DECISION-MAKING

Groupthink and the mediated fantasies it spawns are not new. One of the oldest of mythical tales suggests the persistence of groupthink. The Greek poet Homer first told of it 28 centuries ago. We know it as the tale of the Trojan Horse. During the Trojan War, the Greeks beseiged Troy for 10 years but to no avail. Feigning to depart from Troy, the Greeks left a massive wooden horse outside the city. The horse bore an inscription to the goddess Athena, to whom the Trojans had built a temple in their city. Moreover, because the Trojans regarded the horse as sacred, the wooden figure took on additional religious overtones. Why had the Greeks left the horse? Some Trojan leaders feared it to be a trick. Laocoön, a priest, warned, "Whatever it may be, I fear the Greeks, even when bringing gifts." Others, however, were persuaded by the testimony of Sinon, a captured Greek, who swore it to be an offering to Athena; its huge size was intended to *prevent* its being moved into the city for, once in the city, it would signify Trojan victory. In the end the Trojans, under the leadership of Priam and the council of elders, ignored the pleas of Lacoön and of Cassandra, who warned that the horse "has your destruction within it." Cassandra was restrained when she attacked the horse with an ax and burning brand. Using ropes and rollers, the Trojans pulled the horse into the city. After a drunken revelry of celebration, they fell asleep. Greek warriors hidden in the horse opened the city gates to the Greek army, which quickly entered and sacked Troy.

In this tale are the key characteristics of groupthink. Each characteristic says something about group-mediated politics among governing elites. First, the Trojan elders deluded themselves. After having withstood a 10-year assault on their city, and believing the gods to be on their side, it was relatively easy for the Trojan elite to assume that the wooden horse was a mark of Greek surrender to Trojan superiority, not an act of guile. Such optimism could easily contribute to an untested fantasy of an invulnerable people with right on their side, to whom victory could not be denied. A parallel fantasy was of a Greek people defeated, weak, vulnerable, and evil. Hence, even in calculating the risks involved in accepting the horse, groupthink dismissed them as idle fears.

Second, in spite of the protestations of Laocoön and Cassandra, there was also an illusion of unanimity: "We" who count are in accord. Leaders faced with opposing views often tend to respect one another's opinions so much that if they are of a single mind they assume that because "we all think so" it must be true. Instead of taking seriously the views of outsiders who warn of risks or errors, group members look inward; thus, consensual validation supplants critical thinking. Just as President Gerald Ford's advisers were convinced among themselves that a swine flu epidemic was imminent in 1976, so the Trojans thought the wooden horse a symbol of victory in 1200 B.C.

When people believe themselves unstoppable and united in a quest, it creates another condition of groupthink. That is an environment wherein group leaders dismiss people who voice doubts and, by doing so, send a message to others to remain silent for fear of punishment. Historian Barbara Tuchman, wrote of the legend of the Trojan Horse that it "can tell us only one thing: that Laocoön was fatally punished for perceiving the truth and warning of it."[7] The legend she speaks of involves what happened after the captured Greek, Sinon, had sworn the horse to be an offering to the Trojans. Just as Laocoön starts to refute Sinon, two hissing serpents suddenly appear, wrap themselves around Laocoön, and crush him to death. Today members who dissent from a group's consensus are unlikely to be crushed by serpents, yet a fear of being ostracized by one's colleagues and friends often produces silence rather than forthright dissent in group settings.

In his analysis of modern cases of groupthink, Irving Janis speaks of a fourth characteristic, which he calls "self-appointed mindguards." A *mindguard* is a group member who brings pressure on other members to conform to the group's consensus. The mindguard thus enforces cohesiveness. One form of such pressure is to urge members who dissent from group policy to remain silent. To speak out would merely make a nuisance of oneself by questioning a decision that has already been made. Mindguards insist that the time for opposition is over; now is the time to rally around the group. As a bodyguard protects against physical harm, a mindguard protects against thoughts that lessen the confidence of group members in the soundness of their decisions. Perhaps the mythical serpents were an extreme form of mindguarding, but they made their point: "The appalled watchers," were "moved to believe that the ghastly event" was "Laocoön's punishment for sacrilege in striking what must indeed be a sacred offering."[8]

Third, groupthink can be reinforced by adroit leadership. Members tacitly accept manipulation from a popular leader, especially one highly respected and suave in manner. By controlling the agenda of group discussion, avoiding controversial issues, deciding who—if any—opponents of the proposal may air their views, openly or in private, a leader can unconsciously create the conditions for a single, group consensus on reality rather than fostering the possibility of other visions. Priam of Troy did as much when he paid no heed to the warnings of Cassandra, his own daughter, and bade his followers to ignore them as well. Priam insisted that Cassandra talked "windy nonsense." The consensus cost a high price. Once Sinon crept from the celebration hall and released the Greek warriors to attack their sleeping foe, the only Trojan consensus remaining was a deadly silent one.

Finally, when new members whom other members trust and respect enter a group, a virtual taboo develops against antagonizing them. When new members propose a plan that coincides with the group's thinking or that supports one already determined, the pressure on opponents of groupthink to conform is even stronger. If anything, the newcomers—instead of being regarded as outsiders—serve as external validators of the wisdom and morality of group thinking. Such was precisely the case at Troy with Sinon, the captured Greek warrior. He told Priam and the elders that the Trojan Horse was a sacred offering and a symbol of Trojan victory. In the groupthink climate, Sinon's outsider views prevailed over the warnings of Laocoön and Cassandra. In spite of the fact that they based their views on questionable, even flawed, assumptions, the elders deferred to Sinon's word. In the end all these assumptions about Sinon's trustworthiness were wrong. His treachery doomed the Trojans.

The tale of the Trojan Horse is mythical. Yet, as many scholars have noted since, there have been many instances in history when groups have substituted wishful thinking for realistic analysis. There is a litany of examples of group-mediated realities among governing officials who have substituted groupthink for individual critical analysis.[9] Janis, for one, finds evidence that the failure to take seriously the possibility of a Japanese attack on Pearl Harbor in December 1941 (even as late as 12 hours before the bombing began) was an instance of groupthink. So, also, he argues, was the disaster in 1961 when the United States supported a landing at the Bay of Pigs in Cuba in an aborted effort to topple the regime of Fidel Castro. (It is from Janis's study of the Bay of Pigs fiasco that he extracted the characteristics of groupthink discussed earlier.) The U.S. conduct in the Korean War that resulted in intervention by the People's Republic of China and the 1960s escalation of the Vietnam War were also examples of groupthink. Without the detailed evidence Janis and others marshal, one can only speculate about the pervasiveness of groupthink in government circles at other times. Was, for example, the abortive rescue attempt to free U.S. hostages held in Iran in 1980 the product of groupthink in the advisory circle around President Jimmy Carter? Or, on matters of a less publicized nature, how often are the political realities that seem to call for budget cuts or increases, tax increases or reductions, the ever-rising price of first-class postage stamps, registration for a military draft, or other policies the mediated derivatives of groupthink?

This is not to say that all cases of group deliberation and decision are fantasythink. However, the examples are sufficiently noteworthy and recurrent to indicate that when group members talk only to each other, they may live in an isolation of their own making—one just as hard to penetrate as a tamper-proof medicine bottle, which remaining unopened in a source of pain, not of balm.

GROUP WRESTLING: FANTASY-BUILDING THROUGH INFORMED DISCUSSION

According to the tenets of groupthink, the gathering of policymakers itself gives the decision-making process a life of its own that influences the political realities of group members. Policymakers are not alone in mediating politics through groups. Persons whose livelihood depends on the reporting and interpretation of political decisions also think in groups. When they are journalists and they take part in group discussions before large radio and TV audiences, the views that emerge from their groupthink sessions are the bases for massthink.

In his study of myth Roland Barthes distinguishes between professional boxing and professional wrestling.[10] The former is a contest; boxers compete for victory and the outcome is uncertain. Thus, boxing is a contest much like that for the presidential nomination discussed in Chapter 2. Professional wrestling is another matter. There is no contest; the outcome is preordained. What counts is the celebrated melodrama, much as that found in "Liberty Weekend" (Chapter 1) or national nominating conventions (Chapter 2). Professional wrestling matches are ritual performances between good and evil, handsome and ugly, "legal holds" and "death grips." Billed as "wrestlemanias," televised wrestling spectaculars have brought celebrity status to its professionals—Hulk Hogan, Macho Man, the Beautiful Elizabeth, and many others.

Televised group discussions between journalists reporting and interpreting political events for large audiences—that is, mediating political realities for viewers—possess the characteristics of professional wrestling. Performances are ritualistic, interactions contrived, and conclusions foreordained. Put differently, the dramatic logic of journalistic panel discussions about politics is akin to the logic of professional wrestling. As with any mediation (see the "Introduction") that logic constitutes an imperative that privileges certain political fantasies over others. To illustrate the groupthink imperatives that inform journalists' interpretations, let us compare three regularly televised public affairs programs. Although none of the three has high TV ratings, each is mandatory viewing for political junkies and elites across the nation. Each mediates political realities for the most involved and better-informed of Americans.

"Washington Week in Review": Contrived Consensus

As a journalists' talk show, "Washington Week in Review" (WWR) is a prototype. On a weekly basis five journalists—a moderator and four invited guests—sit around a table in a TV studio in Washington, DC. There are both task and social dimensions to their gathering. The task is to describe, review, and interpret the meaning of the major political news event of the past week. Socially, the panelists know one another well. The moderator, Paul Duke, is a permanent member, and the same invited members appear with only slight variation from week to week. All are national correspondents from the nation's elite press: *The Wall Street Journal, The Baltimore Sun, The Los Angeles Times, The Washington Post, The New York Times, The Richmond Times-Dispatch, Newsweek,* and *U.S. News and World Report.* Although not a top-rated program in size of weekly audience, the Public Broadcast Service's (PBS) WWR is a prestigious half-hour of commentary—"mandatory viewing for much of official Washington."[11]

The discussion between group members on each week's WWR 30-minute program follows a dramatic format; indeed, it has many of the attributes of a ritual drama.[12] The moderator offers a brief introduction, taking note of the top news stories of the week and presenting the members of the panel. He then asks a leading question of one of the panel members. This is the cue for that panelist to make a short presentation (with or without prepared notes) regarding the news item in question. Each of the other three panelists engages in a brief question-and-answer (Q&A) colloquy with the reporter. Although promotional spots for WWR speak of "frank," "candid," and "heated" exchanges, the questions raised by panelists are rarely critical or argumentative. Instead, they clearly assist the reporter to present a consensus view regarding the topic in the news. After the colloquy has been completed with one panelist, Duke then moves to a second panelist. The ritual is repeated until all panelists have spoken on a particular news story and responded to inquiries. From time to time the moderator exercises a suave leadership, reinforcing the group consensus and moving the discussion along. Throughout the ritual drama, social bonding receives as much, if not more, emphasis as does news interpretation. There is far more emphasis on the bonding than on the controversy. So, there is much in WWR that reflects groupthink: Regular panelists know each other well.

- They support rather than criticize one another's views.
- They defer to the occasional newcomer to the group.

- They respond to suave leadership.
- They conform to the imperatives of the ritual drama.

What political realities does WWR offer viewers? To answer that question we looked at the principal fantasies in the content of weekly airings of WWR in a six-week period, February 2 to March 15, 1988. That period coincided with the early contests for the presidential nominations of the two major parties in that year (recall Chapter 2). Specifically, we looked at WWR programs for the period beginning one week before the Iowa caucuses; through the New Hampshire primaries; the primaries and caucuses in South Dakota, Minnesota, and Maine; and to one week following Super Tuesday when 20 states across the nation—the bulk being in the South—held contests. At issue were fantasies developed about the progress of the presidential race on WWR.

The programs presented three major fantasies. One was the Family Feud fantasy, which pertained to the Republican contest. Although six candidates vied for the presidential nomination in the early contests (see Chapter 2), WWR focused primarily on a principal conflict within the GOP family. It was the "nasty race between the vice president and the senate minority leader" (i.e., George Bush and Robert Dole). Panelists viewed this as a bitter contest, one of attack and counterattack that, in the end, "could possibly backfire on the vice president." With Dole's victory in Iowa and Bush finishing a "distant" third, the backfire prophesy seemed vindicated. Going to New Hampshire the next week panelists saw Bush "literally fighting for his political life" and Dole "perhaps overtaking Bush." Dole was clearly getting the better of Bush in the feud. Bush, said panelists, "doesn't have a very clear message"; there was even "a valedictory quality" to Bush's performance in a New Hampshire presidential debate. By contrast Dole "seemed leaderly" and a "more leaderly figure." In the closing hours of the New Hampshire campaign, Bush attacked Dole with negative TV ads. Dole did not respond because he was "sitting on a lead." Again "nasty" was the WWR label describing the contest; there was "no love lost" between Bush and Dole, "Never!" Bush's "astonishing" victory in New Hampshire put him "back on top" but did not end the feud. WWR's moderator summed up the GOP New Hampshire results as "feuding, fighting, and muddling." Panelists analyzed a postprimary TV interview in which Dole demanded that Bush "quit lying" about Dole's record: Bush's people were "gleeful" that Bush could now take the "high road" in the face of Dole's bitterness. After Super Tuesday, the WWR panelists looked back on Dole's all-but-vanquished candidacy and judged that he "blew it in New Hampshire," reeling as a victim of his own "floundering," "disorganization," "confusion," and "too cautious" approach.

A second WWR fantasy involved the Democratic party contests. This was the Brokered Nomination Fantasy. Although Richard Gephart "won" the Iowa Democratic caucus contests, WWR discerned that a "weeding out" (i.e., narrowing of the field of eight Democratic candidates) was "not happening." Asked one panelist, "Are we going to see a thinning of the field?" No, "few will drop out," was the reply. The WWR prognosis after Iowa was for victory in New Hampshire for Michael Dukakis by a "pretty wide margin," with Gephart and Paul Simon "fighting for a distant second," which "down the line" could produce a "possible deadlock"; Super Tuesday primaries would be indecisive. Then the "search begins anew" for a viable candidate, probably New York Governor Mario Cuomo. Given that preview of New Hampshire, the actual results made for a self-fulfilling prophesy. Dukakis's victory over Gephardt produced "co-frontrunners," no grand themes, and a "race for the White House" that "remains as unclear and muddled as ever." After New Hampshire it would be a "war of attrition" for "each candidate just wants to survive." Panelists openly debated possibilities of an "open" Democratic convention that would choose the nominee. The aftermath of Super Tuesday found WWR largely convinced that the nomination race would go to "the wire." Gone were the frontrunners Gephart and Dukakis. Super Tuesday had made for "upheaval." An "eastern liberal" was now the leader (Dukakis), a "black liberal" now a true contender (Jesse Jackson), and a "southerner" had come "to prominence" (Albert Gore). Panelists expressed "doubts" about the "electability" of Dukakis and thought it unlikely he would get to the convention with the "delegates to lock up the nomination." Jackson was "not the likely nominee" (even though he would possibly go to the Democratic convention with "more delegates" than anyone else). Gore had "weakness with workers," and Cuomo had to be taken at "his word" as not interested. Hence, the Brokered Nomination Fantasy took seed; it was not to vanish completely from WWR until Dukakis's nomination was assured.

Finally, WWR offered a He Must Be Taken Seriously Fantasy. There were Republican and Democratic variations. On the Republican side the "He" was Pat Robertson. A second-place finish in Iowa suggested the strength of Robertson's "invisible army" in states where turnout for caucuses and primaries would be low. He "has potential" was the consensus of WWR. At the least he was a "great question mark for Super Tuesday." Panelists speculated that Robertson might win six to nine southern states and have one-third to one-half of the delegates to the Republican convention. That would yield Robertson "profound influence" on the GOP platform and the vice presidential nomination. The Robertson fantasy faded quickly with his poor showings in Super Tuesday. No longer to be taken seriously, WWR judged that there was a "personal rejection of Pat Robertson by the wider Republican constituency." Robertson's candidacy had "imploded," observed one panelist.

The other "He" to be taken seriously was Jesse Jackson. It was not, however, until the telecast before Super Tuesday that WWR even mentioned Jackson. Once WWR did so, however, the Jackson fantasy flourished. "A new Jesse Jackson stumps the Old South," said the WWR moderator, setting the tone. Jackson, the "most liberal" candidate, might even emerge from Super Tuesday with the "most delegates" and be the "Big Winner." The only question, said one panelist," is not "What does Jesse Jackson want?" but

"How much is he going to take?" He had already won votes of whites in northern states; why? WWR supplied several answers: Jackson's "message has mellowed"; he has "moderated his rhetoric"; among a "dull lot of candidates" he bridged the "passion gap"; and, the "press is being kind to Jackson," but that "will change." On Super Tuesday Jackson won the most popular votes, but it was Dukakis who won the most states and delegates. Undaunted, WWR shifted into high gear: A "strong possibility" existed that Jackson might be the nominee! Why? Jackson's "explosive message" crosses racial lines. Yet, there is a difference between the "politics of passion" and the "politics of final choice." Hence, Dukakis remained for WWR the "logical nominee." Win or lose, however, the "fate of the Democratic party in 1988 and years beyond may well rest with Jesse Jackson."

Such were the political realities mediated for viewers of WWR. Their accuracy or lack thereof is not the issue. Rather, WWR illustrates how groupthink occurs in a small group, contributes to the fashioning of rhetorical vision, provides a key link in the chaining of derived fantasies to larger audiences, and thereby joins group- and mass-mediated political realities. WWR generates specific fantasies. So too it generates a fantasy of what political discussion is all about, that is, an amiable, friendly sharing of information in order to attain social consensus. As when professional wrestlers contrive the outcome of their match beforehand, then pretend they don't know it, WWR presents politics as something already known and simply to be revealed.

The McLaughlin Group: Contrived Conflict

Like WWR, the McLaughlin group is a 30-minute panel discussion telecast weekly by PBS. Promotional ads give it a "Federal Authorities" label: "well-informed journalists on the Washington scene" who "provide riveting commentary," an "informative, yet fiesty political talk show." As with WWR, there is a featured moderator, *National Review* editor John McLaughlin (after whom the show takes its name). Four regular panelists represent prestigious news publications. If WWR is an amiable exchange of information, the *Group* is something else. *Group* discussions often lack civility. The moderator practices groupthink leadership, but in the guise of challenging group wisdom, he shouts questions at panelists. Whereas "turn-taking" is the rule at WWR (each person speaking when called on and yielding to questions with courtesy), interruptions, yelling, guffaws, and bickering fill the air on the McLaughlin program. Panelists employ exaggerated gestures, vivid colloquialisms ("that's a lot of garbage"), and compete to outshout each other rather than listening politely. The overall fantasy of political discussion that the *Group* pictures is of spirited disputation and contention bordering on open hostility. The *Group* is a no-holds-barred wrestlemania match.

Does such a match negate the likelihood of groupthink? No. Much of the conflict of the *Group* has precisely the same contrived quality displayed by professional wrestlers when they shout at and intimidate one another outside the ring before and after the televised match. The show and the spectacle become the thing. With the *Group,* contrived conflict between panelists, agitated by rather than moderated by the leader, overrides the topic at issue. In the end, groupthink fantasies build in much the same way as they do on WWR. Thus, we look again at the same six-week period discussed in conjunction with WWR. What fantasies did the *Group* construct? Basically, they were the Clear Message Fantasy, the He Blew It Fantasy, and the Dismissal Fantasy.

Before the Iowa caucuses, *Group* viewers learned "a frontrunner has surfaced in the contest in Iowa." It was Richard Gephardt (with Paul Simon "zeroing in"). The size of Gephardt's likely Iowa win did not matter. He communicated a clear message (protect the United States against unfair foreign trade), could stay the course, and would emerge with Michael Dukakis after New Hampshire as one of the principal contenders (Dukakis was "boring" and without a clear message, but he did have "organization"). With Gephardt's victory in Iowa secured, the Clear Message Fantasy continued to New Hampshire. The *Group* all thought Dukakis would win in that state because he was from Massachusetts, but they thought Gephardt would finish second (he was getting all the press after Iowa). After New Hampshire, it would be "bye-bye Simon," who was the Iowa runnerup. A week later the moderator opened the telecast with the announcement, "Duke nukes New Hampshire." Yet, the focus was on Gephardt. He would "come out of the South strong," had an "excellent chance in the South," was "bad news for Gore," was "ahead," and had a "thematic message" argued individual panelists. On the eve of Super Tuesday, the *Group* repeated the story line that Gephardt was the only candidate with a "consistent, coherent message." There would be no brokered convention; Gephardt was the likely nominee. A week later the Clear Message Fantasy evaporated. "Gone," "gone," "gone but not forgotten," and a "swan dive"—thus the groupthink wrote the epitaph to the Gephardt candidacy (he finished behind Jackson, Dukakis, and Gore in votes, an event the moderator called a "three-headed monster").

The He Blew It Fantasy was the *Group* explanation of George Bush's nomination. The "He" was Senator Robert Dole. The fantasy construction began after Dole's Iowa victory. Of Bush, individual panelists observed that he "will lose the nomination," is "fighting for his political life," there "is not a lot there," and his lead in the polls before New Hampshire is "meaningless." Of Dole: "Momentum" is his. But Dole lost in New Hampshire. Why? He blew it! How? His message had "no vision." With no vision he could not appeal to voters, hence lost, and having lost acted like a "sore loser" in TV interviews. Dole had only "momentum out of Iowa" going for him and no clear theme beyond. Verdict? It was "all Dole's fault."

The Dismissal Fantasy refers to the treatment of Jesse Jackson's candidacy by the *Group.* Whereas WWR thought he should be taken seriously, the *Group* apparently did not. It was not until two telecasts before Super Tuesday that Jackson's candidacy received notice, a scant reference that he showed "strength but is not going anywhere." Prospects for Jackson's success were scarcely mentioned the week before Super Tuesday. And even after his showing then, the Jackson candidacy received notice only as part of the "three-headed monster" alluded to earlier. At least for the *Group* Jesse Jackson would wait several weeks before being other than an invisible candidate (see Chapter 2).

Journalists' Roundtable: Contrived Conversation

Each week the Cable Satellite Public Affairs Network (C–SPAN) airs a panel discussion featuring a moderator (Brian Lamb) and journalists based in Washington who represent such publications as The New York *Daily News, The Washington Times, The Los Angeles Times, The Wall Street Journal, The Nation, U.S. News and World Report,* and others. *Roundtable* differs from WWR and the *Group* in particulars: It is a 90-minute program, the first half devoted to discussion, the second to telephone call-ins; guest panelists do not reappear frequently on later programs; the pace is leisurely and relaxed—even to the sipping of coffee from clear mugs; and there is less information-sharing, as in WWR, or dispute, as in the *Group.* Dispassionate observation, opinion-sharing, and chitchat are the order of the day. Brian Lamb controls the agenda by playing the friendly host to visitors in contrast with the avuncular style of Paul Duke or the shouting protagonist of John McLaughlin. The program offers an image of political news as a matter of casual conversation, rather than as information already known and to be shared (WWR) or debated (*Group*). Call-ins add a mud-wrestling feature to what is otherwise a conversation about holds, grips, takedowns, and bouncebacks.

During the six-week period under consideration, *Roundtable* constructed fantasies about the 1988 presidential nominating contest. Some paralleled those of WWR and the *Group.* Others did not. For instance, the *Roundtable* took Jesse Jackson seriously from the beginning. Jackson, "a phenomenon in 1984" was a "major contender in 1988." The panel discussed the bitterness in the Bush-Dole campaign, as was the case with competing panel shows. But the fantasy most consistently related to those on other journalist talk shows was that of the Brokered Nomination. It originated and persisted in response to Lamb's "Where will the campaign end up?," "Who will it be?," and similar queries. As with WWR and *Group* journalists, those on *Roundtable* fantasized about George Bush's "problems of electability" following his Iowa loss. However, Iowa victor Bob Dole had his problems too—fuzzy about what "he really stands for," a "gap" between his rhetoric and performance, and a tendency to "tailor messages" to the moment. The voiced prospects were for a Bush loss but no knockout in New Hampshire, strength for Bob Dole in advance of Super Tuesday, and a "long-drawn-out battle." It was "Bob Dole's to lose," but more likely there would be "no nominee" by the time of the

GOP convention. Bush's New Hampshire victory did not end the brokering fantasy, only prolonged it for indeed Dole had lost it. Dole's "several image changes throughout his career, lack of a consistent message, and lack of substance," said panelists, cost him. And there was still Pat Robertson, who had been "underestimated" and could "get crossover conservative Democrat" votes in southern primaries. George Bush, always "diminished by TV," had a fragile candidacy throughout the campaign. Naturally Bush's Super Tuesday success ended the Brokered Convention Fantasy with respect to the GOP. Not so for the Democrats. After New Hampshire's primary, one panelist speculated that the nomination would go to a brokered convention, another to a "brokered nomination" before the convention, but the conversational consensus settled on a brokered nomination because a "brokered convention" would not be a good TV ad for the party!

As noted with respect to the Jackson candidacy, not all *Roundtable* fantasies paralleled those of other journalistic talk shows. *Roundtable* conjured up a Megacampaign Fantasy. Instead of talking about the nominating campaigns, panelists discussed how "the press" (i.e., journalists of all kinds) generally described the campaigns—like an ape contemplating itself in a mirror, they said. For example, was there a bias in the news media? No. To be sure, journalists use shorthand labels such as "leftist" or "moderate" in referring to people, but such labels are not biased. At most the labels reflect only a "mindset." And reporters use their own judgment in writing stories; if they are not impartial, their "bosses" will correct it. Is campaign coverage adequate? No. It is "top heavy"—that is, winners and runnersup in contests are covered and other candidates are not. The candidacies of Jack Kemp and of Jesse Jackson should both have had more coverage. What of TV's effect? Questionable. The "inability to communicate" on TV hurt Bruce Babbitt; Richard Gephardt "hit the button on economic issues" on TV; too much TV campaigning for Super Tuesday cut interest and turnout.

WHOSE FANTASIES, WHOSE REALITIES?

Groupthink may develop in any setting—among people living everyday lives, among public officials, even among political journalists. When it does, there are intriguing consequences. Individual judgment yields to group pressure to agree, do the same thing, perhaps to put on an entertaining TV program. Tough-minded critical thinking gives way to tender-minded wishful fantasy. The potential for human fallibility, something the framers of the U.S. Constitution took for granted and sought to control, is enhanced. One reason is that it becomes increasingly hard to find sources of mediated reality that are grounded in firsthand experience of political events rather than in talk about events.

Such is the case with political talk shows. To compare panel shows featuring political journalists with matches featuring professional wrestlers is not intended to demean journalists and certainly not the wrestlers. It is simply to call attention to the ritualistic qualities of journalists' talk, the fantasies constructed by it (sometimes similar, sometimes different from program to program), and the contrasting images of political discussion implied in various TV formats. Professional wrestling, like astrology (see Chapter 8), has its adherents, its believers. Yet, there are others who are skeptical of professional wrestling, deeming it appealing TV entertainment but not crediting it with involving "real" sporting contests. Granted that journalists engaged in televised political discussions are serious about their purposes and their subjects, could it still be that the requirements of the TV entertainment imperative so remove journalists' talk shows from firsthand political experience that they too, like professional wrestling, are more contrived than confrontational? If so, is it possible that the range of mediated realities—in spite of the numerous talk shows available on network, cable, and satellite TV—is restricted and narrow, rather than diverse and broad? For that matter, how much diversity reflecting overlapping, contradictory political realities is in any of various forms of group mediation? We examine that question as we turn to political fantasy-making by inside-dopesters, religious movements, and believers in conspiracy.

NOTES

1. For a discussion of the swine flu and related cases of decisionmaking with fantasy overtones see Richard E. Neustadt and Ernest R. May, *Thinking in Time: The Uses of History for Decision Makers* (New York: Free Press, 1986).
2. Robert F. Bales, *Interaction Process Analysis: A Method for the Study of Small Groups* (Cambridge, MA: Addison Wesley, 1950).
3. Jerry B. Harvey, unpublished lecture, "A Trip To Abilene," presented at a national conference of the Society for Research Administrators, Boston, MA, October 12, 1988.
4. Irving L. Janis, *Groupthink* (Boston: Houghton Mifflin, 1982), p. 9.
5. Ernest G. Bormann, "Fantasy and Rhetorical Vision: The Rhetorical Criticism of Social Reality," *Quarterly Journal of Speech* 58 (December 1972): 396–407.
6. G. P. Mohrmann, "An Essay on Fantasy Theme Criticism," *Quarterly Journal of Speech* 68 (May 1982): 109–132.
7. Barbara W. Tuchman, *The March of Folly: From Troy to Vietnam* (New York: Ballantine Books, 1984), p. 41.
8. Ibid., p. 40.
9. See Janis, *Groupthink;* Neustadt and May, *Thinking in Time;* Tuchman, *March of Folly.*
10. Roland Barthes, *Mythologies* (New York: Hill & Wang, 1972), pp. 15–25.
11. Elizabeth Peer, "Washington's Press Corps," *Newsweek* (May 25, 1981): 92.
12. The discussion of the "WWR," "McLaughlin Group," and "Journalists' Roundtable" in this section is based on a content analysis conducted by the authors.

CHAPTER 8

Inside-Dopesters: The Mediated Realities of Political Celebrities

More than four decades ago a trio of social scientists proposed a theory that something was happening to the social fabric of America. There was a shift, they said, in "social character."[1] By character they referred to a person's orientation to the world, a set of socially and historically acquired motives and desires. Social character consists of the orientations people share. It is the sharing that makes them members of social groups—not policy making or elite journalism groups whose members interact with one another, as discussed in Chapter 7, but groups whose members have common drives and pleasures even though they may not know or encounter one another directly.

Put briefly, the theory was that in some societies social character develops as a result of conventional conformity to widely held tradition. In these societies the power relations among rulers, clans, castes, professions, and so forth are fixed and rigid; the individual obeys the rules and commands carried in the cultural heritage. The people are tradition-directed, that is, traditions mediate realities. Societies may change, however; population increases, new ways and techniques for making a living develop, people become more geographically and socially mobile. Traditions weaken. They no longer prescribe what people should and should not do, especially when they fail to cover novel situations never before experienced. So instead of learning traditions of the tribe, children learn from their elders—family members and teachers—who have encountered newness and change. They learn their lessons early in life, that is, they *internalize* them. Thereafter, the internalized motives and desires, not custom and convention, provide orientation to the world. Such persons are inner-directed; the lessons learned in childhood mediate realities.

The United States has long since ceased being tradition-directed, if it ever was, and for a long period people were inner-directed. But society experienced striking changes in the mid-20th century: Goods, services, education, and leisure were easier to come by; the pervasive automobile, less expensive jet travel, and attractive job opportunities away from home lessened the hold of the family. And the mass media—movies, radio, TV, and popular culture rivaled families and schools as teachers of motives and desires. As tradition yielded to childhood learning, childhood learning yielded to another shaper of social character: cues received from other people. Unlike the internalized principles acquired in childhood by inner-directed persons, these cues have a transitory, short-term quality. A new social character appears, that of the other-directed person whose sources of guidance are contemporaries, *"either those known to him or those with whom he is indirectly acquainted, through friends and through the mass media."* [2] Other people, not tradition or self, mediate realities.

The theory thus described has a political component. Each type of social character gives rise to a distinctive political style, a way of approaching politics. Because custom and convention dictate solutions to political problems for the tradition-directed, the dominant style is the indifferent. With political matters foreordained by tradition, why bother? The inner-directed person wishes to achieve principles and goals inspired by upbringing. The inner-directed person wants to create a political environment to promote acquired self-interests, or at least to protect them. The style is that of the moralizer seeking to reform institutions, to advance vested interests, or to conserve institutions that enhance them. The other-directed person constantly seeks direction by keeping a finger to the social winds; neither indifference to nor moralizing about politics suffices. The other-directed person must *know* what is going on, both to adjust and to adapt to trends and to gain stature in the eyes of others by confiding such inside knowledge. This is the style of the inside-dopester. "Politics, indeed, serves the inside-dopester chiefly as a means for group conformity. He must have acceptable opinions and where he engages in politics he must do so in acceptable ways." [3]

In this chapter we examine the inside-dopesters and their mediation of political realities. Their behavior constitutes group mediation in three respects. First, they reflect the group qualities of the other-directed social character by behaving as inside-dopesters. Second, inside-dopesters are experts who are set apart from others by a reputation, often acquired from other insiders, for knowing things that no one else knows. In this respect, they are like the celebrities discussed in Chapter 3. They are known for being well known, with "qualities—or rather lack of qualities"—that are "neither good nor bad, great nor petty," the "human pseudo-event," who are "morally neutral," but products "of no conspiracy, of no group promoting vice or emptiness." Such a celebrity is "made by all of us willing to read about him, who like to see him on television, who buy recordings of his voice, and talk about him to our friends." And, "his relation to morality and even to reality is highly ambiguous."[4] Finally, political inside-dopesters talk as much to one another as they do to outside audiences, be they on radio or TV talk shows; at conferences or retreats; touring the college lecture circuit; being interviewed on "Nightline," the "MacNeil-Lehrer Hour" or CNN's "Inside Politics"; or commenting in the op ed pages of leading newspapers or in the opinion columns of newsmagazines and journals of political opinion. Who, then, are these insiders?

OFF TO SEE THE WIZARDS!

Insider-trading on the stock market (that is, using privileged information to take advantage of the rise and fall in market prices) has serious legal consequences, but inside-dopestering in politics (that is, pontificating on trends, fashions, and the what-ifs of the times) is not only acceptable but encouraged. Inside-dopestering in politics is a growth industry. To provide the flavor of such wizardry, we focus on a few of the key categories of political seers.

Pack Journalists

Reporters go to official and nonofficial sources for information to support stories. Sometimes though, they rely on gossip, rumor, and one another. This is not surprising; every journalist is out to get a scoop. The competition is often a friendly one; reporters engage in a common endeavor. One inside-dopester of Washington journalism described it this way in writing of campaign reporting: "We are filters," he wrote, and "it is through our smudgy, hand-held prisms that voters meet the candidates and grow to love them or hate them, trust them or distrust them." Like many campaign reporters, he was not modest in claiming, "We are the voters' eyes and ears, and we are more than that, for, sometimes, we perform a larger and, some would say, more controversial function. We write the rules and we call the game."[5] In short, journalists mediate reality.

A reliance on one another in friendly rivalry contributes to a variation on inside-dopesterism called "pack journalism." The phrase is obviously a metaphor; it likens journalists running together in packs to dogs, wolves, or coyotes. In one form or another, the practice is ancient. For example, the first systematic effort to examine how correspondents report political news from the nation's capital described a widespread practice in the tradition of pack journalism.[6] The practice was called *carbon sheeting*. If a reporter assigned to cover a story could not (or simply did not want to) cover it, he would ask a reporter from a rival newspaper for a carbon copy of the competitor's account. Then, with a few minor changes, the reporter would file the rival's story as his or her own. This worked to everyone's advantage—that of the reporter who did cover the story (for if the account appeared in altered form in a competing newspaper, it validated the authenticity of the reporter's account) and that of rival publications (publishing the same details as other journals confirmed not only the facts but also one's news judgment). Presumably carbon sheeting is old-fashioned in the high-tech world of the lap-top word processor; now reporters exchange diskettes instead of carbons. In any event, pack journalism is cooperative competition–competitive cooperation in the news business.

During a presidential campaign, a group of reporters from a variety of news organizations follow a single candidate for several weeks or months. They are, wrote one observer, "like a pack of hounds sicked on a fox."[7] The fox is the candidate; the packlike behavior of the reporters derives from the fact that they travel on the same bus or plane, called the "zoo plane"; eat at the same restaurants and stay at the same hotels; and share notes and impressions. They are friendly rivals both competing and cooperating in efforts to cover the story, namely, the candidate.

Such a womblike coexistence can be a source of conditions of the groupthink described in Chapter 7. The *pool report,* another facet of pack journalism, reinforces packthink. Each day on the campaign trail one or two members of the pack comprise a pool of reporters in close contact with the candidate—say, on the candidate's private plane, at small enclaves, during motorcades, and so forth. The pool constitutes the eyes and ears for the other members of the press entourage who cannot be with the candidate. Members of the pack take turns serving in the pool. The pool reporter writes an account of the candidate's activities that is available to all members of the pack. In filing his or her own article, a pool reporter is not supposed to include anything not included in the pool report. As a result, TV, newspaper, and newsmagazine accounts of the campaign that are derived from pool reports have a uniform quality, as any regular reader or viewer of campaign news knows.

In covering presidential campaigns, the journalistic pack is a group of elite members of the press. There is a pecking order. At the top are national political reporters—experienced correspondents of prestigious newspapers, the wire services, national newsmagazines, and television networks. At the bottom are the representatives of smaller newspapers and organizations. Among the top elite, print journalists have less star quality than do TV network correspondents. Regardless of the identity of the leading actors in the pack drama, there is a packthink atmosphere very much like that first described four presidential campaigns ago: "They all fed off the same pool report, the same daily handout, the same speech by the candidate; the whole pack was isolated in the same mobile village. After a while, they began to believe in the same rumors, subscribe to the same theories, and write the same stories."[8]

Politicians, ever mindful of the folkways of journalists, take advantage of the pack. For example, the good picture is a must for the TV journalist, producer, and news organization. Candidates go out of their way to assure good pictures, which often depict a different reality from what an onlooker witnesses. Thus, raw footage of a typical campaign day reveals what always seem to be crowds much larger than they actually are. Why? Because there is a mediating trick. At campaign stops on the campaign trail, the candidate's staff tries to place a camera platform close to the speaker's rostrum and then to jam the crowd between the two, thus leaving the visual impression of a candidate speaking to a vast throng. The electorate's reality, the visual reality mediated by TV news, is, thus, the reality the candidate's manager wishes it to be.[9]

Pack journalism is not limited to the shared inside dope of political campaigns. A pack can form in reporting any story. Running in packs is most likely to occur when two conditions prevail: (1) when reporters are assigned to regular beats and (2) when they are assigned to cover stories about largely predictable events. The White House press corps, for example, consists of reporters with long-term assignments from their news organizations to cover the scheduled briefings, appearances, and actions that derive from presidential comings and goings. Because such events are scheduled, routine, and predictable in outcome, news organizations plan coverage of them without threat of surprise. Any newspaper or newsmagazine correspondent, any editor, or any TV journalist or news producer is relatively at ease in this daily task of gathering routine news. Politicians recognize this and manipulate both events and accounts to suit their own and journalists' requirements. A close monitoring of political news reveals the result: From one-half to two-thirds of front-page stories of major newspapers or lead stories in network TV news originate from official sources. Thereby pack journalism serves both government and press interests.[10]

Crisis coverage, when authentic accounts of what is happening and why are hard to obtain, promotes pack journalism virtually as much as does the routine coverage of scheduled events. Rumors and speculation abound. Although reported as the inside dope, such tales can be fanciful. For example, during the 444 days of captivity for the American hostages held captive in Iran in 1979–1981 (see Chapter 2), there was much journalistic speculation regarding the likely psychological state of the hostages when they would be released. Would they suffer from the Stockholm syndrome? This malady consists of painful psychological disturbances produced when captives are freed from their captors. Allegedly, after long confinement captives grow dependent on their guards, so much so that ultimately winning freedom produces high anxieties and stress at the very thought of being apart from captors on whom prisoners have been dependent. In news reports, on TV talk shows, in editorials and columns there were dire predictions of such psychological pain for the hostages in Iran. So widely did the inside dope spread—and so widely was the Stockholm syndrome fantasy shared—that the American Psychological Association took a stand. The association noted that the reactions of individual captives would obviously vary greatly and that broad generalizations might be without foundation. Indeed, the whole notion of a Stockholm syndrome derived from a limited study of a few hostages held captive in that city, scarcely grounds for proving a theory. When the released Americans eagerly returned home in 1981 without dependency symptoms, the Stockholm syndrome fantasy evaporated.

Soothsaying Journalists

A journalistic pack by definition has a pecking order; it therefore has leaders—reporter-celebrities who provide pack members with cues. These cues take several forms: privileged information from named and unnamed informants, insights, analyses, predictions, and prognostications. Like soothsayers, the reporter-celebrities prophesy and foretell events. They play crucial roles in creating and spreading journalists' group-mediated fantasies. They are trendsetters who make, unmake, and remake the conventional wisdom of politics.

Such conventional wisdom has become so much a part of our political reality that a national newsweekly in 1988 began a regular feature for its coverage of the 1988 presidential campaign. *Newsweek* inaugurated its "Conventional Wisdom Watch." Accompanied by catchy graphics, the magazine's column informed readers of the ups and downs of Democratic and Republican candidates according to the week's conventional wisdom. For example, three weeks before the selection of a Democratic vice presidential nominee, conventional wisdom (CW) was: U.S. Senator John Glenn (Ohio), "practically a *fait accompli,* to hear some CW-ers talk"; Senator Bill Bradley (New Jersey), "says he's not interested; CW translation: Make me an offer"; Senator Sam Nunn (Georgia), "says he's not interested; CW translation: I'll take it. I'll take it"; Jesse Jackson, "is he playing poker or is he just indecisive? Gossip about his private life revives."[11] Thus the news media reported the insider fantasies it helped to construct in the first place—a mediation of reality and a mediation of the mediation. In CW's case, mediation was flawed; Senator Lloyd Bentsen of Texas won the nomination.

Who are these inside-dopesters, these soothsayers of conventional wisdom? With respect to mediating the realities of national politics, the number is relatively small. Certainly included are national political correspondents and syndicated columnists of major metropolitan dailies (for example, *The Washington Post* or *The New York Times*), national dailies (*USA Today* and *The Wall Street Journal*), and the wire services; political correspondents and columnists of national newsweeklies; principal political correspondents of National Public Radio's "All Things Considered"; hosts of national radio and TV talk shows; anchors, key political correspondents, and analysts of the three TV networks, CNN, and the "MacNeil-Lehrer Hour." When *TV Guide* or the *Washington Journalism Review* has "experts" or "readers" select America's "best journalists," celebrities from these organizations win. For the most part they live and work in the "Big Apple" (New York City), or more likely "inside the beltway" (that is, close to the environs of the nation's capital).

What political realities flow from the insiders? Some soothsayer fantasies take on the status of myth. Others have a far shorter shelf life. An example of the former occurred in the presidency of Ronald Reagan. From the onset of his presidency, journalistic insiders labeled Reagan the "Great Communicator." After his inaugural address inside-dopesters provided reviews: ". . . this speech was most striking for its skilled, faultless delivery and straightforward message"; "Many already are acclaiming him as the most adept communicator in the Oval Office since Franklin Roosevelt." Conferral of Great Communicator status bestowed popularity on Reagan, said insiders. Here is the flavor of soothsaying commentary: Columnist James Reston of *The New York Times* wrote that "the president has public opinion on his side"; Barry Sussman of *The Washington Post* wrote of Reagan's "magnetism"; *Newsweek* found "a blanket of personal goodwill unmatched since Dwight Eisenhower." Yet, the evidence does not substantiate such claims. In fact, during the first two years of office, as he was being mythologized as the Great Communicator, Ronald Reagan's approval rating in public opinion polls was well *below* that of his predecessors. At the end of two years, his rating was 37 percent approval compared with 50 percent for Jimmy Carter, 56 percent for Richard Nixon, 70 percent for John Kennedy, and 72 percent for Dwight Eisenhower. Facts, however, failed to negate the insiders' myth. Throughout his presidency Reagan's reputation for personal popularity and flawless communication skills continued. Perhaps, as insider Haynes Johnson of *The Washington Post* wrote, "Americans do not want to see another failed presidency." Soothsayers did not give them one.[12]

Consider, in contrast, a short-lived soothsayer prophesy. In early 1987 opinion polls indicated that former U.S. Senator Gary Hart of Colorado was the odds-on favorite to become the Democratic party's nominee for president in 1988. He had sought the nomination four years earlier, had run an effective campaign, and had lost the nomination even though he received more popular votes in the primaries than the ultimate nominee, Walter Mondale. In the late spring of 1987, however, Hart withdrew from the Democratic race because of a personal scandal involving marital infidelity. Then, just as suddenly, Hart re-entered the race in December of that year. Here, indeed, was grist for the inside-dopester's mill. David Broder, syndicated columnist of the *The Washington Post* and a widely respected leader of journalistic opinion, speculated in late December that the Democratic party faced trouble: "Its two best-known presidential contenders, Jesse L. Jackson and self-resurrected Gary Hart, are distrusted by so many American voters they are probably unelectable." He went on to say that "unless they find and unite behind" an alternative in the primaries and caucuses—which he now thought unlikely—"the Democrats will lose the White House for the fifth time in 20 years." And, "if the active contenders fail to head off Hart and Jackson, you can be sure someone will be enlisted to do the job." With Hart's re-entry, Broder thought a brokered convention might become a real possibility, something Broder had heretofore thought unlikely. Then, concluded Broder, the Democrats "may find themselves desperate enough to notice" House Majority Leader Thomas Foley of Washington and give him the nomination.[13]

Fellow syndicated columnist and soothsayer, George Will, also thought Hart's re-entry would injure the Democratic party. Hart's presence in the primaries would, thought Will, call attention to the lack of luster among his rivals for the nomination: "The commotion Hart has caused does dramatize the 'none of the above' mood that could produce a brokered convention."[14] It took but a short time for the mediated reality of Hart-the-Party-Heart-Stopper to spread. NBC reported that rivals for the nomination were "being pulled into Gary Hart's soap opera" and ABC noted that Hart had "frozen the Democrats' campaign, stopped it cold in its tracks by becoming once again its primary focus." It was not until stories surfaced of possible financial improprieties in Hart's campaign, coupled with what journalists labeled as "poor" showings in debates with rivals, that the Hart fantasy spawned as the inside dope in December vanished with February losses in Iowa and New Hampshire.

Broder, Will, ABC, NBC, and others caught up in the Hart fantasy hedged their forecasts of a brokered Democratic nomination by sprinkling in qualifiers such as "unless," "if," and "may." In short, they are skilled in the language of "Newspeak." Newspeak is the official language of George Orwell's fictional society of *Nineteen Eighty-Four*. As a set of linguistic conventions, Newspeak consists of an ambiguous and contradictory jargon and style that leaves readers and viewers with a sense that reporters are objective observers who know what is really going on (are inside-dopesters). Any reader of a newspaper or newsmagazine and any viewer of TV quickly recognizes the stock phrases that constitute Newspeak: Insider information comes from "usually reliable sources," a "Pentagon spokesman," "sources close to the White House," "authoritative sources," and so on. Columnists and commentators, always critical of public officials who will not commit themselves on the record, hedge their own analyses with stock phrases: "in the absence of a remarkable turnabout," "unless the president changes his mind," or "if current trends continue." Many journalists mindful of their responsibilities to readers and viewers alert them to "the people's right to know," the "chilling effects" of official news management, and the mischief of politicians who put "spin" on events. Newspeak provides the reporter with an aura of knowing what is *really* going on, of being the eyes and ears of the citizen inside government circles.

Newspeak has a distinctive style as well as jargon. The jargon yields the impression that the journalist is an objective inside-dopester working on the citizens' behalf; so does the style. In fact, the Newspeak style reinforces the image of the reporter as the citizens' representative by saying in effect, "I work on your behalf because I think, write, and talk like you; my reality is your reality." Like everyday conversation, Newspeak is straightforward, to the point, clear, with no room left for apparent ambiguity. Reports are brief, with short, clipped sentences and simple words (aside from the insider's jargon that lends an air of mystery); accounts are succinct, compact, devoid of frills. Metaphors are familiar ones: Elections are horse races, economic conflicts are battles of the budget, weapons systems are hardware, the president's cabinet is his family, political party leaders squabble, and so forth. Editing structures stories (most important information first, secondary information next, details later, interpretation last), balances them to give both sides (as if there is but a two-sided reality), and provides a fast-paced rendering (adjusting in the manner of *USA Today* to the America-on-the-move image).

Newspeak jargon and style also assist soothsayer journalists in dealing with a particularly troublesome kind of happening: the tainted event. Journalists recognize that many alleged newsworthy events are staged solely for their benefit. If the events were not to be reported, they would not occur at all. Political campaigns, presidential efforts at molding public opinion, protest marches, many terrorist acts—all are designed to be reported by the news media. Yet, even though journalists know the event is staged, they cannot ignore it. Editors want copy, TV producers want film, rival news agencies are reporting it, something unexpected might happen, a reporter might get scooped. All these factors pressure the journalist to cover the tainted affair. Like the sleepy young child who will not go to bed for fear of missing something, the reporter must cover tainted events or risk losing the reputation as an insider. To put the best face possible on what should not be covered at all, journalists rhetorically distance themselves from the nonnewsworthy news event. This technique is "disdaining the news," a Newspeak technique by which the reporter says, in effect, "Yes, I define this phenomenon as news. But my story is a bit troublesome for me in my role as a journalist."[15] For example, during hostage crises, the captors frequently stage opportunities for televised interviews with the hostages. Their aim is to publicize their cause. Many correspondents introduce such interviews by stating the conditions set by the terrorists—that the interviews be aired in prime time, that they include a statement by the terrorists, and so on. The correspondent then disavows on behalf of the TV network such restrictions, routinely insisting that the network retains editorial control. The interview appears, then the correspondent asks viewers to decide for themselves what the terrorists' motives are. The journalist as inside-dopester has merely presented "what I could get." In at least one respect the convention of disdaining the news adds a new wrinkle to pack mediation of reality. By alerting readers and viewers to the tainted quality of an event, newspersons imply that it is not real and, thus, by further implication, that mediated versions of other events *are* real. One is reminded of the labeling of foods, drugs, and other substances: "may be dangerous to your health." Does such warning imply that those not so labeled are thereby healthful?

Tea Leaves, Pollsters, and Polltalk

If Newspeak is the language of inside-dopester journalists, polltalk is the language of that group of insiders who claim to know what others do not because they go out and ask them. These are the pollsters who measure support and opposition, opinion trends, and future patterns of preference among the populace. They reinforce a durable political fantasy, that of public opinion. Banner headlines tell us "Public Opinion Supports President" or "Candidate Courts Public Approval." Editorials, columnists, and commentators purport to say what the public thinks. Scholars write texts and monographs defining public opinion and charting its changes. Children learn in school that democracy is government by public opinion. However, public opinion is a shibboleth, a catchword thrown around to cover a range of vastly different things. Certainly people have opinions. Some of those opinions, but not all, are about political matters. And people's views are conflicting, even contradictory. Rarely do they concur, at least to the degree that we can speak with confidence about a single public opinion.

Given the diverse nature of people's views, how can one say what public opinion is regarding a political figure, issue, or event? Many means have been used. One of the most common is to assume that public opinion is precisely what the news media say it is—the *journalistic fallacy,* or the fantasy that any view reported by print or broadcast news as "public opinion," or "public sentiment," is of widespread importance and true. Polltalk is the contemporary version of the journalistic fallacy. It consists of the tendencies of journalists and news agencies to label as public opinion the popular views and sentiments on political questions that opinion polls measure in a statistical fashion.

No major news organization in the country is now without its pollster. Polling may be the in-house operation of the news agency, or more frequently, the agency may hire the services of a prominent pollster. News services often collaborate in conducting polls. CBS joins with *The New York Times,* ABC unites with *The Washington Post,* and so on. Throughout the year, virtually on a weekly, then nightly basis, readers and viewers learn where the people stand on major policy proposals, how much they support the presidency, which candidate leads in a campaign contest—even who are the most respected men and women in American. Says a director of polling for *The Washington Post,* "We've bred a group of political writers who can't write a story without a poll."[16]

How real is the pollsters' reality of public opinion? Opinion polling is both science and art, often so much of the latter that the interpretation of poll results parallels the reading of tea leaves. To begin with, any nationwide poll purports to measure public opinion on political affairs by questioning a small sample (typically 1,500 persons) selected in accordance with scientific criteria that assure a representative cross section of the population. But in any sampling procedure a certain degree of error intrudes. Take, for example, a hypothetical sample of 1,800 eligible voters asked for whom they would vote for president on election day. Assume that 47 percent select Candidate *A*, 44 percent Candidate *B*, and the remainder are undecided or favor another candidate. A sample of 1,800 persons has an error of 3 percent, that is, any reported percentage might be in error by 3 percent plus or minus. Hence, in this hypothetical poll anywhere from 44 to 50 percent might favor *A*, 41 to 47 percent, *B*. The surface reality, then, would show *A* leading; taking possible error into account, however, the reality is one of no difference.

Another problem with poll results is that people do not always have opinions on public affairs, yet they express views under the pressure of questioning. Studies show that when people are asked their opinions on such nonexistent matters as the "Metallic Metals Act" or the "Public Affairs Act," or on such obscure issues as the "Agricultural Trade Act of 1990," from one-third to two-thirds polled will volunteer a view. Crafted into a news item such pseudo-opinions provide a mediated fantasy of public opinions.[17] The way questions are worded makes a difference, too. Faced with the proposition, "The right of a woman to have an abortion should be left to the woman and her doctor," almost three-fourths in nationwide polls agree. But when asked, "Do you support legalized abortion up to three months of pregnancy?" as many disagee as agree.

Nor is it always clear in news polls who the public is that pollsters are talking about. In pre-election polls, for instance, some pollsters sample all eligible voters, others all likely voters, and still others all registered voters. These populations differ substantially from one another, and the mediated realities based on them differ markedly as well. Because we know that Republicans vote in higher proportions than do Democrats, a poll reporting a Democratic lead among eligible voters may foretell an illusory reality because on election day the unregistered and apathetic do not vote.

Problems of error, pseudo-opinions, question wording, and the identity of the public notwithstanding, polltalk abounds in political journalism. Polltalk reinforces the tendency of pack journalism to fashion a reality and hold to it. For example, recall that in Chapter 2 we noted that candidates running in presidential primaries compete not only with one another but also with "Expected," that is, the share of votes that polls show candidates are expected to receive on election day. A candidate not living up to expectations defined by news polls suffers a "crippling loss"; one who exceeds poll-mediated expectations pulls off a "startling upset." Moreover, the widespread use of exit polling (questioning voters outside the election precinct after they have voted) can reinforce pack judgment. Whether, say, "confidence in the integrity of rival candidates" was on the minds of primary voters before they are asked, one cannot say. Yet, pollsters may decide "confidence in government," "integrity," "leadership," or some other factor will be an overriding issue in an election and question people about it. When exit polls stress an item, they not surprisingly find that indeed it "weighed heavily on the minds of voters as they went to the polls on this cold, blustery day in New Hampshire."

Polltalk is thereby often self-fulfilling. During each presidential administration, news accounts assess how well the incumbent performs (for example, Ronald Reagan as the Great Communicator). Sometimes there is the following sequence:

- Soothsaying journalists offer a negative assessment.
- The pack gets the scent and joins in.
- The pack's reports influence the president's standing in opinion polls.
- The pack, then using the president's low standing in polls as evidence, reports the president's "failures."
- The alleged failures then lower presidential popularity, which subsequent polls measure and reporters report.

And the self-fulfilling prophetic mediation goes on.[18]

Sorcerer Consultants

In Chapter 2 we described the role played by paid media consultants in hyping the candidacies of contestants in presidential campaigns. These consultants design the candidate's media campaign; create and produce advertising for newspapers, radio, and TV; endeavor to link a candidate's persona and positions with cherished cultural values; and, through appealing ritual melodramas, tell a story of the candidate's vision for the office and the nation. In carrying out such tasks these consultants mediate the realities of politics by using the candidate's image, performance, and advertising. Taking in all levels of political campaigning—local, congressional, state, and national—there are ample opportunities for media specialists to enter the profession, compete with one another, and prosper through success. The competition is fierce, although the rivalries between consultants are more likely to be friendly than bitter. Given that in any campaign contest there will be only one winner, but one or more losers, victories are difficult to accumulate. Those consultants who consistently manage ("handle") winners are much sought after by potential candidates, so much so that winning consultants have the opportunities to pick and choose for whom to work their magic. Success breeds success.

Something else comes from success: a reputation for wizardry. Because there are so few managers with records of consistent achievement, successful consultants acquire images much like those of the sorcerers of old—that is, they may be thought to have some supernatural insights into the body politic that permit them to see deeper and more knowingly than others. Aspiring political journalists, consultants, and amateurs, as well as candidates, seek out elite consultants in hopes of learning secrets of the craft, of becoming sorcerers' apprentices. The wizards are not hard to find. They eagerly market their insights—not all of their secrets, of course—in a variety of ways. They are featured speakers at meetings of their own professional organizations, the American Association of Political Consultants, and its international body, the International Association of Political Consultants. They are much in demand at workshops, institutes, and conferences sponsored by political action groups and by academic institutions. Reporters prize them as sources of information; newsmagazines, political journals, and Sunday supplements profile the sorcerers and their achievements, secrets, and opinions. They appear regularly on radio and TV talk shows. Many of them publish regular newspapers providing tips and, more important, inside information about politics.

So established do a few elite consultants become as political knowledgeables that their reputations for expertise extend beyond campaign politics. For example, when it became clear following the caucus and primary season in 1988 that the Democratic presidential nominee would be Michael Dukakis, several liberal groups met in Washington, DC, to formulate a policy agenda to be presented to Dukakis should he win election. Featured prominently in news reports analyzing the meeting were remarks by Matt Reese, a consultant to Democratic candidates. His reputation derived from campaigns in which he pioneered voter targeting techniques on behalf of his clients. Somehow campaign wizardry bestowed expertise in policy-related matters: "It's the normal rain dance," he told reporters about the meeting of liberal groups, estimating that liberal impact on a Dukakis administration would depend on the overlap between the constituencies of the liberals and the Democratic party.[19] Other media consultants not only comment on policy questions, they recommend policies. In the early 1980s, educational reform was a prime policy issue at state and national levels. There were proposals for raising teachers' salaries, testing teacher competence, and rewarding promotions and salary increases on merit. These proposals were brain children of a noted member of the media consultant elite. Grooming a client-candidate for re-election as governor in a southern state, the consultant searched around for an appealing policy program. Because citizens cherish education, educational reform was ideal. Who could be against such values as "education," "reform," "merit," and "master teaching"? The consultant drew up the reform proposals, put them in the mouth of the candidate, lobbied the proposals through the legislature (controlled by the opposing party), and successfully won re-election for the governor. The reform package received national attention, thanks to the efforts of the sorcerer consultant, and other states followed suit. Thus was mediated a political reality.

Most elite media consultants, however, confine their mediation to election politics. A principal vehicle for marketing their reputations and expertise is the political newsletter. What does the political world look like in these newsletters? It depends in part on the ideological and partisan persuasions of the consultants who publish them. For example, one elite consultant's newsletter provided a judgment of Michael Dukakis's first-term performance as Massachusetts governor. The newsletter, published two weeks before the governor became the Democratic presidential nominee, claimed that Governor Dukakis had been "anti-business, anti-growth and pro-taxes and regulations"; that he had raised state taxes by 20 percent, moved the state from having the twenty-second to the fifth highest tax burden in the nation, and given the state the third slowest growth in personal income in the United States. The journalistic pack, ear to the ground, made the matter an issue for a brief period.[20]

The content of consultant newsletters is not always so partisan. For the most part it consists of inside dope. The most notable case in point was the computerized newsletter, *Presidential Campaign Hotline,* which appeared in 1987. Two elite consultants, Republican Douglas Bailey and Democrat Roger Craver, developed the idea for this electronic news service. For those persons with computer facilities to access it (and the fee to pay for it), *Hotline* provided summaries of what the major news organizations were saying about candidates and campaigns, opinion polls, reports from candidates' campaign offices, speeches, financial data, and various other commentary and data—even daily polls from Labor Day to election day. In short, the conventional wisdom. A featured segment was "Insider Commentary," described in promotional literature as "the inside analysis of the races prepared by America's most respected pollsters and consultants in both parties." A few samples of *Hotline* mediation: Following the stock market crash of Black Monday in October 1987, readers learned there would be an "inexorable demand for Mario Cuomo" (governor of New York) to be the 1988 Democratic presidential candidate. No such demand materialized. By March 1 "Insider Commentary" reported that the stature gap between potential Democratic nominees and likely Republican presidential nominees had vanished. Cuomo was no longer in "inexorable demand." Three weeks later the column spoke of the "inevitability" of victory—but for Dukakis, not for the phantom Cuomo.

Hotline was not directly available to most voters in 1988, so did this sorcerer's wand thereby not figure in the political realities mediated for them? It did, but not directly. What the service made possible was the continuous flow of inside dope to journalists, the eyes and ears of the voter. *Hotline* helped reporters to cover the presidential campaign *without directly observing* it, thus avoiding rallies, hearing speeches, and boarding the zoo plane. David Broder of *The Washington Post* summed up the potential impact of *Hotline* by saying, "I am very addicted. It goes around the office like hot cakes in the morning."[21] Thus, an electronic newsletter that publishes dope gleaned from insiders mediates the political realities of soothsaying journalists who, in turn, mediate that mediation to provide campaign "realities" for reader and viewers. Political fantasies feed political fantasies.

Pundit Scholars

As a result of the Iran-Contra scandal in 1986–1987, several of President Ronald Reagan's close advisers resigned. One was his chief of staff, who was replaced by former U.S. Senator and Senate Majority Leader Howard Baker. Before the onset of the 1988 presidential campaign, Baker resigned. Following his resignation, news accounts quoted assessments of Baker's tenure:

- Look at Reagan when Baker came in and when he went out—Reagan's position has strengthened in the last year of this presidency.
- It's not that the ship is on the rocks, but it's almost home at port. There are some personnel problems . . . that might dampen the image, but these won't change the impact of the administration.
- He brought a great deal of stature but he was not terribly effective. His skill is to deal with Congress, though I don't see that he was that effective.

Each of the foregoing comments came from a noted scholar-observer of politics. The first from Thomas Mann of Brookings Institution, the second from Stephen Wayne of George Washington University, the third from William Schneider of the American Enterprise Institute.[22] Despite obvious shades of difference in the judgments, they have one thing in common: They exemplify another variety of inside-dopester mediation of politics. In recent years a relatively small number of political scholars associated with leading universities and think tanks (private institutes where writers and researchers can work in congenial surroundings) have achieved a celebrity status that affords them the opportunity to offer their political judgments to nationwide audiences. As do elite journalists, pollsters, and consultants, these scholars appear on "Good Morning America" or "Today," write articles for *TV Guide*, lecture at workshops and conferences, and give interviews to the national media. Like Brahman pundits they are learned and wise, or have reputations for being so, and their views therefore attract media attention.

So persuasive have some of these pundit scholars, generally referred to as the "recognized expert" in news accounts, become in the media that an editor of the *Columbia Journalism Review* satirized them and what they do in an article spoofing their celebrity status.[23] The article consists of two letters written to a fictitious "skilled professional" seeking work not too "mentally taxing." The letters from "DAQ Enterprises" (formerly "Dial-a-Quote") provided hope for the skilled pro. The fictional DAQ is in the business of franchising news, more specifically, placing quotations from its clients in the news media. The purpose of the letters is to explain DAQ operations to the "skilled professional" in hopes of wooing a client who, once having subscribed to DAQ, would no longer need to think, but merely write copy from DAQ releases. DAQ will do the thinking. After an initial letter of inquiry elicits a response, DAQ follows with a second letter that explains that "Washington pundits do the thinking for the press corps. DAQ is the world's largest clearinghouse for punditry," one that will place the "day's conventional wisdom at your fingertips." And, says the letter, "our sole purpose is to be quoted in the news media." The letter goes on to name a "few of the top experts" who can be quoted for their wisdom, their political leanings, and their record for being quoted: William Schneider, American Enterprise Institute, quoted 300 times in 1987; Stephen Hess, Brookings Institution, who responded to 2,880 calls from the news media in a year; Norman J. Ornstein, quoted 600 times in 1986–1987. The letter also explains how DAQ can provide useful clichés to cover all occasions and tells about DAQ's "INSTAQUOTE" service, which even includes 3-D holograms affording "give-and-take conversations with electronic savants."

Remember, the article is a satire, but like so much of satire it says much about its subject. INSTAQUOTE may be fictitous, but *Presidential Campaign Hotline* was not. And, just as the inside dope of the *Hotline* may eventually, although indirectly, reach citizens, so does the punditry of scholar celebrities (in fact, during 1987 William Schneider was the most prominent "expert" appearing on nightly TV newscasts, appearing more frequently than any of the announced candidates for their party's nomination for president!). In an age of mediators mediating what are already mediated political realities, the words of DAQ's second letter are worth pondering: "The more a person is quoted, the more of an expert he or she by definition becomes; the more he or she is defined as an expert, the more that person will be quoted." Then, to the prospective client, "Not to take advantage of this perpetual motion machine would be folly for a fledgling Washington journalist. So step aboard, sit back, and enjoy the ride."[24]

Prophets Honored and Dishonored

There is one other group of people who mediate the political realities of Americans through insider accounts. These are former public officials retired from government. When in office, many such politicians are targets of criticism by soothsaying journalists and pundit scholars. Once no longer actively involved in politics, however, these same individuals take on the status of statesmen, dishonored in office but honored in retirement. This is especially true of former presidents, who do more than appear in celebrity golf tournaments and engage in fly-fishing. Even Richard Nixon, who resigned from the presidency in 1974 fearing impeachment, took on the aura of a sage several years after leaving office. Former presidents are welcome guests on televised public affairs programs, each sharing opinions with fawning interviewers and telling how it "really" was to deal with an issue, policy, problem, or crisis. Articles bearing their names appear in public affairs journals, such as *Foreign Affairs,* and popular magazines, including *TV Guide.* And they publish their memoirs, dutifully promoting their books with appearances on each network's televised morning news and entertainment shows. The rhetorical visions revealed by their insider accounts of life in the Oval Office are often ponderous in tone, controversial, and self-serving, but they offer seemingly credible inside dope by one who once had "a finger on The Button."

A second group of former officials who provide insider accounts are principal presidential advisers and policymakers. Their vehicles for mediating realities are generally lectures, books, and interviews. Depending on the public official, these too may provide self-serving renditions of inside activity, or they may offer different, sometimes competing, versions of what transpired. Memoirs of former presidential speech writers, press secretaries, campaign managers, secretaries of state, and the like (including chauffeurs and maids) fill the shelves of book stores and libraries.

One highly publicized and often controversial form of inside dope consists of the titillating accounts by presidential advisers of life in the White House. Because these accounts written by once-trusted advisers and employees reveal the alleged secrets and foibles of the presidents, First Ladies, and family members, they are called "kiss and tell" books. Such books are scarcely a new form of inside-dopester writing. For example, the personal assistant to Abraham Lincoln claimed that the First Lady was a meddler, manipulator, and haughty. Lincoln, however, had been dead for a quarter of a century before such revelations appeared. More recently, books appear even before a presidential administration concludes. Both Presidents Dwight Eisenhower and Jimmy Carter were subjects of inside-dopester accounts while still in office. The presidency of Ronald Reagan witnessed a stream of kiss-and-tell revelations—in books by a former adviser, a press secretary, a budget director, and a secretary of state, to name but a few. The most highly publicized was former chief of staff Donald Regan's account, *For the Record.*[25] What made it noteworthy was Regan's claim that the Reagan White House often scheduled important events to coincide with astrological predictions. Denials and elaborations from the White House followed: The First Lady, not the president, had a passing interest in astrology; Reagan insisted that no policy decision had ever been influenced by astrology; and the First Family pointedly said they had never even met one astrologer who claimed to spend a lot of time in the White House.

CITIZENS AND SEERS: EXAMINING
THE FANTASIES OF INSIDE DOPE

The melodrama of the Reagan White House ties to the Zodiac generated jokes and serious criticism. Thus, instead of talking of "winning one for the Gipper" (see Chapter 6) wags spoke of "the Dipper." Astronomers attacked astrology as medieval superstition. Religious groups expressed dismay that a president professing deeply felt religious beliefs should be tied to a cult of star worshipers. Shortly, however, the controversy subsided, other matters attracted headlines, and only the jokes remained.

There is an aspect to Zodiac politics, however, that should not be so readily dismissed. The revelations were inside-dope hinting that a whole new set of inside-dopesters—astrologers—might have a political role to play. The criticism of astrology and astrologers quickly banished that thought. Yet, what sets astrologers apart from other individuals is a claim that all inside-dopesters make, which is that they know something other people don't know. Be they pack or soothsaying journalists, tea-leaf reading pollsters, sorcerer consultants, pundit scholars, or prophet politicians, they reinforce this fantasy: that there is a mystery to politics that they can unravel for citizens, that through inside dope politics can be demystified for us. Hence, so the fantasy goes, citizens should pay attention to insider accounts. No matter that the inside dope is frequently dead wrong. As stated in Chapter 3, celebrities have no fear of being wrong, only of being ignored! Still, if the claims of the stargazers are quickly challenged, then why not also the premises of inside-dopesters? The lesson derived from our discussion in Chapter 2 bears repetition and extension. To evaluate the fantastic dimensions of the ritual dramas of presidential contests, citizens must assume the roles of drama critics, sorting the demonstrated from the merely plausible. So too must they challenge the group-mediated fantasies of the inside-dopesters. Otherwise citizens' political futures may indeed be in their stars.

NOTES

1. David Riesman, Nathan Glazer, and Reuel Denney, *The Lonely Crowd* (Garden City, NY: Doubleday Anchor, 1955).
2. Ibid., p. 37 (emphasis in original).
3. Ibid., p. 214.
4. Daniel J. Boorstin, *The Image* (New York: Atheneum, 1962).
5. James M. Perry, *Us & Them* (New York: Clarkson S. Potter, 1973), p. 4.
6. Leo C. Rosten, *The Washington Correspondents* (New York: Harcourt, Brace, 1937).
7. Timothy Crouse, *The Boys on the Bus* (New York: Ballantine Books, 1974), p. 7. "Sicked" is in the original.
8. Ibid., p. 8.
9. Joel Swerdlow, "The Decline of the Boys on the Bus," *Washington Journalism Review* 3 (January/February 1981): 6.
10. Leon V. Sigal, *Reporters and Officials* (Lexington, MA: Heath, 1973).
11. *Newsweek* (June 27, 1988): 5.
12. Elliot King and Michael Schudson, "The Myth of the Great Communicator," *Columbia Journalism Review* 26 (November/December 1987): 37–39.
13. David Broder, "Flawed Primary System Likely to Assure Democratic Defeat," *Dallas Times Herald,* December 23, 1987, p. A–13.

14. George Will, "GOP Mirth Over Hart Could Turn to Frowns," *Dallas Times Herald,* December 23, 1987, A–13.
15. Mark R. Levy, "Disdaining the News," *Journal of Communication* 31 (Summer 1981): 24–31.
16. Barbara Matusow, "Are the Polls Out of Control?" *Washington Journalism Review* (October 1988): 16–19.
17. George F. Bishop, Robert W. Oldendick, Alfred J. Tuchfarber, and Stephen E. Bennett, "Pseudo-Opinions on Public Affairs," *Public Opinion Quarterly* 44 (Summer 1980): 198–209.
18. David L. Paletz and Robert M. Entman, *Media Power Politics* (New York: Free Press, 1981), pp. 74–75.
19. Quoted by Donald L. Rheem, "Ideas for President Dukakis," *Christian Science Monitor* (June 23, 1988): 3.
20. Bradley S. O'Leary, "Tearful Taxachusetts," *The O'Leary/Kamber Report,* 3 (1988): 2.
21. See Mickey Kaus, "Fresh Baked Political Wisdom," *Newsweek,* November 2, 1987: 83.
22. Quoted in the *Christian Science Monitor* (June 15, 1988): 32.
23. William Boot, "Capital Letter," *Columbia Journalism Review* 26 (March/April 1988): 16–17.
24. Ibid.
25. Donald Regan, *For the Record* (New York: Harcourt Brace Jovanovich, 1988).

CHAPTER 9

The Fantasies
of Religious Movements
Political Perspectives
of Contemporary Evangelicals

The year was 1620. A small band of Pilgrims approached the shores of what was to become Massachusetts. On the evening before landing, their leader John Winthrop told them, "For the work we have in hand, it is by mutual consent through a special overruling providence, and a more than ordinary approbation of the Churches of Christ to seek out a place of Cohabitation and Consorteship under a due form of Government both civil and ecclesiastical." He exhorted the faithful, "the eyes of all people are upon us," for "we shall be as a City Upon a Hill." The scene now shifts forward in time about 350 years. Ronald Reagan accepts the nomination of the Republican party for the presidency of the United States in 1980. He says, "Can we doubt that only a Divine Providence placed this land, this Island of freedom, here as a refuge for all those people in the world who yearn to breathe freely?" In his campaign Reagan promises to restore "the city upon a hill." After taking the oath as fortieth president he says, "We are a nation under God, and I believe God intended for us to be free."

For over 350 years the refrain has continued: "Divine Providence," "city upon a hill," "a nation under God." Both major party candidates in 1988— George Bush and Michael Dukakis—used one or more such phrases in their speeches accepting their nominations. So close has been the tie between political and religious rhetoric that one can hardly ignore the importance of organized religion as a mediator of political realities.[1] Yet many Americans do. While they lead their daily, secular lives in a rough-and-tumble and often unfair world, they still tend to think that America is a blessed land that links the political community with the Almighty. Those same people label government as corrupt, politicians as crooks. Real politics and ideal religion are divorced, not married, in the minds of many citizens.

This is not the case, however, for groups intensely committed to a theological view of the world. Such groups elaborate, for their own and the world's benefit, an explanation of all things, including politics, entirely in rhetoric derived from religious belief. Scripture and revelation combine in a rhetorical vision of history and politics—past, present, and future. The world of politics is part of a cosmic melodrama, an agent of God's purposes and design in history. What nations and politicians do reveals the workings of Divine Providence. The wicked, as agents of Satan, also have a role in the grand drama. This revelatory and apocalyptic articulation has been a strain in Christianity since St. Augustine. It survives in many religious groups in America today, such as the Mormons, Jehovah's Witnesses, and Southern Baptists. This chapter focuses on the rhetorical vision of that contemporary religious movement in America variously labeled the Christian Right, fundamentalism, the born-again Christians, and the evangelicals. The discussion permits an account of both the techniques by which that movement mediates political realities and of the overriding rhetorical vision involved. Moreover, it serves as a brief prologue to a consideration in Chapter 10 of another form of group-mediated politics, that is, conspiratorial politics.

The revelatory and apocalyptic vision of politics is most associated with evangelical churches and and movements. The evangelical branch of American Christianity is ancient and tenacious, often more a social movement than a church. American revivalism—the great awakenings in our history—come and go, often in conjunction with, and in reaction to, social change and mass disillusionment. Thus the 1920s, 1950s, and 1970s witnessed the revival of evangelical Christianity, including the elaboration of a rhetorical vision that simplified confusing social and political changes for the benefit of the faithful. In the period of repeated turmoil and repeated crises of recent decades, evangelical Christianity, with its simplistic and powerful message, acquires new salience. Although very much in the tradition of the nondenominational, fire-and-brimstone, repent-for-the-end-is-at-hand tradition of Dwight Moody and Billy Sunday, the most recent evangelical movement adds new features and new twists, including a higher degree of politicization, to the old rhetorical visions of politics.[2]

The current evangelical Christian movement is theologically not much different from its "sawdust trail," tent-meeting evangelical predecessors. Early proselytizers were usually fundamentalist, believing in the inerrancy of the Bible, active soul winning, and being born again, contemptuous of mainstream churches, the social gospel, and ecumenism. They proclaimed, yet again, that the world was in the premillenial last days. The group fantasy evoked a Christian drama that has survived since Augustine. The character of the faithful in most recent movements has differed, however. Rather than rural folk flocking to large tent meetings to hear the Word, they are now urbanized members of the industrial and technological society. And the new evangelicals are not linked by their physical presence in the tent but by a technology: television.

THE MASS-MEDIATED WORLD
OF THE ELECTRONIC CHURCH

The group drama of religious revival is no longer enacted primarily in tent meetings, riverside baptisms, or remote country churches of the Holy Rollers. The most recent Great Awakening that began in the 1970s increased the membership of evangelical churches located now in urban and suburban areas across the United States. Its most visible form is the electronic church that became widespread and powerful in the 1980s. The spread of communication satellites and cable TV gave birth to the electronic church—televised broadcasts from religious sanctuaries to the faithful who enjoyed watching religious programming. The more successful religious broadcasters understood the media logic of television; they employed professionals to develop well-choreographed shows appealing to TV audiences. TV evangelists, dubbed "prime-time preachers," sensed that audiences wanted to hear certain kinds of religious messages presented in an attractive orchestrated style and setting.

The most successful electronic churches accumulated staggeringly large audiences and great wealth. Although estimates vary, the usually reliable arbitron TV ratings figures in early 1988 had evangelist Jimmy Swaggart's broadcasts attracting 2 million households, Robert Schuller's, 1.5 million, and Oral Robert's approximately 2 million. Televangelists Pat Robertson and Jerry Falwell had audiences of hundreds of thousands. Financial figures are less precise: TV evangelists are secretive and virtually unaccountable about the disposition of contributions. Estimates are that at his peak of popularity Jimmy Swaggart's ministry brought in $140 million annually, and that Jim and Tammy Bakker's "Praise the Lord" (PTL) ministry brought in around $120 million. For a while, the major TV ministries were so prosperous that their estimated total annual revenues reached 2 billion, largely in donations from the 65 to 70 million people in the United States who identify themselves as born-again evangelical Christians. With this money, religious broadcasters built empires of crystal cathedrals, amusement parks, prayer towers, universities, state-of-the-art communications facilities, and lavish lifestyles.[3]

The advent of Christian television dominated by fundamentalist ministries evoked the fantasy of a Christian community identified by television ministries, a social bloc that could be mobilized for a conservative movement. For viewers of Christian television, it was easy to fantasize an evangelical subculture of power, wealth, and growing size. In fact, telechristianity was not uniform in theology or politics; it was a pseudo-community that was more a product of fantasy than of fact.[4] There were inherent divisions and rivalries built into the TV ministries that made for warring camps. To outsiders, many televangelists seemed to be preaching the same brand of old-time religion and social reaction to modernity that goes back to Billy Sunday and Dwight Moody. There were often, however, subtle, yet key, theological distinctions between evangelicals, fundamentalists, Pentecostals, and charismatics that produced rivalries. Perhaps more important, the largest TV ministries were led by preachers with egos sometimes as large as their followings; rivalries and jealousies abounded. Critics likened the "holy wars" and scandals involving teleministries to corporate struggles between religious entrepreneurs trying to monopolize the market by driving competitors out. In any case, the close of the 1980s witnessed highly publicized scandals, the disclosure of financial mismanagement, and bickering involving the most prominent of TV ministers— Swaggart, the Bakkers, and Roberts. The fantasy of an evangelical movement whose values would transform the nation into a "Christian America" began to evaporate.

Not only were TV evangelists divided by doctrines and ambitions; they collided over what rhetorical vision to convey. Some were highly politicized; others avoided politics almost altogether. The most popular TV ministries saw no contradiction in using a godless entertainment medium (TV) to join discussions of delicate religious, social, and political matters such as abortion, school prayer, homosexuality, and AIDS. Instead, they were impressed with the power of TV to convey their politico-religious message. If Jesus Christ were on Earth today, said PTL's Jim Bakker, he would have to be on TV because that would be the only way he could reach God's people. After a decade of Christian TV and the rise and demise of various minister-celebrity stars, it was no longer clear that evangelists' appeals were actually contributing to the growth of TV's Christian community. Evidence accumulated that the effect of TV ministries was to reinforce the faithful already committed to evangelical religion, not to expand the pool of "God's people." Indeed, it appeared to some students of religious movements that generational attrition and disillusionment were contributing to shrinking audiences, making competition between televangelists to retain supporters and contributors all the more fierce.[5]

The rhetorical visions of the electronic superchurches varied, but such visions were all driven as much by the melodramatic imperatives of TV (see our "Introduction") as by nuances of gospel preachments. To appeal to large and dispersed TV audiences, televangelists became entertainers, employing the styles, formats, and values of show biz. Television is a profane and secular medium, subject to the whims of fickle audiences who use it in leisure time for entertainment. It is difficult to sustain mass interest, even among those many who are born again, while discussing complex theological doctrines or conducting solemn liturgy. Religious programming turned necessarily to the conventions and formats of television entertainment, measuring success by ratings and donations. Thus did TV ministries contribute to another fantasy: the gospel of success. By its very nature, the marriage of popular religion and popular television preached a gospel of success. Electronic ministries programmed religion as television spectacle, mixing the sacred and the profane in ways that not all Christians approved. Some viewers criticized selling religion as entertainment, exchanging sacred gospel for loot, and becoming marketers of the gospel. Jim Bakker typified a televangelist view, boldly stating, "We have a better product than soap or automobiles. We have eternal life." Such was the mediated blend of the sacred and profane.[6]

The relationship between the several large TV ministries and their constituencies is a vicarious one, wherein the viewer seeks a TV ministry with which to identify, and the minister-celebrity seeks to communicate a message that induces widespread identification. As noted earlier, the relationship is a fantastic appeal to a pseudo-community that doesn't exist, broadcast from a stage conforming to TV's fantasy world—the talk show set of the "700 Club" or lavish cathedrals filled with pageantry, pomp, and ceremony. The sacred drama the viewer witnesses suggests an idealized Christian community, one created, structured, and edited for television. In the midst of such orchestrated order, beauty, and peace, the directly experienced church in one's hometown appears much less inviting, beset as it is with ambiguities, human failings, unmet budgets, and failed ambitions. Thus, identification with a TV superchurch allows people to enjoy the entertaining play of the sacred drama without the responsibilities of actually taking part, without going to church.

The Structural Fantasy of TV Religion

There are two fantasy processes at work in electronic religion, what we may call a *structural fantasy* and a *participatory fantasy*. By structural fantasy we mean that religious programs, like any other kind of mass communication, have a dramatic format and progression satisfying to audiences. The very format of the religious programming provides audience messages, both explicit and implicit, with which they can identify. For example, the highly formal show structure of programs such as Jerry Falwell's "Old Time Gospel Hour" and Dr. D. James Kennedy's "Coral Ridge Ministries" communicate an idealized and orderly Christian community, a welcome respite from the turbulence of, say, news programs. The fantasy is communion in a primary group, the electronic church, that is part of a wider, unified, and cherished community of faith. The congregation depicted in TV ministries consists of solemn, pious members. For example, the people in Falwell's pews are quiet, deferential, and prayerful; the choir is youthful, scrubbed, and respectful of their elders; the ministerial hierarchy in the pulpit exemplifies the expectation of piety. Dozing, yawning, quiet gossiping, flirting, and day-dreaming (all common to congregations of many a local church) are, by contrast with TV ministries, impious. The format of the TV service thus offers a vicarious piety.

The structure of teleministries such as that of Falwell or Kennedy also communicates authority. Aside from a few invoked and approved responses, the audience is expected to listen to the authoritative preacher. No one disputes his preachments on God and government, history and culture, constitutional law and moral behavior. By asserting the authority of the Bible and himself, such a minister communicates a confident certainty that for many in his audience is a welcome alternative to the moral confusion and secular activity of the outside world. In the formal structure of the televised service and the authoritative rhetorical vision of the minister-celebrity, one may find an imagined pious community headed by an authority figure that assures believers of moral and, indeed, political superiority.

The Participation Fantasy in TV Religion

The fantasies of vicarious piety and unquestioned authority provided by the orchestration of "Pray TV"—that is, derivations of the structural fantasy—can be sustained only if viewers feel personally caught up in the cause or vision of primetime preachers. This sense constitutes the participation fantasy. The style and content of televangelists' performances help to promote a sense of personal involvement in the TV-mediated cause, which becomes for the faithful a group-mediated experience.

Enthusiastic and dynamic preachers such as Jimmy Swaggart, Dwight Thompson, and Kenneth Copeland—throwbacks to the exhortatory style of tent meetings—exemplify teleministries that communicate participation by appealing to the ecstasy of faith. Before his fall from grace in a widely publicized scandal involving a prostitute, Swaggart typified the appeal. An intense and athletic performer on stage, perspiring freely, he contemptuously condemned the sins of the world in his TV services. Swaggart invited identification with the dynamics of faith, sharing the fantasy of the imminent evangelizing of the world and the defeat of both secular and sacred enemies (liberals, Roman Catholics, and so on). Jim and Tammy Bakker's PTL offered the same type of participatory fantasy but with a lower-keyed style. Their ministry employed a talkshow format to communicate consensus among evangelical Christians and the *joy* of the faithful. They chatted with celebrities, sang, cooked, planned grandiose building schemes, ran tours and parades, built a theme park with shops selling Tammy's records, cosmetics, and other items. The park even had a water slide. They presided over the creation of an evangelical metaphor of Heaven as a talk show, boutique shop, and ice cream parlor.

As each of the major TV ministries sought to offer viewers a sense of participation in an eternal cause, each created a distinct miniuniverse to set it apart from competitors in the TV marketplace of faith. Along with Bakker's Heritage Park was Falwell's Liberty University, Robertson's Christian Broadcast Network (CBN), Swaggart's Louisiana-based operation, Schuller's crystal palace, Oral Roberts's university—all offering a spectacle of a sanctified place, a respite from the world and a model of heavenly Christian utopia devoid of problems and strife to which the faithful could come and participate.

As with the original Christian story, it came to pass that there was trouble in each TV paradise. Claims to moral superiority were difficult to sustain in light of revealed sexual and financial excesses (and even sins) by the more celebrated TV evangelists. Both Jim Bakker and Jimmy Swaggart lost much of their following after disclosure of sex and financial scandals. Critics were quick to ridicule the once-self-righteous preachings of both men. Oral Roberts embarrassed many followers when he announced that he had seen a 900-foot-tall Jesus in the desert and had fought the devil in his bedroom. He also claimed that God told him that He would "call him home" by a certain date if Roberts didn't raise the requisite $8 million for Roberts's medical missionary program. Critics questioned the accountability and financial practices of the new evangelical empires. A former employee of Pat Robertson claimed that Robertson's CBN was a cult built around a false prophet. Falwell's Liberty University came under fire for isolating students in a rigid, disciplinary cocoon and indoctrinating them into right-wing political orthodoxies dictated by Falwell. There were accusations that Swaggart routinely demanded polygraph tests of employees suspected of disloyalty and divergent views. Once-pure TV evangelists started to appear as petty martinets who ruled over their own self-enclosed worlds as absolute monarchs, as high priests without fear of challenge or contradiction.[7]

Whatever the truth, televangelists built media empires by appeals to the participatory fantasy of their viewers. People seek uses, gratifications, and rewards from watching TV ministers just as they do from other forms of mass-mediated entertainment. They learn religious expectations, find gratifying comfort and inspiration, and view televangelists as sources of active power for life in the here and hereafter, but at the heart of the participation fantasy lies another activity. To give tangible effect to personal identification with the media pseudo-community, the faithful take part in a direct way: They contribute money to the sacred cause. Contributions sustain the various projects and broadcasts of the ministries.[8]

The participation fantasy is thus that one is part of an accessible and perfect Christian community, a community acting with and for "me." The televangelists' success suggests that people seek something that local churches and mainstream denominations do not provide. Perhaps directly experienced churches emphasize too much the burden and agony of faith, whereas the electronic churches offer instead promises of material and moral prosperity, including the fantasy of being part of a movement destined for political power and national regeneration. TV evangelists often preach and often exemplify a gospel of prosperity, the fantasy that if one invests emotionally and financially in the TV ministry, it results in God-given financial, spiritual, and even physical rewards. (This "health-and-wealth Christianity" has been condemned by many Christian leaders, including Falwell.) Investment in a TV ministry promises, at least implicitly, access to a divine power that intervenes in one's life. At their most blatant, TV ministers promise a relationship with God—contributions in exchange for heavenly rewards. Pat Robertson's "700 Club" regularly broadcasts cases of prayers for miraculous healing or financial salvation being heeded. Robertson formulated what he called "Kingdom Principles," a form of Christian charity that suggested divine reciprocity: Invest in Robertson's ministry and receive divine blessing with interest. Although critics argued that such appeals made God into a stockbroker that paid off for the right investment, the fantasy provided to the believer was clear: "I have been rewarded with a healthy body or bank account because I invested."

Religion and Politics after the Fall

Recent TV evangelists have implied through structural and participation fantasies that divinely given affluence is legitimate. Televangelists tout themselves as exemplars of the Horatio Alger story, citing their ministries and fortunes as proof of the legitimate rewards God gives to the faithful. A large following, an impressive physical plant, mansions, private airplanes, and richly appointed facilities communicate implicitly that "God's people" should enjoy the finer things in life. Thus, there is no conflict between Christianity and capitalism, or between godliness and success. After the fall of Bakker, Swaggart, and TV evangelists of lesser celebrity status, there were questions about whether power and fame had gone to these celebrity-preachers' heads and whether contributions were justified. In 1986, for instance, Jim Bakker's PTL raised $129 million in revenues, of which the Bakker family collected $1.6 million in salaries and bonuses; only 2.9 percent of total revenues went to charity. When Oral Roberts asked followers for $8 million for his medical mission program (pleading on TV, "Will you help me extend my life?"), critics noted that he lived in a mansion near the university campus, owned a $3.5 million mansion in Beverly Hills and four Mercedes-Benz cars, held membership in two country clubs, owned two $550,000 resort houses in Rancho Mirage, California, and that his son, Richard Roberts, was moving into a mansion in the Roberts family complex. Lindsay Roberts, Richard's wife, reported that she, like Oral and Richard, accepted expensive gifts to avoid insulting the giver: "Even Jesus might have worn a Rolex if somebody had given him one."[9] Other major televangelists had similar lifestyles. Swaggart lived in a million-dollar estate, paid himself and his relatives huge sums (he had 12 relatives on the payroll), and refused to reveal how he disposed of his $140 million annual revenue. Falwell paid himself over $100,000 a year, lived in an antebellum colonial mansion, and had unlimited access to airplanes, limousines, and the president of the United States. Robertson lived in a handsome and spacious Georgian estate on the grounds of his 685-acre Virginia Beach complex, kept a stable of horses, and flew the country in his private jet.

Both the TV ratings and the donations to teleministries began to decline in the late 1980s. The practitioners of "crisis Christianity," appealing to audiences for just one more donation to meet just one more manufactured crisis, began to suffer very tangible ratings and financial crises of their own. Televangelists made drastic cutbacks in staff, projects, and telecasts. Arbitron estimated that in the first half of 1988, Swaggart's audience had gone from 2.1 million in February to 923,000, Roberts's dropped from 2 million to 635,000, Robertson had lost 45 percent of his 440,000 households, Schuller had lost 500,000 viewers, PTL was not only bankrupt but down to 105,000 viewers, and Falwell's audience had declined 30 percent in one year [10]

It was in this setting that Pat Robertson launched his bid for the presidency in 1988. Although there was mounting evidence that no evangelical vote could ever constitute a majority, Robertson and his supporters thought otherwise. God, said Robertson, directed him to run for president: "There is an enterprise the Lord set me on a year or so ago—running for president of the United States." He promised to run again in 1992: "That is His plan for me and for this nation." As a candidate, Robertson envisioned an evangelical "invisible army" that would score victories for him in Republican primaries. It did not happen. Even though an ABC poll found that 39 percent of all Republican primary voters and 33 percent of all Democrats identified themselves as born-again Christians, they did not become soldiers in Robertson's "invisible army."[11] In states with large evangelical populations, Robertson still fared poorly. He didn't help his cause by appearing testy and mean-spirited, and expressing views that often appeared bizarre. He claimed that Margaret Sanger, the founder of Planned Parenthood, wanted to create a "master race" by sterilizing "blacks, Jews, mental defectives and fundamentalist Christians," and that American women needed to have more babies as a patriotic duty to the country to prevent decline in our (presumably white and Protestant) "culture and values." He claimed to be a direct descendant of one of the founders of Jamestown, of a signer of the Declaration of Independence, of two presidents (the Harrison family), and of ancestors of Winston Churchill. And Robertson suffered setbacks in his campaign—charges that he had used the influence of his father (a former U.S. senator) to shirk combat duty in the Korean War; that his first son was born 10 weeks after he and his wife were married; and that his campaign biography contained misrepresentations (he never did "graduate study" at the University of London, as he claimed).

Despite these very worldly embarrassments, Robertson held firm in his conviction of divine destiny, maintaining the core belief that the Secret Kingdom of God is at hand, and that it is the responsibility of Christian leadership to assume positions of power in anticipation of the imminent time when the true believers will reign jointly with Christ over the earth during the Millenium. Even then, God will apparently need the help of Christian leaders like President Robertson to rule. Thus, the true Christians must "educate" themselves for the Kingdom, preparing to rule justly by rewarding the faithful, punishing the wicked, and defeating the forces of Satan. A Robertson presidency would certainly be guided by a vision.[12]

The future of televangelism as a mediator of political realities is problematic. TV ministries have created enclaves (Liberty University, PTL, Oral Roberts University) evoking fantasies of an ideal Christian community, but these heroic dramas of creation may be important only to loyal followers, not to outsiders. Critics portray televangelists as suspect figures in a very unheroic melodrama, either as childish fools unable to control their lust for women and lavish living, or as exploitative villains preying on the elderly to sign over their retirement money in exchange for the hope of Heaven.

In some respects both heroic and unheroic portrayals derive from the same source—the TV imperative. The same technology that promoted tele-ministries also contributed to their decline. TV ministries benefited from the spectacle, show business, and entertainment values of the medium. They cele-brated their celebrity. Television favors the immediate, the colorful, the excit-ing, and the novel, however, and no successful TV series runs forever. Sooner or later audiences grow bored, press their remote controls, and switch chan-nels. Beginning in the 1970s, TV evangelists brought something new to TV, something responded to by people with evangelical backgrounds and beliefs. To hold and build audiences televangelists had to adjust to TV. Even as they vowed not to compromise with the Devil, they did compromise with television. The successful ones provided audiences with what they wanted to hear and see, sound theology or not. Faced with the problem of presenting a serious religion in an entertainment medium, many televangelists made Christianity into an object of entertainment and not worship, of play and not piety, of spectacle and not sacrament. Instead of the great mythical themes of ancient faith, they offered the immediate fantasies of ephemeral communities and easy salvation. In all this they were initially successful. They accumulated large audiences, power, and money—commodities that are great sources of temptation. As ce-lebrities, it was easy for them to fall into the trap of idolatry and begin to believe in their own infallibility and destiny, inviting shared fantasies that con-fuse personal ministerial power with godlike power. The center stage of televi-sion transformed the evangelist into a celebrity, then into a mass-mediated god. But we all remember that the ancient Hebrews had a name for idol wor-ship. They called it blasphemy.[13]

THE RHETORICAL VISION OF THE CHRISTIAN RIGHT

The intellectual roots of the Christian Right are in the Augustinian vision of the Christian drama of history, in which the Elect of God suffer and struggle through history as a Church Militant against Satan's Hordes, eventually de-feating evil in an apocalyptic triumph at the end of history and the beginning of the Millennium. This millenial view imbues the believer with a sense of righteousness in a fight against the forces of darkness, justifying zealous action to destroy or convert evil and redeem the world. In its American version, this vision sees America as a "redeemer nation" whose national mission it is to fight zealously against evil at home and abroad, to ensure the inevitable victory of the right and holy. For church people whose beliefs stem from Calvinism, the war against evil often takes the form of a crusade of the holy against enemies who are stigmatized as demonic forces. The descendants of the original Calvinists have long been social crusaders, arguing that Christians should apply moral standards to society to control vice and folly. In some ways American Calvinism was the source of both traditions of liberal reformism (feminism, abolitionism, and progressivism) and conservative reforms (Sunday closing laws, book bans, movie censorship, and Prohibition). But in the 19th century, evangelical pietists developed a political agenda based on the redemptive mission of creating a Christian commonwealth with the votes amassed by a Christian party that would elect to office only converted Christians who would enforce Christian morality. Such morality would work "to outlaw the Masons and the Mormons, to enact activist laws, to enforce prohibition, to censor immorality, to prevent birth control, to maintain a Christian Sabbath, and eventually to restrict immigration and pass laws preventing the teaching of evolution."[14] These are many of the same social goals of cultural and behavioral orthodoxy sought today.

Even though times have changed, the dramatic vision and logic of the Christian Right have not. Adherents see themselves as a community of saints who are "saved," involved in a theological moral drama, fighting a holy war against Satan and his agents. Satan's hordes include a wide gallery of villains and fools—liberals, feminists, homosexuals, and "prochoice" abortion activists; the creators of popular music, movies, and TV programs; and so on. Some of Satan's agents wittingly contribute to the satanic purpose by purveying or justifying evil; such are the publishers of *Playboy* and *Penthouse*, the sponsors of soap operas, and the creators of "heavy metal" rock music. Others are merely misguided or duped people—often the consumers of popular fare—who foolishly believe soaps, rock, X-rated movies, and the like to be harmless. The former indoctrinate or corrupt the latter into un-Christian and thus demonic thought and conduct. For example, critics of rock recordings argue that they contain subliminal satanic messages and sex- and drug-advocating messages (often "back-masked," discernible only if the record is played at a different speed or backward). One fundamentalist minister claimed that the theme song to the old rerun TV show "Mr. Ed.," if played backward, contains a satanic message: "Someone sung this song for Satan!"[15]

The End Is Near

If such charges about popular culture and politics are true, clearly America has fallen on hard times. Why? Because the nation and its people have turned their backs on social and political fundamentals. There has been a national fall from grace. America was once a godly nation in some nostalgic golden age in the past. The country was founded by people dedicated to creating a Christian nation. Both the Founding Fathers and the founding documents (such as the Constitution) were imbued with Christian principles. America was blessed because she was governed with that Christian intent. However, at some obscure point, the nation fell from grace and is now cursed. The wicked and those who tolerate wickedness now govern. America is close to an apocalyptic end, or at least a crisis, that will determine whether it returns to Christian foundations and is again blessed, or continues in decline, like Babylon and Rome, because of unrepented sins and rule by the unrighteous.

This, then, is a romantic vision of national restoration, returning us to a dream state that never existed, yet it remains a compelling, if only nostalgic, vision. This image of a romanticized past is one that the Christian Rights' predecessors among past evangelical pietists shared. Ernest Bormann has pointed out that when 19th-century speakers "looked about them and found times of troubles, sinfulness, and societal ills that required reform, they cast their solutions into a mighty panoramic drama of history that essentially portrayed the successful reform as requiring first a *restoration* of society to its original foundation." Bormann goes on, "Many American reformers began their journey forward into a better society by moving backwards towards the true foundations, by a restoration of the original dream of the founding fathers."[16] The Christian Right imagines a kind of apocalyptic restoration, a crusade that in the future will return all to a state of original purity redeemed in the postlapsarian world (see Chapter 5). "We're fighting a holy war," Falwell once said. "What's happening to America is that the wicked are bearing rule. We have to lead the nation back to the moral stance that made America great. . . . We want to bring America back . . . to the way we were." Like ancient Israel, America has had plagues visited upon the country in recent years because we had turned away from biblical tenets and godly government. Major national ills of past decades—loss of the war in Vietnam, Watergate, drugs, crime, AIDS, uprisings—all resulted from turning away from God. The recurrent appeal on a national level is much like the appeal of the televangelists on an individual level: If we seek national repentance, stop our ungodly activities (legal abortions, the ban on state-sponsored prayer in public schools, even deficit spending), then God will restore us to power and prosperity in the world.[17]

The Christian Right enumerates a set of political, economic, and social fundamentals, derived from and justified by biblical teachings and precedent, from which America fell and to which it must aspire again. The nostalgic fantasy is of a once and future union between God and government, church and state, conjuring up images of the Mayflower compact, thankful Pilgrims, Washington at prayer in the snow at Valley Forge, schoolmarms reading from the Bible in one-room country schools, or family Bible study around the fireplace in the log cabin. A widely circulated book, *God and Government,* says that "the political choice before us is Christ or chaos." The Bible is the "Great Political Textbook," so "No governmental institution can govern properly apart from following the commands of God's Word as they are set forth in both the Old and New Testaments." The function of American government is clear: "The central focus of all realms of government is the regenerating work of Jesus Christ." From this premise flows severe restrictions on the activities of secular government: "The state is not to assume the role of educating children" nor social welfare for the sick and needy, because the church, through the tithe and the voluntary generosity of Christians, can provide, without "statist corruption and misappropriation." Not only was the Constitution designed to promote Christian principles and law, the First Amendment does not mandate the separation of church and state: "The First Amendment does not require the federal government to be secularized." However, since the fall away from biblical restrictions on civil government, statism has grown to the point at which it threatens the proper role of the church and the undermining of the state's role of furthering the creation of a "Christian nation."[18]

The political goal, therefore, of the Christian Right is to *re-Christianize America*. Fantasies of a Christian past blend into fantasies of the restoration of a Christian future that transform America from a secular and pluralistic society into a sacral and monistic one. Capitalism, justified as biblical, should be led by Christian businessmen who will transform it into a force of benevolence and prosperity. Schools should have Christian curriculums, dress codes, strict discipline, and rote lessons. Some familiar objects of popular taste—adult movies, TV soap operas, sex-oriented magazines, hard rock music—must be prohibited. Like the Marxist utopia, the vision of a "Christian America" is vague in the details but clearly a very different place from contemporary America.

The holy war to Christianize America includes the *identification of the archenemy*. One candidate for archenemy consists of secular humanists. According to Christian Right author and activist Tim LaHaye, secular humanism is a philosophy of "man's attempt to solve his problems independent of God." Included among such secular humanists are Aristotle, Machiavelli, St. Thomas Aquinas, Rousseau, Marx, Bertrand Russell, and John Dewey—indeed, a breathtaking array of talent and intellect more frequently identified as the intellectual core of Western civilization. Nevertheless, their godless approach to life has had totally negative effects and is responsible for virtually every social ill imaginable, from drug addiction to low reading scores. "Most of the evils in the world today can be traced to humanism, which has taken over our government, the UN, education, TV, and most of the other influential things of life." Although there only about 275,000 humanists in the land, nevertheless "they occupy key positions of leadership, where they exercise an inordinate influence on America." The archenemy is everywhere—in churches and universities, public education and private endowments, the publishing industry and TV networks, and most of all, in government. "We must remove all humanists from public office and replace them with pro-moral political leaders." They must be stopped in their subversive, if ambitious, goal "to so weaken our national character that we would lose our American identity and merge with the other countries of the world in the creation of their carefully planned new world order—by the year 2000.''[19] Critics of such a view may regard the search for secular humanists as yet another of the many witch hunts that have sprung up throughout American history. For those gripped by the fantasy of a Manichean struggle against an insidious archenemy, however, the secular humanist conspiracy is as real as Satan.

The holy war to purge the wicked from the restored American Garden of Eden is made all the more urgent by the fact that we are now in the prophesized apocalyptic *last days*. This poses a fantastic paradox. The end is at hand because of a divinely ordained disintegration of moral and political order, yet we are enjoined to prepare America and the world for precisely the inevitable about which we can do nothing. A vast literature exists attempting to apply the prophecies of Revelations to present events, usually a gigantic nuclear war centered in the Middle East involving Israel, the Arab states, and the Soviet Union. For some, signs and omens portend the imminence of the end—earthquakes, wars, famine, changes in weather, the appearance of false prophets and cults. They see a final battle, Armageddon, involving the world's major powers in a nuclear holocaust that will kill a large portion of the human race. However, Christ will return at the peak of the battle. There are different versions regarding where, when, and how all this will happen, but believers agree that the time is near. They were no doubt heartened in their faith when in 1983 President Reagan speculated thusly: "You know, I turn back to your ancient prophets in the Old Testament, and the signs foretelling Armageddon, and I find myself wondering if—if we're the generation that's going to see that come about." Others see such eschatalogical speculation as but a historical fantasy climaxing with the revenge of the just on the wicked, with believers finally getting to see their enemies in high places get what has been coming to them all along. One observer terms this version of the last days "The Gunfight at the Armageddon Corral," in which Jesus returns like a Western gunslinger to zap the bad guys and rescue the good guys who have upheld virtue and faith.[20]

Whither the Right?

As the 1980s closed, political observers speculated about the actual political potency of the Christian Right. Rightists were active in GOP politics and involved in numerous issues at local levels—picketing abortion clinics and stores that sell adult magazines, attempting to get "creationism" taught along with evolution in public school biology classes, banning books from public libraries, and so on. In a few instances, the political activities of the Right proved bizarre, including requests for deaths of "opponents" (such as Supreme Court justices, state attorneys general who prosecuted Christian ministers for abuses at church schools, and former Secretary of State Alexander Haig). Falwell's Moral Majority opposed a civil rights act in Congress on the grounds that passage would require the employment of "homosexual drug addicts with

AIDS as youth pastors in local churches." Still other Rightists were involved in an attempt to prove that the Nazi destruction of European Jews, commonly called the Holocaust, did not happen, fantasizing that an ostensibly Christian nation such as Germany could not have done such a thing and that the Holocaust was a myth that served insidious Jewish interests.[21]

Despite all these and other activities, it is unclear how much electoral or group strength the Christian Right can muster. Some studies indicate that the power of prestigious religious broadcasters on voting is minimal. Even though one in every five adult white Americans identify themselves as evangelicals, they do not constitute a voting bloc of consistent support for Christian Right candidates.[22] Supporters of the Christian Right, however, assess the movement's influence as greater than that and mount political campaigns to exploit it. *The Presidential Biblical Scoreboard,* for example, in 1988 rated the presidential contenders of both parties on several questions in hopes of influencing party primaries. Among the rating items were "biblical-family-moral-freedom issues," and "God's and humanistic anti-God values." Such ratings are useful, the publication claimed, because of the "70 million Christian voters—the largest voting block in America."God's people have "the biblical mandate" to oust the conspiratorial "Liberal Minority" from power, thwart the agenda "to remove Judeo-Christian values and influences from American life," and bring about the passage of "godly legislation" based on a "truly Christian agenda for the political world." That agenda covers an astonishing array of specific issues allegedly "biblical," including supporting aid to the Nicaraguan Contras, "privatization" of Social Security, and the Strategic Defense Initiative; opposing sanctions against the apartheid government of South Africa and "comparable worth" pay for women.[23] The fantasy of a biblical agenda that speaks to every contemporary issue, a biblical test for every candidate, and a Christian society with unamimous consensus on values and policy is the core of the Christian Right's political vision.

The Christian Right has always been more of a movement than a church, hence bound to be beset by sectarian squabbles and power struggles among ministerial leaders. In many ways, the Christian Right is the American manifestation of the current march of fundamentalisms—be they Jewish, Moslem, nationalist, or even Marxist—that are "militantly antimodern, fanatical, and hold in contempt the separation of church and state."[24] The American version is a reaction against all forms of modernity perceived to be caused by a satanic conspiracy to undermine Christianity and the traditional national values believed to stem from it. Modernity is in fact a creation of the ultimate secular force, capitalism; yet Rightists are unwilling to say that business is satanic. Nor will they entertain the thought that a combination of fervent religious faith, unquestioning patriotism, and belief in a superior national destiny may breed a fanaticism that is intolerant and even idolatrous. Nor do they concede that large numbers of Americans simply do not share the view that religion and politics can be so easily mixed. Most Americans accept the separation of church and state as part of the social contract between private and public spheres, and they are suspicious of claims to a "biblical covenant" that gives power over others to one segment of the spectrum of Christianity.

THE QUEST FOR REDEMPTION

Ultimately, the romantic political vision of the Christian Right, as with many of the congregations of the electronic TV church, is that social and political problems can be handled only by "the godly." Small wonder, then, that there are a longing and a search for a tested heroic leader who will emerge from the shadows to redeem a fallen nation. Armed with a sense of righteousness and a holy agenda—so goes the wishful thinking—the leader enacts a drama of purification aimed at nothing less than the integration of American society into a sacred community. The scenario is simple: Identify, punish, and purge agents of Satan from our midst; and complete the moral drama with a sense of restoration through purification of thought and deed, all happily enforced through "godly legislation." The desire for a redeemer with the heroic qualities of zealotry in pursuit of a godly calling and commitment to rule as a "rod of iron" on behalf of the holy doctrines of the evangelical elect is seductively tempting. But it is seductive in a demonic way for realizing that vision of a Christian America would require a commitment to power and to political idolatry beyond the scope and restraints of either the Bible or the Constitution.

Segments of the Christian Right thought they had found such a leader in Lt. Col. Oliver North. In 1988, Jerry Falwell brought North to Liberty University to honor him with an honorary doctor of humanities. North spoke to the enthusiastic assembly (after the singing of "The Marine's Hymn") standing in front of a huge American flag. Falwell introduced him as a "true American hero" and compared his ordeal to that of Christ, saying, "We serve a Savior who [also] was indicted." Falwell initiated a petition drive to urge the president to pardon North for any illegalities connected with trading arms for American hostages, covert arms sales, and covert aid to Nicaraguan Contras. The televangelist applauded efforts to get North to run for public office. On the "Old Time Gospel Hour" Falwell noted that North was born in a small American town, had grown up with solid American values, had served his country with valor, had undergone a conversion to Christ, and had zealously obeyed a "higher law" by defying Congress in fighting godless communism—all essential ingredients for a fantastic zealous redeemer hero. If North will prove to be savior of Christian America, only time will tell. But for the moment, many of the Christian Right thought that they had found their man.

Fantasies of a purified and perfected Christian America die hard. And the fantasy of a Christian "shining city upon a hill" remains a shimmering ideal even as the processes of secularization inexorably make it a virtual impossibility. Those persons tempted by the desire to impose such a vision should recall what happened to Winthrop's original "city upon a hill":

> Massachusetts failed as a "Model of Christian Charity" at the same time that it achieved worldly success: the generations which followed Winthrop's concerned themselves less and less with the perfection of souls and the achievement of salvation, and what had begun as a community dominated by religious purpose rapidly became a society with a secular orientation. . . . Fifteen years after Winthrop's death, Roger Williams predicted: "Sir, when we that have been the eldest, and are rotting . . . a generation will act, I fear, far unlike the first Winthrops and the Model of Love: I fear that the common Trinity of the world (Profit, Preferment, Pleasure) will be the *Tria omnia*, as in all the world beside . . . that God Land will be (as it is now) as great a God with us English as God Gold was with the Spaniards."[25]

NOTES

1. Roderick P. Hart, *The Political Pulpit* (West Lafayette, IN: Purdue University Press, 1977) discusses the rhetorical dimension of civil religion in the United States. See, too, Russell E. Richey and Donald G. Jones, *American Civil Religion* (New York: Harper & Row, 1974); Cushing Strout, *The New Heavens and the New Earth* (New York: Harper Torchbooks, 1974); Lois P. Zamora, *The Apocalyptic Vision in America* (Bowling Green, OH: Bowling Green University Popular Press, 1982). More theoretical works on religion include Mircea Eliade, *The Sacred and the Profane* (New York: Harcourt, Brace, & World, 1959), and Peter L. Berger, *The Sacred Canopy* (Garden City, NY: Doubleday Anchor, 1969).
2. See Marshal Frady, *Billy Graham: A Parable of American Righteousness* (Boston: Little, Brown, 1979); for Finney, Moody, and Sunday, see Tazelle Frankl, *Televangelism* (Carbondale: Southern Illinois University Press, 1987), pp. 23–61; see also Robert Bahr, *Least of All Saints: The Story of Aimee Semple McPherson* (Englewood Cliffs, NJ: Prentice-Hall, 1979).
3. The figures are from "TV Preachers on the Rocks," *Newsweek* (July 11, 1988): 26–28.
4. Various writers have cast doubt on the existence of an evangelical community that thinks and votes alike: Peter G. Horsfield, *Religious Television: The American Experience* (White Plains, NY: Longman, 1984); Jeffrey K. Hadden and Charles E. Swann, *Prime Time Preachers* (Reading, MA: Addison-Wesley, 1981); George Marsden, *Fundamentalism and American Culture* (New York: Oxford University Press, 1980); Perry Deane Young, *God's Bullies: Power Politics and Religious Tyranny* (New York: Holt, Rinehart and Winston, 1982).
5. Frankl, *Televangelism,* pp. 147–151.
6. Franklin B. Krohn, "The Language of Television Preachers: The Marketing of Religion," *Et cetera: A Review of General Semantics* 38 (1981): 55.
7. See the profiles in Marshall Fishwick and Ray B. Browne, eds., *The God Pumpers: Religion in the Electronic Age* (Bowling Green, OH: Bowling Green State Univer-

sity Popular Press, 1987); on Falwell, see Frances Fitzgerald, *Cities on a Hill: A Journey through Contemporary American Cultures* (New York: Simon & Schuster, 1986).

8. Donald Horton and R. Richard Wohl, "Mass Communication and Para-Social Interaction: Observations on Intimacy at a Distance," *Psychiatry* 19 (1956): 215–229.

9. *Newsweek,* "TV Preachers," p. 28.

10. Arbitron figures, cited in *Newsweek,* "TV Preachers," p. 26.

11. ABC News poll, cited in Everett C. Ladd, *The Ladd 1988 Election Update* 1 (1988): 2.

12. Pat Robertson with Bob Slosser, *The Secret Kingdom* (Nashville, TN: Thomas Nelson, 1982).

13. This criticism is developed by Neil Postman, *Amusing Ourselves to Death* (New York: Penguin Books, 1986), pp. 114–124.

14. William G. McLoughlin, "Pietism and the American Character," in H. Cohen, ed., *The American Experience: Approaches to the Study of the United States* (Boston: Houghton Mifflin, 1968), p. 44.

15. Frank W. Oglesbee, "The Devil, You Say? Back-Masking in Contemporary Christian Music," paper presented to the Popular Culture Association Annual Meeting (April 1987).

16. Ernest G. Bormann, *The Force of Fantasy: Restoring the American Dream* (Carbondale: Southern Illinois University Press, 1985), p. 17.

17. The Falwell quotation is from Eileen Ogintz, "Evangelists Seek Political Clout," *Chicago Tribune,* August 31, 1980, Sec. 2, p. 1–2; on national redemption, see Carol Flake, *Redemptorama: Culture, Politics, and the New Evangelicalism* (New York: Penguin Books, 1985), pp. 215–239.

18. Gary DeMar, *God and Government: A Biblical and Historical Study* (Atlanta: American Vision Press, 1982), pp. ix, x, 5, 18, 33, 172.

19. Tim LaHaye, *The Battle for the Mind* (Old Tappan, NJ: Fleming H. Revell, 1980), pp. 9–10.

20. Ronnie Dugger, "Does Reagan Expect a Nuclear Armageddon?" *Washington Post,* April 8, 1984, p. C-1.

21. On the holocaust fantasy see the publication *Christian News* (New Haven, MO: Lutheran News, Inc., Herman Otten, Publisher).

22. Corwin Smidt, "Evangelicals in Presidential Elections: A Look at the 1980s," *Election Politics* 5: 2 (Spring 1988): 2–11; and Smidt, "Evangelicals and the 1984 Election: Continuity or Change?" *American Politics Quarterly* 15 (1987): 419–444.

23. David Baisiger, *Presidential Biblical Scoreboard* (Spring 1988), published by Biblical News Service.

24. Martin E. Marty, "Fundamentalism Reborn: Faith and Fanaticism," *Saturday Review* 7 (new series) (May 1980): 37.

25. Lawrence J. Towner, "John Winthrop, a Model of Christian Charity," in *An American Primer,* ed. Daniel J. Boorstin (Chicago: University of Chicago Press, 1966), pp. 23–24.

CHAPTER 10

Devils and Demons
The Group Mediation of Conspiracy

On November 22, 1963, the nation was stunned by the news that the young and vigorous President John F. Kennedy had been assassinated in downtown Dallas. Police arrested a suspect named Lee Harvey Oswald. He too was felled by a killer. Subsequently, a commission investigated the assassination and concluded that Oswald was guilty and had acted alone, but questions lingered. Many people were not satisfied with the possibility that a single, deranged individual could so randomly alter the course of history. A large body of literature, a movie entitled *Executive Action*, and TV docudramas emerged to feed one of humankind's most durable fantasies: that things are not what they seem, that events such as the Kennedy assassination are not random events, that such an act must be the work of an elaborate plot masterminded from some hidden conspiracy. As evidenced by the spate of TV shows and written features marking the 25th anniversary of the Kennedy assassination, the fact that no conclusive evidence has ever been produced linking Oswald to a larger conspiracy has little relevance. Many people still believe that he acted on the directions of a secret cabal—the Soviets, the Cubans, the Mafia, right-wing tycoons, you name it, even his successor, Lyndon Johnson.

This is not to say that there are never conspiracies in history, but those persons who think that everything that happens is engineered by a conspiracy succumb to "smoke-fire" logic. For the conspiratorial mind-set, there is no possibility that Lee Harvey Oswald could have acted alone. For them to make sense out of Kennedy's death, Oswald *must* have been part of some grand design or evil scheme. Any coincidental or strange facts surrounding him and the assassination are smoke that proves the existence of conspiratorial fire.

Conspiracy theories are a form of popular history based on a fantasy of hidden determination: that events are caused by the manipulations of hidden and powerful elites who control or influence the course of history to their own selfish advantage. The recurring fantasy of historical change simply ignores the apparent multiplicity of factors that seem to affect social developments. Building such gothic castles in the air may be the result of a too-vivid imagination; nevertheless, it is a popular way of giving structure and meaning to a world that seems complex and unfathomable. Conspiracy theories are part of our fantastic knowledge, allowing people to share with others their understanding of what's *really* going on.

Because many people are skeptical about the validity of such theories, those persons drawn to conspiracy notions tend to seek like-minded people willing to share the fantasy. For many of us, political reality consists of the palpable and immediate events we read about in the papers or see on TV—the interplay of parties and interests, the coming and going of leaders, deals, speeches, and conflicts. Groups of people who believe in a conspiracy behind the apparent have mediated a political reality among themselves that conjures up a shadowy but unseen world that guides for its own purposes the world we see. Even though government seems to be conducted in some measure in the open, with powerful leaders identifiable, for believers in conspiracies really important matters are decided in unknown settings by parasitic and venal powers that do not want their complicity known. This shared conviction gives believers a sense of their own moral and epistemological superiority. A member of a formally constituted group that believes in a conspiracy theory (such as the John Birch Society, the Liberty Lobby, or the "Larouchies") or an informal gathering of like-minded friends can feel morally righteous in their joint identification of evil. Since "We" alone know the awful truth of the extent of the perversity, we can define ourselves as the group of the good and wise who will expose and someday defeat the infamy. We can also see ourselves as alone possessing a knowledge of the wheels within wheels that explains what is really going on; the vast uninformed majority is in the dark.

We cannot here define the psychological frame of mind that leads people to conspiracy fantasies. (Perhaps in some cases pathologies are at work.) We can, however, speculate. For many people, the world they experience through the media is both complicated to the point of incomprehensibility and fearfully out of control to the point of chaos. Instinctively believing that there must be a way to explain the perplexing course of events and that some force must be in control, they project on some group, real or imagined, the power to control from behind the scenes. In their fantasies, they imagine a lurid melodrama of illegitimate and venal power exercised by a group to which they attribute a wide variety of negative traits. If the country is going to hell, then someone must be responsible and because the visible people of power seem ordinary enough, real power must be secretly exercised by hidden powers. History must be a grand conspiracy of the immoral few against the moral many. Those who think they have discovered the hidden truth of history acquire a sense of righteousness and mission, to expose and defeat the evil designs of the conspirators. Persons who feel powerless and on the fringe of mainstream politics may well be drawn to affiliate with a group that elaborates a fantasy satisfying to those longing to believe. In some cases, participation in such fringe groups may merely function to soothe anxieties by making them feel moral and knowledgable. Fantasizing about world power is heady stuff, however, and may have more drastic consequences.

To understand the appeal of conspiracy theories, we must make a distinction between political ideology and political folklore. A political ideology is an articulated and abstract perspective on the political world, elaborated for forensic political debate and involving a program of action. We expect mainstream conservatives and liberals in America to espouse an ideology that formulates what they believe government is and should do. Most people, however, do not have an ideology in this restricted sense. Their ideas about politics more likely stem from everyday sources—conversations, gossip, rumors, groups, tabloids, tracts, popular media, and so on—not abstract doctrines. A lot of what people believe about politics is folklore, popularly derived ideas and images of politics that are diffuse and transitory. Conspiracy theories are part of our political folklore and are expressed through informal channels of communication as a popular explanation of what's happening in the world. Persons drawn to conspiracy notions articulated by a group may well have been exposed to folkish expressions that make belief congenial. If we hear and accept prejudices against Jews, for example, then we are likely to be more receptive to popular theories that there exists an international Jewish conspiracy undermining our values or possessions. The Nazis articulated in their party ideology the culpability of this nonexistent Jewish conspiracy. The power of the fantasy derived from the exposure of millions of Germans to popular prejudices against Jews, which made many Germans receptive to such nonsense in threatening times. Popular prejudice combined with Nazi ideology to produce a potent fantasy that led to a policy of mass murder. Conspiratorial folklore was not ever, nor is it now, just idle talk, for it has the potential to introduce into politics the spectre of demons.[1]

THE DEMONIC MELODRAMA IN THE POPULAR MIND

A wag once remarked that the Genesis account of mankind's first family must be true because it is all such a bad melodrama that no one could possibly have made it up. True or not, it has a powerful grip on many people, not only those in the Judeo-Christian tradition. Many other religious, economic, and political movements have drawn on this simple and powerful myth to cast themselves as the heroes in a mighty historical struggle pitting good and evil, the forces of the godly against the forces of the ungodly. This story, with its roots in the apocalyptic thought of the ancient Middle East, still colors the politics of the region with the belief in divine destiny to defeat one's enemies in a holy war, a view shared by orthodox Moslems and Jews. In St. Augustine's formulation, Christian history is a cosmic drama of a Manichean struggle between the children of light and the children of darkness culminating in an apocalyptic *dénouement,* namely, the triumph of righteousness and the defeat and punishment of organized evil. In the biblical version, the demonic forces that subvert and destroy good are agents of a satanic conspiracy. Since these satanic agents are ingenious and energetic, they can be defeated only by righteous vigilance and militance that identify and thwart their lure among the unwary. Even though the struggle is fearful, at the end of the history the victory of good will be complete and final. In sum, for those of whatever belief who share such visions, history is literally a fight against the demonic.

The appeal of this story is evidenced by the fact that it is not confined to any one doctrine but has been adopted, perhaps quite subconsciously, by groups other than Christians. For example, one of the major political movements of the past hundred years has been communism. Marxist communism, both out of power and in, is a movement with an elaborate ideology and policy goals deriving from an articulate philosophy. But the appeal of communism surely is in part because of the power of the story it tells, which is an elaborate historical drama of class conflict between evil masters and virtuous workers, personified as "My Lord Capital" and "The Collective Worker." The respective personifications correspond with the ancient forces of conspiratorial darkness and the oppressed force of common virtue. The power exerted by conspiratorial forces against mankind is unfathomable, yet there works a mysterious providential force (dialectical materialism) that ensures the ultimate triumph of the proletariat over evil capitalism. The triumph is a happy ending to history's long drama.[2]

Whatever secular or sacred form it takes, the essence of the group fantasy at work in such stories is that history is conspiracy. Christian or Moslem, Jew or gentile, communist or Nazi, nationalist or internationalist—all imagine that they are involved in an epic struggle against an unregenerate enemy, eternally cunning and resourceful, and with whom compromise is impossible, even fatal. Thus, politics is not a cold conflict over mere money, territory, and power. Rather, political realities mediated by groups believing in conspiratorial theories reflect a moral struggle of lofty principles threatened by incarnate evil, a conspiracy so vast and overwhelming that only a concerted effort as dedicated and ruthless as the demons themselves can defeat it. Here is an eternal contest of the angelic against the demonic: The evil that is in "Them" is hidden and must be discovered and exposed; the evil that is in "Us" is of "Them," threatening "Us" with possession by "Them." Both evils, in "Them" and "Us," must be exorcised. (Compare this with the alien fantasy in Hollywood movies of the 1950s as discussed in Chapter 5.)

In the medieval Christian version of the story, for example, various figures were identified as the Antichrist who led the infamy on Earth. People created and shared elaborate fantasies about demons of the enchanted world—societies of witches, witches' Sabbaths, devil possession, the ritual sacrifice of Christian virgins. Community guardians held inquisitions, pogroms, and other forms of persecution to root out such demons, even though the demonology was the product of vivid and demented fantasies, not demonstrable fact. The accused executed in the infamous Salem witch trials, for instance, were social scapegoats, conveniently labeled as demonic agents in an atmosphere of social change and hysteria. Long after, in the 20th century in Josef Stalin's Soviet Union—allegedly ruled by a secular and scientific ideology—purge trials branded prominent Bolsheviks as enemies of the state, agents of foreign satanic nations with powers and designs no less demonic than the witches of old. Indeed, in the United States after World War II, various congressional committees, caught up in the Red fantasy of the time, labeled witnesses as "communists," a stigma accepted as no less satanic than those used to brand supposed demons in earlier inquisitions. The political community in power labeled and persecuted victims as living proof of the existence of satanic powers in one case and conspiratorial subversion in the other.[3]

In recent centuries, popular conspiracy theories have become more secular and earthbound, although still retaining the power of the old story of the contest of cosmic forces of good and evil in an apocalyptic struggle to the death. No matter what form the tale may take, it still is a variation on the original *demonic melodrama.* Each variation on the demonic tale has standard features: The characters are representations of good and evil, and the plot unfolds the intense peril of the possible victory of evil, holds out a sentimental faith in the triumph of good, and appeals to popular desire for sensational and even lurid adventure, mystery, romance, and nightmare. In conspiracy tales throughout the ages, the adventure is the heroic quest to defeat demonic powers; the mystery is the recognition and exposure of a secret cabal; the romance is the triumph of cherished values over sinister expediency; the nightmare is the monstrosity of the evil that threatens. The demonic melodrama of conspiracy has breathtaking scope and eternal appeal.[4]

If such folktales were just idle conversation, they could do no harm. Unfortunately, some people believe that conspiracy fantasies explain what's happening in the world. Somewhere, someone is pulling the strings behind the scenes, and "We" (adherents of conspiratorial political realities) know who it is. As an example of the consequences of conspiratorial beliefs, consider the venerable myth of the international Jewish conspiracy that has persisted through the centuries. Originating in the religious anti-Semitism of Christian Europe, the recurrent fantasy of a Zionist conspiracy consists of several themes: a secret league of Jewish bankers and financiers; diabolical ritual practices that rededicate Jews to the cause of world domination; secret cabalistic themes in Jewish theology that unite conspirators. No innocent folktale, this. Recall that the Nazis used the fantasy of international Jewry as the explanation for their losing World War I and the subsequent economic deprivation. Anti-Semites concocted bogus documents such as the infamous forgery *The Protocols of the Elders of Zion* that "proved" the existence of the conspiracy, thus justifying punishment of the Jews. Hitler once remarked, "Behind England stands Israel and behind France and behind the United States."[5] Wherever there is some major social change that threatens vested interests in the world, there is likely to appear an updated version of the well-worn Jewish conspiracy.

People caught up in social and political movements frequently find solace in conspiratorial theories. Feeling powerless, they join others in a search for the cause of their powerlessness. They find it in a powerful force inimical to popular interests. Once movement members identify the conspiratorial enemy, they associate with the conspiracy all the negative and fearful attributes traditionally associated with devils and demons. That accomplished, the members of the political group combating conspiracy seek perfection, but a strange sort of perfection. As noted earlier, the demonic melodrama casts "Us" as the soldiers in the Great Cause, the defense of good and right; and it casts "Them" as the perfected opposite, a form of pure corruption and malevolence. For instance, Nazi rhetoric perfected the image of Nazis as the bearers of "Aryan" racial purity and the bringers of the "Thousand Year Reich," and equally perfected the negative image of the Jew as the polluted and corrupted inferior enemy.

Perfection of the enemy produces a paradox. On the one hand, the enemy is inferior to "Us," for our superior goodness and purity of motives places "Us" above "Them." On the other hand, the enemy is cunning and mendacity perfected—an awesome, albeit inferior, opponent. Hence, unless "We" superiors are eternally vigilant, "They" will get the upper hand, making "Them" superior, "Us" inferior. Thus, the perfection principle leads to demonic irony. The conspiracy is of such magnitude and strength that it must be fought on its own terms—that is, with techniques of cunning, mendacity, corruption, and malevolence—lest pure good succumb to pure evil. This justifies the forces of good using the tactics of the demonic, fighting fire with fire to be equal to the task. Ironically, the good must imitate evil by being as ruthless as the unprincipled enemy. Why? To conquer the enemy and then to advance superior moral and political principles! Indeed, many crusaders against conspiracy admire the amoral ruthlessness of the fantasized enemy. Satan's hordes, Jews, Masons, the Papacy, whoever—crusaders perceive them as more disciplined, dedicated, and single-minded than "Us," endangered as "We" are by lack of vigilance, purpose, and zeal. Thus, the Jesuits tried to be more ardent and merciless than Satan's hordes, the Nazis more ruthless than the Jews, the anticommunist more persecutory than the communist.

The rhetorical vision of those who believe in conspiracy views of history and of politics receives substance in a wide assortment of well-developed theories. However, all such theories assume that what people see on the surface is not what is "really" going on. Indeed, surface events, as described in news accounts or in scholarly works, are but diversions intended by conspirators to hide from the populace their nefarious efforts to control politics for their own evil ends. In a world that cannot be taken at face value, how then do people know what reality is, what to believe? The answer to that question is a leap of faith, belief in the conspiracy, belief that "They" are out to get "Us." Let us now consider how people have made that leap of faith in America, both in the past and in contemporary politics.

THEY'RE HERE: CONSPIRACIES AND THE AMERICAN POLITICAL TRADITION

Contemporary political groups of the Right or Left whose members crusade against conspiracies continue a long tradition in America of mediating political realities through demonic melodramas. Historian Richard Hofstadter has called this the paranoid style in American politics. He refers not so much to the clinical, pathological sense of a paranoid and persecution mania as to a more generalized perception of the way the political world works and the melodramatic features attributed to it.[6] Americans have been receptive to conspiracy theories throughout history. They are adept at creating rhetorical visions of conspiracies. From the beginnings of the Republic, pamphlets and books exposed the alleged conspiratorial activities of Catholics, Masons, and other groups. John Robison's book on "the Illuminati conspiracy" in 1797 was an early example.[7] Political groups, often with patriotic or nativist impulses, constructed fantasies of conspiracies; the anti-Masonic party, the Know Nothings, and the Klu Klux Klan espoused beliefs in foreign cabals bent on controlling the United States.

The tradition received considerable impetus with the advent of the Soviet Union as a world power and the spread of communism as a 20th-century political ideology. Communism, of course, did espouse world revolution and calculated means to obtain power. In the demonology of many Americans, communists have replaced Masons, Catholics, and Jews as the source of the grand conspiracy of tradition. Reds were an easily perfectible enemy. Centered in a vast and mysterious land (Russia), advocating values that were economically and socially repugnant, politically aggressive and calculating, alleged to commit atrocities and enslavements—all in all, the communists made a good candidate for demonic conspiracy. After World Wars I and II, America had two Red scares fed by monstrous fears of domestic communism. When President Ronald Reagan in the early 1980s accused the Soviet Union of being "the focus of evil in the modern world," he but drew on a rich tradition of Red baiting.

Out of the Red scare following World War II, the rhetorical vision of the American Right evolved. Like the witches of Salem in the 17th century, Red enemies seemed everywhere. Rather than explain the widening appeal of communism as being derived from long-range historical forces, the fears of the Right dramatized the doctrine as an insidious conspiracy with tentacles reaching to the heart of America. Senator Joseph McCarthy accused Secretary of State George Marshall in 1951 of being part of a "conspiracy so immense, an infamy so black, as to dwarf any in the history of man."[8] J. Edgar Hoover of the Federal Bureau of Investigation (FBI), always quick to pick up on a popular issue of the moment, abandoned the fight against organized crime for the fight against domestic communism.[9] The scare gradually abated as a popular concern, but the fears it generated added impetus to the zeal of persons attracted to conspiracy theories. The Red menace and godless communism helped to create and sustain such groups as the John Birch Society, the Liberty Lobby, the Christian Anti-Communist Crusade, and others. In the best tradition of conspiratorial rhetorical visions, these groups developed distinctive theories of a demonic conspiracy and elaborate and intricate theories of political conspiracy. In any consideration of the political realities of conspiracy theorists in America, these groups must be considered.

The membership corps of groups such as the John Birch Society have facile, complex explanations for why the political world they fancy exists. Monolithic communism, they argue, is a secular but demonic force, a perfected enemy of uncanny guile and zeal, whose historic scheme is to undermine the United States by isolating it abroad and subverting it domestically from within. The communist conspiracy, directed from Moscow, has had such success that most of the world is, or soon will be, in the Red orbit, they say. Only a few staunchly anticommunist states—Chile, Taiwan, South Africa—have stood firm against the tide, but they, too, are threatened. Here at home communist infiltration into the government was rife, or so it seemed to conspiracy theorists in the 1950s and 1960s who even thought that such figures as President Dwight Eisenhower, Chief Justice Earl Warren, and Secretary of State John Foster Dulles were conscious agents of international communism. Leaders of major church bodies, corporate and banking executives, mass-media moguls, and labor unions were also included in the conspiracy. In 1973 Robert Welch, the founder of the John Birch Society, said that the "scoreboard shows that the United States is 60 to 80 percent influenced by communism."[10] Every major policy innovation—Medicare, the Occupational Safety and Health Administration, environmental protection—existed in part to expand government control and the overall aims of the conspiracy. Every foreign policy involvement aided only the communists. America fought the Vietnam War, for example, to help the communist cause in Asia. Every moment for social change (e.g., civil rights) and every popular fad (e.g., rock 'n' roll) were communist-inspired, designed to undermine order and morality.[11] Thus was communism a perfect enemy for a conspiratorial rhetorical vision: a force with demonic overtones, conspiratorial ubiquity, a historic mission, and the power to manipulate events, institutions, and elites.

The original Bircher rhetorical vision was "documented" in John A. Stormer's widely circulated *None Dare Call It Treason*.[12] Published during the Goldwater movement of 1964, it codified the fantasy of widespread communist influence in virtually every facet of American life. Throughout the book, the formula is the same: Some area of life—churches, media, unions, government—is infiltrated by communists. The infiltrators are readily identifiable as former members of procommunist organizations or supporters of procommunist positions. The infiltration explains why social changes have been inimical to U.S. interests. Good people get duped by communist cunning into supporting programs that the Kremlin wants. Villains worm their way into positions of power to subvert institutions and morals. For example, theologians with "records of support for communist causes" advocate destructive changes in the Revised Standard Version of the Bible.[13] Mental health programs are not really designed to help the mentally ill but to "re-educate the world's population using psychological procedures to create a new breed of amoral men who will accept a one-world socialistic government. They hold the weapon of commitment to a mental institution over the heads of those 'reactionaries' who rebel at accepting the 'new social order'."[14] The private, elite foreign policy organization, the Council on Foreign Relations, controls American foreign policy and aims at a world government that will expand the Communist empire.[15] And so it goes. It is a conspiracy of design in which each part fits the blueprint for takeover and control. "The communists," we are told, "are extremely close to total victory."[16] The demonic threat is imminent; only a holy crusade can defeat it now.

In the 1960s the Birchite conspiracy fantasy grew more ambitious and inclusive. Birch literature integrated the communist menace into a larger and longer-running conspiracy. Robert Welch noted:

> In the upper circles of this conspiracy, there is not the slightest trace of noble purpose, or of the misguided idealism by which members of the lower echelons are sometimes deceived. There is only sordid self-interest of the most Faustian variety. For two centuries ruthlessly ambitious criminals, whom we shall call the "Insiders" have been helping themselves, and each other, to the prestige and wealth and power which were the only real objectives of their lives. They have been held together in all of these activities, however, and their efforts have been given coherence and direction, by their concerted dedication to the ultimate goal of world leadership for the "Insiders" of a later day. And that day is now almost upon us.[17]

The "Insiders" are an international elite attempting to control the world. It can be traced at least to the Bavarian Order of the Illuminati, formed in 1776 and dissolved by the Bavarian government in 1785. (American Opinion Bookstores of the John Birch Society carry reprints of Robison's 1797 book on the Illuminati.) Birch researchers have tried to document the activities of the Illuminati and its founder, Adam Weishaupt. The Order appears to have been an Enlightenment rationalist movement with links to Freemasonry. Both Robison in the 18th century and Welch in the 20th entertain the fantasy of moral degradation as both practice and goal of the Order. Robison saw the Illuminati as "a libertine, anti-Christian movement, given to the corruption of women, the cultivation of sensual pleasures, and the violation of property rights."[18] Welch charged that Weishaupt seduced the sister of another leader of the Order and then had her murdered.[19] Such gossipy tidbits about the fantasized immoralities of the enemy provide a recurrent theme in conspiracy theories, dating at least to the medieval fantasies of orgiastic activities during the witches' Sabbaths.

In the Birch theory, the Illuminati survive and prosper, all in virtual secrecy, save for a few who see through their scheme. The Illuminati were behind the French Revolution, hired Karl Marx to write *The Communist Manifesto,* engineered Bismarck's social legislation in Germany, and brought about the Federal Reserve system, the graduated income tax, and the direct election of U.S. senators—all to further nefarious schemes. They financed the Bolshevik Revolution in Russia, planned all the major wars of the 20th century, started the United Nations for ultimate purposes of a world government, are responsible for every great upheaval, including the civil rights movement and assassinations of key political figures. Their domestic agenda in the United States is subversive, to corrupt and eventually control through a variety of means, including fluoridating water, destroying religion, teaching socialism in the schools, presenting morally undermining fare in the movies, music, and other entertainment media, managing the news, inflating currency, even spreading disease. (Russian flu was germ warfare!) The Illuminati success is truly fantastic, a triumph of secret organizational manipulation and co-optation.

This international power elite has no national or ideological loyalties. Nations are destroyed to realize conspiratorial goals; ideological agendas are simply tools in the conquest. In the widely circulated update of the conspiracy theory, Gary Allen's *None Dare Call It Conspiracy,* the author wrote that "finance capitalism is the anvil and communism is the hammer to conquer the world."[20] The Council on Foreign Relations remains the key American institution for the conspiracy, but international bankers, such as Rockefeller and Rothschild, are now at the top of the great conspiracy. The conspirators (dubbed Bilderbergers, after the hotel where the Council on Foreign Relations first met in Holland in 1954) meet annually in secret. They include politicians, industrialists, intellectuals, and others united in covert loyalty to the conspiracy. The meetings plot the latest moves. That being the case, conspiracy theorists have no difficulty linking subsequent world events to the grand design. For instance, when President Richard Nixon introduced wage and price controls in 1971, conspirators received advance notice; they used such "insider" information to profit from the policy move. Every recent American president, apparently, from Woodrow Wilson on (with the exception of Warren Harding and Calvin Coolidge), has been under conspiratorial control. Thus, President Carter was "taken inside" by the Rockefellers while still governor of Georgia; Reagan "sold out" at an unspecified time.

The institution that is key to the conspiracy is the Trilateral Commission formed in 1972. The commission is, in the views of many conspiratorial theorists, the foreign ministry of the Council on Foreign Relations. It carves out spheres of influence around the world. When Jimmy Carter became president, his appointment of people with Trilateral Commission ties to high office fed the fantasies of conspiracy theorists. Although President Reagan was not a member, Vice President (later President) Bush was, as was Secretary of Defense Caspar Weinberger and others in Reagan's administration. Bush and Secretary of State Alexander Haig attended a meeting of the Trilateral Commission the night before an attempt on President Reagan's life in March 1981, stirring speculation that the power elite wanted him dead. Notable American members have included Henry Cabot Lodge, Margaret Mead, Edward Kennedy, Marlon Brando, Otis Chandler (publisher of the *Los Angeles Times*), and William Paley of CBS. Important foreign leaders involved in the conspiracy include such strange bedfellows as Nikita Krushchev, Mao Tse-Tung, Josef Tito, Charles de Gaulle, Fidel Castro, and other closet conspirators.[21]

Conspiracy theory casts U.S. Senator Edward Kennedy as one of the ultimate villains, a man conspirators hoped to make president of the United States. Zad Rust's book *Teddy Bare* says that "the Force of Darkness" conspired to cover up the Chappaquiddick affair because Kennedy is "one of the prominent operators chosen by the Hidden Forces" to lead us (returning to a traditional image) to "the enthronement of the Antichrist."[22] There is often speculation among Birchers that events occur because of internal conflicts and intrigues *within* the conspiracy. Thus, two Kennedys (John and Robert) were killed for reasons internal to the conspiracy. Watergate occurred because of a split within the conspiracy. Even wars, the speculation goes, occur because of internal conspiracy disputes.

The conspiratorial elite approach ever nearer to victory. The John Birch Society stands alone—with the heroic symbol of John Birch, a missionary in China, who was apparently executed by the communists—as a strong force with a sense of crusading rectitude. The Society alone recognizes the immediacy of the climactic apocalypse, the approaching secular Armaggedon in which the Grand Conspiracy will emerge victor or vanquished. Action alone will defeat the enemy—educating youth to the "truth" in summer camps, becoming active in local politics, holding seminars and lectures to educate the public, and so forth. The contemporary political world is drama in which the hidden villains must be unmasked if the great mass of fools (the public) are to see the existence and perfidy of the conspiracy.

How do we evaluate such a grandiose theory? As with any fantasy, it feeds on assertions that seem true enough or are at least credible: It is true that there is an international power elite; there are secret meetings of international figures in secluded spas and nobody really knows what is discussed; there is a Trilateral Commission with ties in high places. But that this constitutes proof of a "conspiracy" is debatable. How a vast conspiracy could make such gains and exercise such power without anyone ever really breaking the silence is puzzling. The theory assumes a causal and controlling force in history. Yet it is equally plausible that the world is disorganized with no one in charge. If a conspiracy is running the world, people might well say it is doing a pretty bad job of it! If it is not, that may be even worse, proving no one can deal with the vast problems besetting humankind.

We can understand the appeal of such a theory to many persons. Persons drawn to conspiracy theories do not fit any particular psychological profile, so the appeal of a conspiracy theory cannot be explained solely as mass paranoia. People gather in groups, we have said, and through fantasizing create a satisfying rhetorical vision of the world. For a variety of reasons, persons attracted to political groups crusading against conspiracies have developed a common fantasy about the political world. It provides them with a powerful dramatic explanatory device. Ernest G. Bormann writes as follows:

> Against the panorama of large events and seemingly unchangeable forces of society at large or of nature the individual often feels lost and hopeless. One coping mechanism is to dream an individual fantasy which provides a sense of meaning and significance for the individual and helps protect him from the pressures of natural calamity and social disaster. The rhetorical vision serves much the same coping function for those who participate in the drama and often with much more force because of the supportive warmth of like-minded companions.[23]

Orrin Klapp, speaking of crusading groups in general, notes that *dramatic rituals* enhance the solidarity and satisfaction of group members.[24] It is likely that an elaborately articulated conspiracy, discussed and applied within the group and disseminated to the world outside, is such a ritual drama. As group members dream a collective fantasy about the conspiratorial structure of the political world, they achieve the kind of satisfaction that theater provides— identification of the nature of the world, personification of roles, and catharsis through the knowledge the play brings.[25] The group dramatizes political reality, giving it a sense of "inside dope" (see Chapter 8), of knowing what's "really" going on, transforming the impersonal world of historical change into an understandable drama, pitting "Us" against those archfiends, "Them," who threaten what "We" believe in. The group can take considerable satisfaction in identifying and personifying itself as the hero of the drama; members can experience a thrill from knowing the true nature—and for some, even the outcome—of the play; and they can share anxieties over the satanic challenge they face.

The John Birch conspiracy theory is a bad melodrama. It is a rhetorical vision in the demonic tradition with the villains clearly unregenerate, even satanic, and morally degraded in every way. The Rockefellers, Kennedys, and other villains could scarcely be more nefarious if they played the vile landlord in a 19th-century stage melodrama. The richest and most privileged men in the world, the greatest beneficiaries of Euro-American capitalism, are ironically the ones who are trying to destroy it. But someday the first shall be last, and the last first. The moral force of ordinary people will topple the temples of Mammon, slay the Philistines, and restore the moral community. The *adventure* of the melodrama is the quest to expose and defeat the conspiracy; the *mystery* is who is in the conspiracy and what they are up to; the *romance* is the preservation of the values of family, church, town; the *nightmare* is the possibility of the conspiracy gaining control of the world. The *logic* of the conspiracy drama impels it toward a *deñouement* very soon, the children of light versus the children of darkness; and the *perfection* of the conspiracy's villainy and the extent of its power lead to the advocacy of demonic means to fight against its world; the saviors, imbued with the logic of their own rhetorical vision, will become as demonic as those they fantasize as the conspiratorial enemy. Armed with rhetorical vision, political groups sometimes gain the power to impose their fantasies on reality whether they are true or not. The logic of the vision leads to a quest for redemption through the victimization and purging of the conspiracy; reality must live up to the logic of the mediating rhetorical vision.

OLD WINE, NEW BOTTLES: CONTEMPORARY RESPONSES TO CONSPIRACIES

The John Birch Society and similar anticonspiratorial groups carried the torch against devils, demons, and hidden monsters in the 1960s and 1970s. As indicated earlier, such groups inherited a long tradition of conspiracy fantasy and fighting in the American political tradition. In the 1980s they were joined by new groups sharing conspiratorial visions. These emergent groups espoused a blend of tastes from previous conspiracy theories, combined them with contemporary vintages, and bottled them as another explanation of what was wrong in the world, why, and what to do about it. If they differed from their predecessors, it was in the breadth and outrageous quality of their claims. A few anticonspiratorial groups advanced their views through propaganda, fund-raising, and political agitation. Others, as we shall see, took more extreme measures.

Is the Queen in Her Counting House?: The "LaRouchies"

Among the less violently inclined of the most prominent new political groups elaborating a conspiracy theory were the followers of Lyndon LaRouche, called in news accounts the "LaRouchies." LaRouche, a former Marxist, recruited a small but dedicated following. LaRouchies distributed literature at airports, raised funds, and ran candidates for public offices. Elements of the LaRouche doctrine are familiar conspirational fantasy. Once again the Rockefeller-financed Trilateral Commission is at the center of things—the power behind not only all recent American presidential administrations but the world narcotics traffic as well. LaRouche claims that conspirators tried to assassinate him when he exposed their identities. They were "leading scions of the Eastern Establishment banking families . . . the Swiss and British oligarchy, and the Catholic 'black' oligarchy, which has its coordinating center in the Knights of Malta. . . . [T]he Episcopalians were determined to employ the Jews against the LaRouche-led anti-drug campaign." LaRouche forces stood alone against the international conspiracy to spread drugs, understanding the scope of the crime: "[T]he Soviet Union is up to its ears in the spread of the drug trade, and that trade represents one of the ingredients that glues the Trilateral Commission crowd, and the Soviets, into a political alliance. . . . [I]nternational bankers had turned their economies into virtual drug plantations . . . the bankers and the IMF [International Monetary fund] encourage dope growth and traffic." Most astonishingly, one of the key conspirators is Queen Elizabeth of England: "[T]he British monarchy's illegal drug traffic into our nation" is " . . . aided by those leading elements of the Zionist Lobby which have controlled organized crime in the USA and the Caribbean since the early 1920's." We must fight illegal drugs as a "war against Britain, to the purpose of saving our youth and our nation from the destruction the British monarchy has projected for us."[26]

LaRouche sees plots and hidden relationships in many quarters. Henry Kissinger he views as a Soviet agent; bankers from Hong Kong to Zurich "hate him [LaRouche] bitterly, because of the wide circulation of his proposals for establishing a new, gold-reserved-based monetary system"; the International Monetary Fund was the instigator of the AIDS epidemic; the Department of State does "the work of the Soviet empire"; Jesuits, communists, bankers, Establishment bluebloods, Zionists, Episcopalians, drug dealers, liberals and conservatives, the Club of Rome, indeed virtually every major institution is bent on destroying LaRouche and the world. Philospher Bertrand Russell was "the most evil man of the 20th century," because he forged an agreement with the Soviets for British and American power elites "to divide the entire world between two world-empires, the first to be ruled by the wealthy and the powerful financial families of the so-called Liberal Establishments . . . ; the second part of the world-empire, the Russian Empire, would be made much larger than Russia's division of the world negotiated during the war-time Yalta Conference."[27] LaRouche's account of the structure of world power is almost a compendium of all past conspiracy theories. As in the film *Casablanca,* all the usual suspects have been rounded up, and virtually every major world or national institution is complicit. If LaRouche is correct, then Joe McCarthy was right long ago when he envisioned an immense conspiracy and black infamy that dwarfed all previous conspiracies.

Not everyone agrees that the LaRouche fantasy is nothing more than that. In 1986, the Anti-Defamation League (ADL) of B'nai B'rith, which conducts studies of such groups, published a report entitled "The LaRouche Political Cult: Packaging Extremism." They accused LaRouche of perpetuating a "paranoid theory of history" based on a fantastic network of worldwide conspiracies that simply do not exist but that appeal to the gullible and fanatical. They found his worldview to be "bizarre and often incoherent" and his own organization to cloak extremism and character assassination in a "secretive strategy of deception."[28] As if determined to provide unwitting support for the ADL's charges, LaRouche accused them of working with Soviet intelligence, the Reuters News Agency, the FBI, and a host of others to target LaRouche as being behind the assassination of Swedish Prime Minister Palme. All this is "part of the same package" as the Iran-Contra operation. Directing the plot are Department of Justice officials, "the official link to the Moscow Procurator" who "framed" both LaRouche and Austrian President Kurt Waldheim. Justice officials were "attached to the Soviet network of influence now operating inside the Reagan administration" and directed by such tycoons as Armand Hammer, "Lenin's financial agent." The entire directorate is connected to the "European arms-merchants" and "Israeli weapons-suppliers" selling arms to Iran's Khomeni. All this, LaRouche says, "is only the piece of the yarn, which, if pulled continuously, will unravel many things overdue to be brought to the light of day."[29]

If this fantasy is what Richard Hofstadter meant by the paranoid style in American politics, by 1987 Lyndon LaRouche and his followers had much to be paranoid about. He was under investigation by the Federal Election Commission, the Internal Revenue Service, the Secret Service, and the Federal Bureau of Investigation. LaRouche headquarters and operations had been raided by police, he had been declared bankrupt, and he defended himself against charges that zealous followers had bilked large sums of money out of elderly supporters, falsified credit card charges, and had destroyed evidence and obstructed justice. Perhaps much yarn indeed was unraveling. In late 1988 he was convicted and sent to prison.

Surviving the Survival Right

The 1980s witnessed not only the Larouchies but a far more frightening and violent set of crusaders against alleged conspirators, namely, vigilantes associated with the Survival Right. These groups had links to various Klu Klux Klan and neo-Nazi sects but took traditional conspiratorial themes and gave them a new application. Many such groups were located in the Midwest and West, often in areas hit hard by the farm crisis of the decade. For whatever reasons, persons attracted to the movement sequestered themselves in rural communes in Nebraska, Idaho, and elsewhere, developing within the isolated groups an elaborate theory of world conspiracy and racial supremacy.

In one commune in Nebraska, for example, commune leaders required members to listen to tapes spelling out how the U.S. Constitution had been personally revealed by God, how a cabal of international Jews had amended the document in violation of God's law by giving the vote to blacks and women and establishing an income tax, and how "Yahweh our father is at work setting the stage for the final act against the Christ-murdering Jews and their father Satan."[30] There were also required viewings of the movie *Red Dawn* wherein Soviet troops invade the American heartland and establish a Soviet-style state, one opposed by local young people who fight a guerrilla war against it. The Survivalist Right movement spread across the West, sharing a commitment to internal group ideological and behavioral discipline enforced by humiliation, beatings, torture, and even death. In one case a 5-year-old boy was hanged with a dog leash. Members acquired a cache of weapons and money (in some cases by theft) and engaged in violence (including murdering a Denver talkshow host who baited them).

The various neo-Nazi and white supremacist groups within the Survivalist Right hold many tenets of conspiratorial folklore: an international Jewish conspiracy connected to bankers taking over the U.S. government (referred to by one group as the "Zionist Occupied Government"); a belief in white racial superiority and destiny; and an apocalyptic vision of final struggle against evil that is currently underway. These vigilante groups give themselves varied but pretentious titles: Posse Comitatus, The Order, Aryan Nations, The Covenant, the Sword, the Arm of the Lord, the Silent Brotherhood, the Christian Defense League, and the Arizona Patriots. Those of them who are prone to violence are apparently inspired by a fantasy novel, *The Turner Diaries*, a novel that describes a future war by native patriots against the international conspiracy. The novel's episodes include a bombing of the FBI building in Washington, a mortar attack on the "Zionist-held" U.S. Capitol building, and the execution of dozens of prominent Jews and blacks. Whether acting out such a story line or not, many such crusaders have been involved in murders, bank robberies, weapons, heists, and counterfeiting. Plans for violence against the U.S. government are ambitious: According to a federal indictment these plans include murdering federal judges, machine-gun attacks on IRS offices, destroying public utilities and water supplies, and training a guerrilla army in secret camps.[31]

These crusading groups are bound together by a miasma of political fantasies loosely shaping an extremist perspective. There is apparent admiration for Nazism and Hitler. One group, Aryan Nations, has a church in Idaho with a stylized swastika in a stained glass window behind the altar along with romanticized portraits of Hitler and Rudolph Hess in the vestry. Others among the Survivalist Right share a belief called "Identity Christianity," which maintains that the true chosen people are Nordic Caucasians, the "true Jews" who migrated to the British Isles. Those normally known as Jews, says the doctrine, are the descendants of Satan who seduced Eve and produced the lineage of Cain, "the seed of Satan" and the source of all evil. Yet, these "soulless" inferior races, the pseudo-Jews, somehow managed to gain control of the world. Now they are engaged in the struggle to destroy the true Jews. The survivalists will resist by retreating into armed enclaves, then retake the Zionist-controlled world for those of Christian identity. In the mediated political reality of Identity Christianity, Armageddon, which is near, may occur in Nebraska.[32]

The Survivalist Right is in the tradition of American nativism, fantasizing that remote groups and powers are a threat. To defend "the American way," survivalists adopt the Nazi way, promote a bizarre theology, justify criminal actions, and live in isolated paramilitary camps. Recruited largely from areas hit hardest by the farm crisis, they frequently hold bankers responsible for their misfortunes. The potential seductive quality of such a conspiracy fantasy is illustrated by a Lou Harris poll (commissioned by the concerned Anti-Defamation League) in 1986 taken in Nebraska and Iowa. It found that 28 percent of those polled in a representative sample agreed that a "Jewish-inspired conspiracy of international bankers" was causing the farm crisis (32 percent disagreed, 40 percent said they never heard of it).[33] Faced with poverty and powerlessness in the wake of the decline of rural America, conspiracy theories became a way of projecting blame onto a fantasized enemy and reasserting some belief in "native" grass-roots superiority. The rise of the Survivalist Right in these areas of economic depression and social decay remind us that such fantastic folklore is not easily dismissed. Goaded by similar beliefs about Jewish bankers, other extremist groups have secured power in places where similar conditions prevailed.

BAD MELODRAMA AS ENTERTAINING THEATER

The penchant to leap to faith in conspiracy theories is obviously not confined to groups on either right or left of the political spectrum. Our focus in Chapter 9 on doctrines of the Christian Right and in this chapter on those of such rightist groups of recent decades as the John Birch Society, the LaRouchies, and the survivalists is not meant to ignore leftists. There are dedicated and highly ideological leftist groups whose members also fantasize about conspiracies by political elites. Such elites, say group members, prevent intellectuals, the unprivileged, and common folk from achieving their true potential and destinies. Leftist crusaders struggle against a reactionary power elite that includes many of the same culprits that rightists confront—the Trilateral Commission, large banks, international power brokers, multinational corporations, and so on. Like anticonspiracy vigilantes on the Right, they assume that these elites are essentially united behind ulterior aims, goals that exclude or subvert the interests of people outside conspiratorial circles. For conspiracy theorists of all stripes, the people in charge are inherently evil; the powerless identified in conspiracy doctrine as pure are the last hope of the world. Right and Left crusaders share the melodramatic view that truth is forever on the scaffold and mendacity forever on the throne.

As we approach the end of the 20th century, will conspiratorial fantasies increase and, if so, what does that imply? Recent examples suggest a "Yes" to the first question. A controversial former governor of Arizona impeached for campaign irregularities, Evan Meacham, believed that a socialist conspiracy, largely directed by bankers with "foreign entanglements," works behind the scenes to amend the U.S. Constitution and destroy the nation. An aide to the mayor of Chicago with links to black nationalist groups gave public lectures to Louis Farrakhan's Nation of Islam. The aide claimed that there is a powerful international "secret society" whose goal is the oppression of blacks and the creation of a Jewish-run world government; that mandatory schooling is enforced so whites can make money on inoculations and Jewish doctors can inoculate black children with the AIDS virus; and that the conspiracy wants to bankrupt every American city.[34] Clearly, any number of people of any political persuasion can play the conspiracy game. And if the number of people, influential or otherwise, who believe that conspiracy is on the increase, then we can look forward to an era in which conspiratorial fantasies may undermine hopes for political rationality and tolerance. We have seen all too many times how easily the theater of group experience of fantasy becomes the theater of group action. Persons gripped by the self-delusion of conspiracy fight most bitterly against unseen foes and imagined enemies.

The group impulse to dramatize history by transforming it into a grand conspiracy and a struggle of heroes, villains, and fools in a demonic melodrama personalizes, simplifies, and renders understandable confusing and complex contradictory realities. Groups yielding to that impulse explain history in an entertaining way by imbuing it with the attributes of a theatrical play in which history is seen as an uncompromising war in which the source of evil and travail has been unmasked, the causal power has been identified, and the victory or defeat of the conspiratorial enemy is imminent in the apocalyptic present—the closing curtain, the culmination of history. It is good theater even if bad melodrama. To the skeptic, it may all be irrational delusion, but to others, it has considerable appeal.

Philosophers of history vigorously debate how history works. Most speak of history as blind, as a chaotic succession of events over time, as a process of impersonal forces and chance elements that propel history toward no discernible goal. Such a view of history is not too satisfying and not a little frightening. To explain historical chaos as being simply chaos does not appeal to dramatic sensibilities. History is much more understandable, interesting, and exciting if it is a grand romantic melodrama, full of adventure, mystery, peril, and threat and with a moral to the story. Conspiracy theories of devils and demons have all these qualities, qualities that make them and those who believe in them potent mediators of political realities.

NOTES

1. The consequences of belief in the demonic has produced several analyses. See, variously, Robert Jewett, *The Captain America Complex* (Philadelphia: Westminster Press, 1973); Ernest Becker, *Angel in Armor* (New York: George Braziller, 1969); Dan Nimmo and James Combs, *Subliminal Politics* (Englewood Cliffs, NJ: Prentice-Hall, 1980); Lionel Rubinoff, *The Pornography of Power* (New York: Ballantine, 1968); Paul Ricouer, *The Symbolism of Evil* (Boston: Beacon Press, 1967); Stoddard Martin, *Art, Messianism, and Crime: Sade, Wilde, Hitler, Manson* (New York: St. Martin's Press, 1985).

2. Robert Tucker, *Philosophy and Myth in Karl Marx* (Cambridge, MA: Harvard University Press, 1961), pp. 221–224.

3. See Norman Cohn, *The Pursuit of the Millenium* (New York: Oxford University Press, 1970); Hugh Trevor-Roper, *The European Witch-Craze of the 16th and 17th Century and Other Essays* (New York: Harper & Row, 1969); Norman Cohn, *Europe's Inner Demons: An Inquiry Inspired by the Great Witch Hunt* (New York: New American Library, 1977); Michael Kunze, *Highroad to the Stake: A Tale of Witchcraft* (Chicago: University of Chicago Press, 1987); Carlo Ginzburg, *Night Battles: Witchcraft & Agrarian Cults in the Sixteenth and Seventeenth Century* (New York: Penguin Books, 1986); for the post-World War II search for Reds, see Victor S. Navasky, *Naming Names* (New York: Penguin Books, 1981)

4. See Earl F. Bargainnier, "Hissing the Villain, Cheering the Hero: The Social Function of Melodrama" *Studies in Popular Culture* 3 (Spring 1980): 48–56; Northrop Frye, *The Secular Scripture: A Study of the Structure of Romance* (Cambridge, MA: Harvard University Press, 1976).

5. Adolph Hitler, quoted in Herman Rauschning, *The Voice of Destruction* (New York: G.P. Putnam's Sons, 1940), p. 237; Norman Cohn, *Warrant for Genocide: The Myth of the Jewish World-Conspiracy and the Protocols of the Elders of Zion* (New York: Harper & Row, 1969); L. J. Rather, "Disraeli, Freud, and Jewish Conspiracy Theories," *Journal of the History of Ideas* XLVIII: 1 (January–March 1986): 111–131.

6. Richard Hofstadter, *The Paranoid Style in American Politics* (New York: Random House, 1964), pp. 3–40.

7. John Robison, *Proofs of a Conspiracy Against All the Religions and Governments of Europe* (1797).

8. Senator Joseph R. McCarthy, "America's Retreat from Victory," *Congressional Record,* June 14, 1951, 9A Reprint, p. 1.

9. Richard Gid Powers, "J. Edgar Hoover and the Detective Hero," *Journal of Popular Culture* 9, (Fall 1975): 257–258.

10. Phillip Nobile, "Welch Still Sees Lefties on the Right," *Chicago Sun-Times Midwest Magazine,* September 16, 1973, p. 38.

11. Seymour Martin Lipset and Earl Raab, *The Politics of Unreason* (New York: Harper & Row, 1973), pp. 248–287.

12. John A. Stormer, *None Dare Call It Treason* (Florissant, MO: Liberty Bell Press, 1964).

13. Ibid., p. 128.

14. Ibid., p. 155.

15. Ibid., pp. 209–217.
16. Ibid., p. 229.
17. Robert Welch, *Birch Society Bulletin* (July 1968): 4.
18. Hofstadter, *Paranoid Style,* pp. 11, 31–32.
19. Lipset and Raab, *Politics of Unreason,* p. 254.
20. Gary Allen, *None Dare Call It Conspiracy* (Rossmoore, CA: Concord Press, 1971), p. 125.
21. Anthony C. Sultton and Patrick M. Wood, *Trilaterals over Washington* (Phoenix: August Corporation, 1979).
22. Zad Rust, *Teddy Bare* (Boston: Western Islands, 1971), p. x.
23. Ernest G. Bormann, "Fantasy and Rhetorical Vision: The Rhetorical Criticism of Social Reality," in John F. Cragan and Donald C. Shields, eds., *Applied Communication Research: A Dramatistic Approach* (Prospect Heights, IL: Waveland Press, 1981), p. 20.
24. Orrin Klapp, *Collective Search for Identity* (New York: Holt, Rinehart and Winston, 1969) pp. 292–295.
25. See Richard Merelman, "The Dramaturgy of Politics," in James Combs and Michael Mansfield, eds. *Drama in Life* (New York: Hastings House, 1976), pp. 288–289.
26. Lyndon H. LaRouche, Jr., *A Program for America* (Larouche Democratic Campaign, 1985), pp. 176–181.
27. Ibid., pp. 156–158, 235–244.
28. Anti-Defamation League of B'Nai B'Rith, "The Larouche Political Cult: Packaging Extremism" (1986), Kenneth J. Bialkin, Chairman.
29. "Swedish Press Links Moscow to FBI Hounding of LaRouche," *The LaRouche Democratic Campaign,* 1987.
30. James Coates, "Nightmare in Kulo," *Chicago Tribune,* November 16, 1987, Sec. 2, p. 5.
31. James Coates, *Armed and Dangerous: The Rise of the Survival Right* (New York: Hill & Wang, 1987).
32. James Coates, "Faith, Hate Crossbreed," *Chicago Tribune,* July 20, 1986, Sec. 2, pp. 1, 6.
33. James Coates, "Farmers, Jews Join Bias Fight," *Chicago Tribune,* October 23, 1986, Sec. 1, p. 10.
34. See Michael A. Weinstein, "Malign Neglect's Harvest of Bitterness and Resentment," *Chicago Tribune,* May 11, 1988, Sec. 1, p. 19; James Coates, "Governor Steering Arizona to the Right," *Chicago Tribune,* January 11, 1987, p. 17, 24.

CONCLUSION

The Age of Fantasy
Fictions, Facts, and Pipedreams

Miss Sherwin of Gopher Prairie, whom we first encountered in the "Introduction" to this book, was a fictional character. Still, she represents all of us who live in a mediated world. Largely unable or unwilling to experience firsthand and directly the rich complexities of politics, we substitute mass- and group-mediated realities. Like Miss Sherwin, we accept simplifications: Unable to imagine the millions of people who might die in nuclear warfare, we think instead of the loss of cities, "Kansas City," "Chicago," "Washington." And, like Miss Sherwin, we want our expectations fulfilled: Presidential candidates speak of the threat of nuclear war, but never, if they are truly "presidential," do they threaten a first strike to start such a war.

We have seen that many people are involved in many ways in mediating our political realities, in creating and communicating fantasies about politics. Thus mass-mediation occurs in TV news, the melodramatic rituals of election campaigns, the re-presentation of history, popular magazines, movies, and sports—to recall but a few such mediators. We receive group-mediated fantasies from elites, inside-dopesters, religious and political groups, and other sources. The persons involved in both mass- and group-mediation of politics are mindful of our Sherwin like desire to simplify and fulfill our expectations. So, as we have seen many times in preceding chapters, they provide us with appealing, condensed political visions. Are these visions, like Miss Sherwin, also fictional? And if fictional, are they still so plausible as to appear factual nonetheless?

At least one set of reality mediators, advertisers, rely on our readiness to accept fiction as fact. Thus the origins of "counterfeit news." As an example take "Legal Action Hotline." To a TV viewer, "Legal Action Hotline" appears to be a typical public affairs program, very similar to "Washington Week in Review," "The McLaughlin Group," or "Journalists' Roundtable" (see Chapter 7). Instead of journalists conducting a forum on events and issues in the week's news, "Legal Action Hotline" features three attorneys and a host discussing how citizens can take full advantage of their legal rights. The attorneys exchange views on the legal options open to people injured on the job, ill-treated by a physician, or involved in an auto accident. If viewers want added details and advice, the program provides a toll-free hotline number. Behind this façade of helpful discussion, however, is yet another reality. If viewers call in for advice, operators provide instead names of attorneys who have paid to be listed as members of a referral service, and they charge for any legal advice they give. The TV discussion that appears to be a news and public affairs program is actually an extended TV commercial, one of a growing number of program-length commercials (PLCs), now a staple of televised advertising. PLCs hype not only legal advice but diet plans, balms to reduce unsightly cellulite, hair restorers, and magic potions unknown to the traveling medicine men of early America.[1] By using the conventional formats of TV newscasts, PLCs meet many viewers' expectations as to what is real: "I saw it on the news." The reality is not merely mediated but counterfeited as well.

In our "Introduction" we spoke of a form of counterfeited reality, the designed experience, which in exchange for hard cash provides people with opportunities to live out their fantasies by blurring the boundaries between fiction and fact in imaginative, creative ways. As the merchandising of designed experience becomes a booming industry, what implications does this novel form of mediating realities have for popular understandings of politics?

DESIGNED POLITICAL EXPERIENCE
IN THE AGE OF FANTASY

Historians faced with the task of simplifying long, complex periods in the unfolding of human experience often condense the years into identifiable eras, or ages. Thus, they write of the Classical Age, the Age of Empire, the Middle Ages, the Age of Kings, of Reason, of Romanticism, of Revolution, and of Science. Given that so much of what we know about the contemporary world reaches us as plausible, taken-for-granted fantasy that is assumed to be real and never seriously challenged, perhaps we now live in an Age of Fantasy. There are at least indications that this might be so. Let us look at a few.

Recurring Political Fantasies

We noted in the "Introduction" that some visions of political reality repeat themselves from one year to another, one decade to another, one generation to another. So recurrent are these fantasies that they may take on the character of myth—dramatic, sometimes credible accounts accepted at face value but that cannot be proved true or false. The durability of recurring fantasies is indicative of the fantasy age in which we live. We have introduced several such recurring fantasies. The following is a list of the major ones considered and the chapters discussing them.

RECURRING FANTASIES IN AMERICAN POLITICS

Chapter 1
The News as Enlightenment Fantasy
The Great Crash Fantasy
The Land of Liberty Fantasy
The Fantasy of Experts in Control (CBS-TV)
The Fantasy of the Populace as Victims (ABC-TV)
The News as Demystification Fantasy (NBC-TV)
The Fantasy of Heroic Conquest
The Captivity Fantasy

Chapter 2
The New Face Fantasy
The Beauty Pageant Ritual Fantasy
The Great Debates Fantasy
The Endless Campaign Fantasy
The Presidential Vision Fantasy

Chapter 3
The Cult Fantasy
The Calvary Charge Fantasy
The Nuclear Holocaust Fantasy

Chapter 4
The Celebrity Fantasy
The Fantasy of Celebrity Immortality
The Popular Royalty Fantasy
The Cinderella Fantasy

Chapter 5
The Populist Fantasy
The Prelapsarian Fantasy
The Commitment Fantasy
The Red Scare Fantasy
The Fantasy of Transcendence

Chapter 6
The Fantasy of Athletic Heroism
The Edenic Fantasy
The Eton Fantasy
The Sportsmanship Fantasy

Chapter 7
The Rational Decision-Making Fantasy
The Fantasy of Free-Wheeling Political Discussion

Politics as Designed Experience

Designed experiences flourish in the Age of Fantasy. Recall from our earlier discussion that so long as people find it increasingly possible to acquire material possessions, they turn to seeking new experiences instead. Opportunities to escape the routine of everyday living by experiencing the unusual take on a high priority. The designed experience industry exists to fulfill such desires. For a fee experience brokers find out what people want to experience, then engage experience design firms to create and arrange whatever experience the consumer cares to purchase. Does a middle-aged male wish to fulfill his boyhood fantasy of playing major league baseball with the Chicago Cubs? No problem. A one-week Cubs' camp in Arizona provides the opportunity (see Chapter 6). Does an amateur explorer want to join a scientific expedition? Again, there is no problem; experience design firms offer more than 75 such expeditions to points throughout the world. Any fantasy, any dream vacation, any experience is within reach.

Designed experiences thus take mediated realities, that is, fantasies, and turn them into experienced realities. They offer a means to make our fantasies more real than the secondhand realities encountered through mass and group mediation. It is farfetched to argue that contemporary politics is a series of designed experiences, but there are signs that many aspects of politics have taken on the character of designed experience. Consider television news, a subject we discussed in Chapter 1. Many TV organizations—local stations, cable operations, even national networks—routinely engage the services of high-priced consultants to conduct research into the viewing needs and desires of potential audiences. These consultant–experience brokers ask, for example, what people in viewing areas want to see on newscasts. Good news, crime and mayhem, local color, their neighbors? With that information, consultants acting in effect as experience brokers advise TV executives regarding the most appealing format, structure, anchors, correspondents, and content for news shows. Designed news (political and otherwise) thus fulfills audience desires, increases viewer ratings, and attracts advertising revenue. There *are* authentic, newsworthy happenings in the world, and the news reports them. But the report is a designer report, not all that different as a packaged product from designer jeans! Do the viewers pay for that experience? They do, indirectly, in the purchase of advertised merchandise.

Increasingly, as we saw in Chapter 2, political campaigns, both for candidates and voters, are designed experiences. Many candidates for local, even statewide, office come to electoral contests with a record of private achievement but lacking experience with political parties, campaigns, or public service. Hired political consultants—media consultants, pollsters, and the full range of hypesters described in Chapter 2—serve as experience brokers and designers. Thus, for a price a citizen can purchase the experience of a designed political campaign, either the "thrill of victory or the agony of defeat" (a fantasy borrowed from another mediator of realities, ABC-TV's "Wide World of Sports," as described in Chapter 6). The voter, listening and viewing the campaign of the consultant/candidate, opts to join in the designed experience of the ritual contest or turn elsewhere for the unusual.

In the era of telepolitics, the quadrennial conventions of the Democratic and Republican parties have taken on the character of designed political experiences. In 1988, for instance, more that 30,000 people participated directly in the designed experiences of the two national conventions—15,000 journalists, almost 10,000 delegates and alternates, party officials, convention staff, entertainers, businesspersons, and tourists. Convention planners, acting as experience designers and ever-mindful of the requirements for a good TV show for audiences throughout the world, carefully orchestrated convention activities with preset schedules, timed events, and scheduled interviews for journalists. They even wrote and rehearsed scripts for "spontaneous" floor demonstrations. Delegates, some with political backgrounds and some with none, paid large sums to attend what for them was an experience designed by convention managers who told delegates when to rally and march, wave banners, placards, and flags, and adorn themselves with hats, shirts, buttons, and other paraphernalia of their party and candidate.

As technology develops, there are reasons to believe that politics can become even more of a designed experience than it is now. For example, before long TV screens will be large, all-encompassing surfaces that curve around entire rooms, with viewers at the center. Viewers will be able to experience the sensation of being in the middle of any scene projected on the screen—a throng of people eagerly trying to shake the hand of the president, the assassination of a political leader, the crowd of spectators watching a coronation or the explosion of a manned space vehicle, on the floor of the U.S. Senate during a momentous debate, or at a congressional hearing into official wrongdoing. And the possibilities do not end with TV screens that envelop viewers. Through the technology of holography it is possible to project three-dimensional images at various points within a room. Entire scenes, say, from a play, may be projected so that the various characters appear lifelike and real. Thus, instead of simply viewing a taped summit meeting between world leaders, a person would have *the sense, the fantasy, of being there.*[2]

Such are the possibilities for mediated political realities as the Age of Fantasy unfolds. But designed experiences, no matter how much enhanced by technological wizardry such as wraparound TV screens and holography, are just that, *mediated* realities. They are not direct, firsthand experiences but designs substituted for them. As with the other means of mass- and group-mediation of realities that we have discussed in this book, designed experiences provide an illusion. It is the illusion that there is only one reality to experience, one way to experience, and that it is through the designed experience. Slavish acceptance of that illusion (we can call it the ultimate fantasy, or the *Fantasy of Single Realities*) has tyrannical implications. When people act on the basis that they do so in a single reality of the moment, then to control their behavior it is necessary only to control their perceived mediated realities, to control their fantasies. There is a potential for such carefully calculated and manipulated fantasies. George Orwell's fictional utopia *1984* (see Chapter 8) was one expression of that potential. That the potential exists need not dictate its certainty. At least, it need not if we are willing to surrender the illusion of single realities and step into a world of plural possibilities.

MEDIATED POLITICAL PLURALITIES, NOT REALITIES

In the 17th century the philosopher Francis Bacon speculated about the tendency of humans to hold beliefs that were simply not true. He called these "false notions" and reasoned that there were four chief sources of such "idols."[3] First, he wrote, there are *idols of the tribe.* These idols spring from the false assertion that human senses and perceptions are valid sources of beliefs. Such idols are similar to those we have likened to the pluralistic ignorance that marks group-mediated politics in our contemporary nation of tribes of inside-dopesters (Chapter 8) and of religious and political movements (Chapters 9 and 10). Persons who reject the human senses and perceptions as a touchstone of beliefs and instead think that the private reasoning capacity of the individual offers a better source of reality worship what Bacon called the *idols of the cave.* If one can but look into one's self, think such worshipers, true knowledge will flow not from mediation but from meditation. A third source of false notions derives from the *idols of the marketplace,* that is, social intercourse, group discussion, and group decision-making. This is what we have described as groupthink (Chapter 7). Finally, the source of reality for

CONCLUSION: THE AGE OF FANTASY   **229**

some people consists of beliefs passed down from generation to generation through tradition, philosophy, ritual, custom, convention, and so on. These are the *idols of the theater* and very much in the character of the melodramatic imperative of mass-mediated political realities (recall especially Chapters 1, 3, and 5).

Bacon provided no particular advice for how to escape such idolatry. That people still base their political beliefs on superficial impressions, meditation, groupthink, and dramatic portrayals is testimony to the endurance of the idols of tribe, cave, marketplace, and theater. The fantasies derived from the mediation of political realities constitute our modern day idols of politics. Giving up such fantasies, no longer embracing such idols, is not merely difficult; it is sometimes too painful to contemplate. This was the lesson learned by the clientele of Harry Hope's hotel and bar.

In 1946 Eugene O'Neill, one of America's greatest dramatists, published one of his last plays, *The Iceman Cometh,* a drama about fantasies tenaciously held.[4] It teaches us something about how the fantasies of our politics beguile and, if taken for granted as reality, enervate, devitalize, and perhaps even immobilize a body politic. All the action of the drama occurs in a back room of a combination hotel and saloon in New York City owned and operated by Harry Hope. It is the summer of 1912. Gathered in the bar in the early hours of the morning are Harry and a host of regulars, most of them roomers at Harry's hotel. The regulars are not actually customers because each and every one is down on luck and has no money to buy anything. So, in a daily and nightly ritual, each sits in the back room of the bar hoping that either Harry or a rare stranger from off the street will stand them to free booze.

The cast of characters is a strange combination: Harry's brother-in-law, an unemployed one-time circus man; a one-time police lieutenant kicked off the force; an alumnus of Harvard Law School who never practiced law; a former proprietor of a gambling house; a former Boer War commando; a one-time captain of British infantry; a perennially unemployed news correspondent; a former editor of anarchist publications; a weatherbeaten anarchist; and another one-time revolutionary who fled to Harry's after informing on fellow conspirators, including his own mother. The only gainfully employed regulars are two bartenders and three prostitutes, all also residents of Harry's hotel.

A strange place. Says one of the aging patrons: "It's the No Chance Saloon. It's Bedrock Bar, The End of the Line Cafe, The Bottom of the Sea Rathskeller!" He surveys the others as they sleep off their drunks at dimly lit tables. He notes a "beautiful calm in the atmosphere." He remarks, "No one here has to worry about where they're going next, because there is no farther they can go. It's a great comfort to them." But, he says, "Even here they keep up the appearances of life with a few harmless pipe dreams about their yesterdays and tomorrows."[5] These pipe dream fantasies, however, are the meaning of life for each person. Harry, a former ward politician, has not been outside his building since his wife died 20 years earlier. He dreams about taking a walk around the ward "tomorrow" to reclaim his political power as though he had yielded it only yesterday. His brother-in-law fantasizes a return to the circus. The former police lieutenant plans to seek exoneration "tomorrow." Also "tomorrow" the lawyer will practice law, the gambler will get a new establishment, the commando and infantry officer will return to the Veldt, the news correspondent (nicknamed "Jimmy Tomorrow") will reclaim his job, the prostitutes will quit walking the streets, and on and on. And, of course, everyone will pay Harry past-due bills "tomorrow." "The tomorrow movement is a sad and beautiful thing," says the cynical old anarchist.[6]

Today, however, everyone is awaiting the arrival of Theodore Hickman ("Hickey"). Hickey is a hardware salesman who occasionally drops in (on his "periodicals"), throws down a wad of money, buys drinks for the house, gets smashed, and indulges the regulars in their pipe dreams. The patrons eagerly await Hickey's arrival on this particular day for it is Harry's birthday. Hickey is always especially generous in buying booze each year on Harry's birthday.

After a long wait, especially for those suffering from the withdrawal symptoms of not having had a drink, Hickey arrives. He enters in the normal glad-handed, boisterous manner of "good ol' Hickey." The bartender brings drinks. There is a toast. Everybody drinks, everybody but Hickey. "You'll have to excuse me, boys and girls, but I'm off the stuff. For keeps," he declares. The regulars stare in amazed incredulity. He assures everyone that he will still buy them rounds, to their relief, but that he will have none of it: "I finally had the guts to face myself and throw overboard the damned lying pipe dream that'd been making me miserable, and do what I had to do for the happiness of all concerned—and then all at once I found I was at peace with myself and I didn't need booze anymore."[7]

The remainder of *The Iceman Cometh* (the iceman of reality) concerns Hickey's efforts to get the regulars of Harry Hope's to face up to their pipe dreams, recognize them for the illusions that they are, and having faced them, be goaded into doing all those things they had promised themselves for "tomorrow." Once they give up the "Palace of Pipe Dreams" they, too, will find "true peace" and happiness. The patrons do not yield without a struggle but slowly some come around. The news correspondent finally admits that he would never be able to get his job back because he was fired for drunkenness. Others begin to face up to their pipe dreams. After years of idleness some even walk (or are shoved) out of the door of Harry's bar. But Harry Hope is the hard case for Hickey. Harry has all kinds of excuses for not surrendering his pipe dream and actually going out to walk the ward—his loss of hearing, his rheumatism, the heavy traffic on the streets, and so on. But in a rage at Hickey, Harry finally relents: "If there was a mad dog outside I'd go and shake hands with it rather than stay here with you!" Out he goes, but soon the bartender sees that Harry is turning around. Says Hickey, "Of course, he's coming back.

So are all the others. By tonight they'll all be here again. You dumbbell, that's the whole point."[8]

And they do all return, but nothing seems the same. They feel shame, especially in the face of Hickey's new-found serenity and peace. They drink and drink but to no effect. "No life in the booze. No kick. Dishwater. Beejees, I'll never pass out!," whines Harry Hope.[9] And at that point Hickey reveals the story of how he rid himself of his pipe dream. As he tells it, *his fantasy* involved his wife's love for him and her misery because of it. All she ever wanted to do, he says, was to make him happy, but she was never happy in return. The reality, Hickey says, to which he awakened, his pipe dream exposed, was deficiency in his own character. There was the source of his wife's sadness. Of what did that deficiency consist? Of his drinking, absence from home, chasing after other women, carousing, and so on. Having awakened to his pipe dream, Hickey asked himself how he could make amends, how he could make his wife Evelyn happy and remove her torment at loving such a louse. "I'd driven myself crazy trying to find some way out for her," he says. Then it came to him, "the only possible way out—for her sake," and "the only possible way to give her peace and free her from the misery of loving me." The regulars chorus "Who the hell cares? We want to pass out in peace!" But Hickey continues, "So I killed her."[10]

Hickey is arrested. It takes some time for things to return to normal at Harry's, but they do. Each patron picks up the old pipe dream. Harry takes another drink, then joyfully exclaims, "Beejees, fellers, I'm feeling the old kick, or I'm a liar. It's putting life back in me!" Then he says, "It was Hickey kept it from—," Harry stops, says Hickey was crazy, possessed with "a lunatic's pipe dreams."[11] Everyone at Harry's, in contrast, is sane. So the pipe dreams are not fantasies, they are reality. That reality reinforced, all sink back into the stupor of their ritualistic lives.

Like Plato's parable of the cave with which we closed the introductory chapter of this volume, *The Iceman Cometh* testifies to the human yearning for illusion. Hickey is but the prisoner freed from the cave to walk out and peer into the sunlight. On his last visit to the cave that is Harry's bar, he is no longer "good ol' Hickey"; now he is a threat to the comfortable reality of the bar and its patrons. Again like the prisoner, he may merely be substituting one illusion for another. *The Iceman Cometh* not only speaks of the seduction and persistence of fantasy; it also tells us something about what happens when one acts on the basis of such illusion. Hickey kills Evelyn because he follows the logic of his pipe dream to its end. His act was no illusion, however, for it had real-world consequences for Evelyn.

It is on this note that we conclude our mediated reality of mediated political realities. The logic of fantasy dictates simplified, single explanations for events; the logic of reality, however, is one of complexities and plural explanations. The logic of fantasy demands consistency or, at least, easily reconciled inconsistencies; the logic of reality is one of contradictions or, at least, of confusion. The logic of fantasy is one of certainties, the logic of reality of equally plausible possibilities. In his "Ivan Turgenieff," which appeared in *French Poets and Novelists* in 1878, Henry James wrote:

> Life is, in fact, a battle. . . . . Evil is insolent and strong; beauty enchanting but rare; goodness very apt to be weak; folly very apt to be defiant; wickedness to carry the day; imbeciles to be in great places, people of sense in small, and mankind generally, unhappy. But the world as it stands is no illusion, no phantasm, no evil dream of a night; we wake up to it again for ever and ever; we can neither forget it nor deny it nor dispense with it.[12]

No manner of premature closure of potential political realities will allow us, despite our store of dramatic and enriched fantasies, to avoid awakening to the political world that "as it stands is no illusion." We hope that readers of this volume will "for ever and ever" seek out and ponder alternative realities to those derived from mass- and group-mediated politics. The security of Harry Hope's is not as appealing as it might seem.

NOTES

1. Jeffrey Chester and Kathryn Montgomery, "Counterfeiting the News," *Columbia Journalism Review,* 27 (May/June 1988): 38–41.
2. Philip Kotler, " 'Dream Vacations': The Booming Market for Designed Experiences," *The Futurist* (October 1984): 7–13.
3. Francis Bacon, "Novum Organum," in Edwin A. Byrtt, ed., *The English Philosophers from Bacon to Mill* (New York: Random House, Modern Library, 1939), pp. 34–35.
4. Eugene O'Neill, *The Iceman Cometh* (New York: Random House, Vintage Books, 1957).
5. Ibid., p. 26.
6. Ibid., p. 50.
7. Ibid., p. 79.
8. Ibid., pp. 195–196.
9. Ibid., p. 235.
10. Ibid., pp. 240–241.
11. Ibid., pp. 249–250.
12. Henry James, *French Poets and Novelists* (London: Macmillan, 1878), pp. 318–319.

Author Index

Subject Index